ANIMAL WARFARE

David Henshaw was born in Huddersfield, Yorkshire in 1946. He began his career in television journalism as a researcher for Granada TV, and has since worked for Anglia TV before joining the BBC where he has produced and presented current affairs programmes for both TV and radio, including *File on Four* on Radio 4 and the *Black and White* documentary series on BBC 1. In 1986, his close work on the extreme, militant edge of the animal rights movement culminated in the well-received BBC documentary for the *Brass Tacks* series.

Broadcaster and journalist, David Henshaw lives in Manchester.

DAVID HENSHAW

Animal Warfare

FONTANA/Collins

First published in 1989 by Fontana Paperbacks
8 Grafton Street, London W1X 3LA

Copyright © 1989 David Henshaw

Printed and bound in Great Britain by
William Collins Sons & Co. Ltd., Glasgow

For Tom and Dan

Is it not crystal clear, then, comrades, that all the evils of this life of ours spring from the tyranny of human beings? What then must we do? Why, work night and day, body and soul, for the overthrow of the human race!

GEORGE ORWELL, *Animal Farm*

CONTENTS

ILLUSTRATIONS

1. Anarchist Ronnie Lee, founder and leading organizer of the ALF. (*Copyright Pixfeatures*)

2. Animal rights activists chain themselves to the railings at 10 Downing Street. (*Copyright Press Association*)

3. The ALF's 'Poisoned' Mars Bar hoax of 1984. (*Copyright BBC*)

4. First 'publicity' shot of the self-styled 'Hunt Retribution Squad'. (*Copyright Jacquie Hughes*)

5. The ALF's version of Father Christmas. (*Copyright ALF*)

6. ALF activists in standard uniform of combat jacket and balaclava, raiding a battery hen run. (*Copyright ALF*)

7. Bournemouth cell of the ALF – the Mars Bar hoaxers – interviewed by the author. (*Copyright Bill Lyons, BBC Manchester*)

8. 'Ben', the ALF organizer of the Mars Bar hoax of 1984. (*Copyright Bill Lyons, BBC Manchester*)

9. Tim Daley, former trainee commercial pilot, and leading animal rights activist. (*Copyright Rex Features*)

10. John Beggs, press officer of the South East Animal Liberation League and BUAV activist. (*Copyright BBC*)

11. Dingles department store in Plymouth, destroyed by an ALF firebomb Christmas 1988. (*Copyright Press Association*)

12. The Hunt Retribution Squad pose for a shot after the desecration of the Duke of Beaufort's grave in 1984. (*Copyright Press Association*)

13. Animal rights demonstrations against vivisection. (*Copyright Rex Features*)

14. Close-up of 13. (*Copyright Rex Features*)

PREFACE

Most human liberation movements conform to a kind of pattern. Whether inspired by race, gender or a sense of nationhood, they are susceptible to reasoned analysis. The story of the animal rights movement, by contrast, is a rambling, contradictory and chaotic saga. Animal liberation, as a revolutionary philosophy, has generated something of an eccentric and peculiarly British hybrid, lurching uncomfortably between low farce and pure terrorism. What follows is a reflection of that chaos.

This book was developed from the BBC Television documentary of the same name: I owe a debt of thanks to my editor Colin Cameron and my producer Bill Lyons for sharing what became an obsessive enthusiasm for a subject that often seemed impenetrably bizarre. Some of the additional research for the book was carried out by Mark Gregory, to whom I am also grateful. But most thanks go to Charlotte Hogwood, who encouraged and cajoled at crucial moments.

DAVID HENSHAW
August 1988

CHAPTER ONE

> Only an all-out war, fought with
> intelligent tactics can offer the animals
> any hope of freedom.
> ALF Supporters Group Bulletin No. 13

On a quiet January morning in 1986 Peter Savage the owner of Shamrock Farms animal, breeding and import centre was getting ready to go to work. A couple of minutes earlier, he had said goodbye to his younger daughter Philippa, but now here she was back on the doorstep, and with her a policeman. What he had to say was barely believable. There had been a phone message about a bomb under the Savage family car. The officer had just had a look and there was, indeed, something suspicious under the petrol tank. The whole family had to get out, and quickly. All Peter Savage could think about, he admitted later, was the neighbours; not so much the embarrassing horror of a bomb scare in sleepy, suburban Steyning, but the indiscriminate slaughter that would have followed an explosion. At half past eight in the morning the street was full of commuters heading off to work in nearby Brighton, and, worse, children making their way to school: innocent people, blissfully unaware that out of the blue they had been placed squarely in the front line of a new kind of war. It was a war being fought in deadly earnest. In the curiously neutral terminology later employed by the police bomb squad who turned up to deal with the object under the Savages' car, the device was 'viable'. It would have blown away half the street.

Half a dozen miles away, dog lovers marched their animals up and down Brighton promenade, past aerosoled graffiti proclaiming 'animal liberation' and 'meat is murder'. Hard to take seriously, that kind of language: after all, the English were a nation of animal lovers, were they not? The great national cliché, it was hardly believable that it should now be grotesquely transformed into a new and bizarre form of terrorism.

1

But just a month after the car bomb in Steyning there were more – and this time they went off.

Three meat trucks at a depot next to the main Brighton abattoir were severely damaged and one was a write off. Twenty thousand pounds' worth of damage was done in one midnight raid. When depot foreman Les Wilsher turned up the next morning, it was 'very frightening. There were smouldering trucks, the firemen were just on the last legs of putting it out ... we'd never known anything like that before.' True, there had been an increasingly vocal picket from local animal rights activists, slogans painted over the depot walls, even superglue in the locks. But this was different. 'The terrible thing is,' said Les Wilsher, 'you often get drivers down who stay overnight, and some of them sleep in the cab. Imagine if the driver was asleep in his cab, and all of a sudden a bomb came through his window or something. I mean, they're talking about "meat is murder", but they could have killed a human.'

The really chilling thing for the men at the meat depot was their inability to grasp that they were now in the firing line, that someone really would try to kill them because of what they did for a living. This was more confusing than Northern Ireland. 'It's all done in the dark,' said a meat packer; 'it's all done without conversation, reason or argument as far as we're concerned.' The gulf in comprehension was more frightening than the Molotov cocktails. All they knew was that these people, whoever they were, meant business. A few miles down the coast they broke into another lorry park: this time they sawed through the safety bolts on the cabs and loosened the wheel nuts. Sudden braking on the motorway would have meant an equally sudden death.

So if it was to be war, the meat depot had to be put on a war footing. Now, bright lights illuminate the compound and security patrols keep it under constant observation. Outside town, in the prosperous farming country round Brighton, these tactics were already in use. The man who owns and runs a large battery chicken farm would talk about security only if he could remain anonymous. He had just spent £5,000 on a high tech system that caused a banshee-like wail to reverberate around the chicken sheds on the detection of an intruder. Perversely, it gave the farm the appearance of what the liberationists say it is, a concentration camp. But the farmer was not playing games; these people were terrorists. 'They can really

2

have no other definition to fit the kind of things they are doing, including explosive devices, intimidation of people, and even threats of killing.' But, again, the sinister thing about them was their silence. 'There's no point of human contact or debate ... it's a secret enemy.'

The local representative from the National Farmers' Union agreed: this was a form of 'rural terrorism' and it was getting worse. Local farmers felt intimidated and increasingly angry: most wouldn't talk openly about what was going on, for fear of reprisals. Only a few weeks before, a concrete block had been hurled through the bedroom window of one of the union members. It had just missed his elderly mother. The situation was getting out of hand. When it came to the issue of animal welfare in farming, things had always been pretty civilized. 'We can talk to reasonable people; we like to show them what we're doing, and we can talk to reasonable organizations ... but these new people we just cannot deal with.' Here was an enemy full of implacable certainty, uninterested in diaglogue.

The closer you looked at this one small section of England, the nastier the situation began to appear. It wasn't just the bombs: there was a constant level of minor acts of violence, carried out with monotonous regularity. Much of the time they never made the papers, but for the people whose homes and businesses were the target this was small consolation. George Street is the main shopping centre for Brighton's sister town of Hove. It looks genteel, where Brighton is raffish; the pavements are crowded by the respectable elderly, come here for peace and quiet in retirement. But the shop owners of George Street now found they had precious little of either. All four butchers had had their windows smashed several times over; Boots the Chemists had been attacked; the delicatessen had been bricked. 'ALF' slogans had been daubed on each of these targets, and 'meat is murder'; chemists were in the front line because they were accused of selling drugs tested on animals. It had got so bad, and the insurance bills so horrific, that one butcher had installed a video camera outside his shop. Everyone else had simply put up metal shutters, but the video butcher didn't like the image: if you made your shop look like Fort Knox, then the enemy had almost won. It made you look as if you were doing something to be ashamed of.

George Groom could see that, but he was a practical man, and if metal shutters were going to do the job, he was going to have them installed. In just twelve months his business had suffered more than enough 'outrages', as he called them. 'We've had broken windows, spray-on graffiti, bricks have broken internal fixtures and fittings . . . all done this year.' The graffiti said that George Groom and his wife were murderers, that what he was doing in his shop was the equivalent of running a Nazi concentration camp. But, once again, he had no idea who was saying and doing these things. 'I haven't a clue. I wish I did, because what I'd like is some kind of civilized argument.' It wasn't just the damage to his shop, it was the implication that he somehow hated and tortured animals. He was actually rather fond of animals, and fancied running a small farm when he retired; as for the joints of meat that decorated his counter and shop window, he didn't class them as corpses. 'They are just meat. If they came into the shop alive, and we had to take them out to the back and slaughter them as they used to in the old days, I might feel differently. But they come to us humanely slaughtered, and not really resembling the animals they were in the field anyway. They've no fur or anything.'

But this was war, and, to George Groom's enemy, these were limp excuses. No one who sold, used, farmed, traded in, exploited or experimented on animals was innocent. Genuinely not having the faintest idea what the aerosoled communiqués of their attackers actually meant was no excuse either. Whatever the deficiencies of their tactics, the midnight raiders were certainly not short on moral certainty.

What most of their targets failed to appreciate was that all this violence was fuelled by an ideology far removed from their own cosy notions of animal welfare. Being kind to animals, in the traditional, rather soppy English sense was irrelevant: this was a liberation movement, and it owed more to the struggles of women, gays and blacks than to the RSPCA. A new 'ism' had been invented to stand alongside sexism and racism: the crime of 'speciesism'. Animal exploiters were 'speciesists', whether they knew it or not. And ignorance was no excuse.

Sometimes the raiders and the bombers claimed their acts on behalf of specific organizations, sometimes they just seemed to be freelance. Most of the more dramatic actions were said to be the work of the ALF – the Animal Liberation Front. You couldn't walk more than a few hundred yards round the streets of Brighton without coming across their logo, usually sprayed in black, often accompanied by anarchic addenda. The bomb that was planted under Peter Savage's car was claimed by a group calling itself the Animal Rights Militia. Three others had been placed under the cars of other prospective victims in different parts of the country on the same night; they had been timed to go off at hourly intervals. Whoever made them, said the police, knew what they were doing.

Like the men at the meat depot and the butchers, Peter Savage had known for some time that he was unpopular with the new breed of animal rights activists. He was used to demonstrations at Shamrock Farms, the business owned by the family he had married into. Shamrock Farms imports animals – mainly monkeys – specifically for the purpose of medical research, in other words, vivisection. If that was never exactly popular with many traditional supporters of animal welfare, it was quite intolerable to the new breed of activist. Over the years, Peter Savage had monitored the gradual shifts in attitude on the part of those who would turn up to demonstrate outside his offices. He'd always been willing to talk to anyone about the rights and wrongs of vivisection; it was not something that he treated lightly, and he welcomed the chance to express his own carefully worked out arguments in favour of medical research on live animals. But by the mid 1980s, polite discussion had given way to chanting and abuse; and then, one day some months before the bomb was placed under his car, there came intimations of a new and distinctly sinister shift in attitude. 'One time during one of the demonstrations outside my offices, I was having a discussion with one of the demonstrators, and we were talking generally about the morals of medical research . . . and the gentleman I was talking to made it clear that although he personally did not condone violent action, he felt certain that some members of his group or supporters of his group would eventually take action against individuals in the industry. Personal action.' The phrase had a sinister resonance.

Having got used to being regularly described as a 'murderer', 'torturer', and 'living off the blood of innocent animals', Mr Savage has now had to get used to the kind of security conscious régime followed by judges in Northern Ireland. 'Well, obviously, I check under my car as regularly as possible. Whenever I walk out of my house I check, and if I ever forget, my wife never does.' But the strain of living constantly under this kind of threat has taken an understandable toll on the family. It is particularly tough on Philippa, his younger daughter. 'She's very nervous about going to bed at night; it's very difficult to get her to leave us and go upstairs on her own. The scars will take a long time to wear off.' And the people who planted the bomb: if they realized they had had that kind of impact on a child, would they have any regrets? 'I don't think so, because of the nature of the people we are dealing with. I do not believe they are concerned with individuals on my side of the fence, only with their own cause and their own feelings.'

The question is, who exactly were these people? Not just the bombers, but the wider group whose broad support the bombers enjoyed. Who were the people in a nice place like Brighton who were now defending violence and intimidation on behalf of animal rights? Not quite what you'd expect. Kenneth and Christine Harrold, for example, live in a highly desirable part of Shoreham-by-Sea. Mr Harrold is a retired senior civil servant in the Treasury; there are twin grey Mercedes saloons parked outside the family home which has an air of unostentatious opulence inside. The Harrolds are polite, reserved, rather old fashioned, they tell you, in their social attitudes: they had lived abroad for some time before recently returning to England. Hardly the sort of people you expect to hear defending the fire-bombing of meat trucks; but that is precisely what you do hear. 'It didn't endanger anyone's life did it?' bridles Mrs Harrold. That's not what the men down at the depot say. 'Well, they always say that don't they? If there's no one within ten miles, they'd say someone could be killed.' So the bombing was OK? 'I can't say I'm opposed to it . . . no, I'm not.' And to those who might be surprised to hear someone of her age and impeccable background defending such an action, Mrs Harrold summons the full moral rectitude of a Gerry Adams. 'I don't mind if people are surprised . . . I'm just very sorry that they can't see it my way. It's the duty of people to learn more about what is going on in this country.' As for people like Peter Savage, and the vivisectors he services, 'they are absolute evil sadists . . . and in my view they should all die in the same way that the animals die.' Mrs Harrold and her husband don't like the word terrorism very much. In their view, firebombing a set of trucks was simply a moral imperative. 'Someone has to make it known that there is a strong determination to get things altered.'

Should you spot the Harrolds walking their dog along Shoreham Sands, you would automatically put them down as a rather touching pair of old-fashioned animal lovers; but even more curious than their allegiance to the bomb squads of the ALF was the nature of their allies along this stretch of coast. A couple of miles back towards Brighton, and set back from the sea front, there's an elegant if rather faded row of red brick terrace houses. It had been taken over as a squat by a group of anarchists, a peripatetic bunch of between twenty and thirty black clad young people. Most of them were very young indeed – late teens to early twenties – with a leavening of rather elderly hippies. These, too, supported the ALF. The first thing you saw as you made your way into the squat, up a dark staircase, was a huge black flag strung across the back wall of the main living-room, with the letters 'ALF' emblazoned across it. The 'A' was encased in a circle, in the common graffiti vernacular of the street anarchists of the eighties.

Yes, said the squatters, there was a war going on in Brighton: 'a war against animal abuse'. A more direct form of action was now having to be taken because cruelty and abuse was always being 'covered up'. Like the Harrolds, the activists in the squat talked the language of conspiracy. The vivisectors and the meat traders hid behind high walls and security fences; what they were doing in the sordid privacy of their laboratories and abattoirs was the equivalent of what the Nazis did to the Jews. This was meant quite seriously. Steve, late twenties, in jeans composed more of holes than material, was talking in an intense monotone. 'The action against the Jews and against animals nowadays is exactly the same. It was people then, it's animals now.' An analogy that would surely offend most Jewish people more than a little? Not if they realized that all species were equal, with equal rights, said Steve.

No one was going to apologize for all the local bombings; people like Peter Savage and the meat traders were asking for it. 'I can totally understand people placing bombs under cars', argued Steve, 'the animal rights people aren't to blame. It's his [Savage's] fault for being a vivisector.' Only the other day, a couple of the squatters had met an old lady in the street who said she was 'quite chuffed' about the bombs being planted, and that while she was on the subject, she was rather pleased about Prince Andrew being kicked by a horse. She was too old to do anything, but she'd support kids who had the guts to do it for her.

What was beginning to emerge in Brighton was a very odd social landscape indeed. Strange coalitions had evolved in the birth of the animal rights movement. And there was nothing very unusual or particular about this piece of south coast England: all over the country local animal rights groups had been established in the eighties, and in each of them you would find curious combinations of class, age and politics. Anarchists and fascists, respectable Tory-voting pensioners and radical socialists – all united by the single and overriding issue of animal rights and by a growing impatience with the cautious gradualism of the old established animal welfare bodies.

Here, the Brighton Animal Rights Group embraced activists and sympathizers right across the spectrum. Meeting in the upstairs room of a pub just off the sea front, you would find rainbow-haired punks sitting next to pensioners who were happy to march with the local branch of the National Front against ritual slaughter in Jewish and Moslem abattoirs; next to them would be hunt saboteurs, and then activists who had taken part in a raid to free animals from a big south coast laboratory complex; in the corner sat the elderly founder of the local evangelical Christian animal rights group, a heroine of the local press and a woman of selfless good works. In between, there would be a large number of ordinary local people, teachers, local government officers and plenty of students. There would be argument and heated debate, but the fundamental issue was animal rights: and somehow that had now become much more significant than hairstyle, clothes, age or background. As a phenomenon it was both very odd and very English.

What was distinctly un-English was the almost millenarian tone of the argument. Time was running out for the animals, for all of us; the situation was desperate, annihilation of the planet imminent. Violence was inevitable. 'I think people involved in vivisection have got to expect more of this,' said Steve, the anarchist. He'd heard about an animal rights activist in Exeter who had poured petrol over his clothes and then set himself on fire. 'He did that because he was mentally depressed at the amount of abuse that was going on. He just couldn't take any more, so he just did it to shock everybody into realizing what's happening.' People were getting desperate, the whole thing was getting desperate. Every six seconds an animal was dying in a British laboratory: the bombs were inevitable.

This was a strange cocktail: the fervour of charismatic Christianity allied to the chilling logic of Sinn Fein (later, ALF leaders talked longingly about the visit to an IRA pub, where everybody sang rebel songs, and knew all the words: some day the ALF would have a place like that, and their own songs . . .). And above all, here was an ideology that brooked no argument, no discussion, no dialogue.

For the liberationists' targets in Brighton it was all very confusing. 'I don't know what kind of person this is,' Peter Savage had to admit. 'I never thought I'd met anybody that would consider placing a bomb under someone's car. It's difficult to envisage what sort of person it is. I can only assume that they're very bitter and very twisted.' George Groom, the butcher, couldn't understand why 'these people' called themselves 'animal lovers'. 'I don't see as they can be . . . not as such . . . the things they're doing don't constitute being an animal lover.' But George was wrong: they didn't call themselves 'animal lovers': to the new breed of activist the term was offensively patronizing to the non-human species they had elected to defend; it was as bad as 'nigger lover'. And some of them didn't even like animals: they could be noisy, smelly, a nuisance – but that wasn't the point. Animals had rights, rights as fundamental and defensible as human rights. No one had bothered to explain this to George Groom: there were just black aerosoled announcements across the walls of his shop – meat was murder. It was a message that made no sense to Les Wilsher and his cutters and packers down at the abattoir. Animals had always killed each other, always would. Was that murder? Lions and tigers ripping their prey to pieces in the jungle, it was the law of nature, surely. If only some of these people would come forward and just talk sensibly. 'It's gone quite far enough what with bombs and sawing bolts on safety cabs,' said Les. 'It's time somebody sat down and did a bit of talking and tried to make some sense of it.'

But the truth was that in a war the cause is served by deeds not words. And by the mid eighties, the deeds committed by animal rights activists were considerable. A conservative estimate of six million pounds' worth of damage per annum, quite possibly, said some policemen, an awful lot more. Many farmers and laboratories wouldn't publicize break-ins, and proper collation of the real figures was difficult. What was clear was that there was a great deal of activity going on; the ALF alone claimed five raids a night, every night, spread across the country. Economic sabotage and personal intimidation were tactics pursued with remarkable success: when activists claimed to have poisoned Mars Bars in 1984, to protest about dental research on monkeys, Mars lost a staggering three million pounds.

These people were not playing games. The things that were happening in Brighton were happening all over Britain: thousands of people, bound up in the same social mosaic, were fighting a campaign for the animals. But it hadn't all happened overnight. The road that eventually led to the bomb under Peter Savage's car went back a long way.

CHAPTER TWO

Someday, someone will get a
screwdriver in the face.

Ronnie Lee, founder member of
the Band of Mercy

In the early part of the 1980s, television viewers became accustomed to the sight of a small bearded man with gold rimmed glasses popping up with monotonous regularity on news magazine programmes. This was Ronnie Lee, self-styled 'press officer' of the Animal Liberation Front. Wearing a determinedly untrendy blue denim cap, Lee would talk authoritatively of the Front's latest 'action', be it the Mars Bar rat poison hoax or arson attacks on farms and laboratories. As the ALF's volume of destruction grew, so Ronnie Lee achieved the status of a minor public figure: when interviewed, he spoke in something of a high, droning whine, as if explaining the perfectly obvious to the irredeemably obtuse. He became something of a figure of fun among journalists, a kind of joke version of Danny Morrison representing a low-rent and perhaps loony version of Sinn Fein. Lee himself was a great admirer of the Irish Republicans; he visited their pubs, and envied the power of myth and ritual in their rebel songs. The ALF should learn from them, he told colleagues.

When the ALF made the papers, Lee's was the face the public put to the organization: yet always he managed to distance himself from the actual events he defended. But the truth was that, from the very beginning, Lee had been the inspiration behind, and the central founder of the movement. The mild, distinctly gnome-like person who never allowed himself to be provoked into losing his temper by interviewers made much of his claim to be a pacifist, and of the ALF's ideals of non-violence. But Lee's background lay in anarchy, and from the moment he became involved in the animal rights movement he seemed to those around him to be an unusually single-minded fanatic. 'In a revolution, he'd have been perfect,' said

11

one of Lee's original comrades; 'he'd have been the one to give the orders if it was necessary to sacrifice someone.'

By the time the violence had reached the kind of level faced by people in the Brighton area in that spring of 1986, the ALF was only one of several organizations claiming responsibility. But names actually meant very little: within the movement, there were a group of activists of varying degrees of commitment to illegality, and they tended to cloak their actions in what were often purely ad hoc acronyms dreamt up for the occasion. As an umbrella, the ALF had for more than ten years been the organization within which both individuals and splinter groups could liaise and function. And Ronnie Lee, most activists had to agree, *was* the ALF.

The story of the Front began back in the late 1960s. Its origins lay in a curious fusion of naïve altruism and the arrogant, messianic anarchism that became briefly fashionable at the end of the decade. In the sixties, if you cared about animals (no one yet talked about 'animal rights' – this was one movement where actions preceded ideology) you joined a tame, respectable organization like the RSPCA, or you offered your services to the Hunt Saboteurs Association. This had started in 1962 as a non-violent but rather more positive means of taking on animal abusers directly: if violence did occur, it was largely the fault of over-zealous and ill-tempered huntsmen and women deprived of their day's sport. The HSA was, and still is, a genuinely idealistic bunch of people, genuinely opposed to violence: but its very nature attracted people of a less gentle disposition.

Ronnie Lee was training to be a solicitor at law college in London when he first went out 'sabbing'. In 1971 he formed a new HSA group in Luton, along with a band of like-minded friends who felt that more should be done, particularly against the practice of 'cub hunting', the method used by the hunters to train young fox hounds by sending them in after baby foxes. Lee and his friend Cliff Goodman quickly made their reputation in the 'sabbing' world; according to the ALF's 'official' history, published in the Front's Supporters Group magazine, the Luton gang 'successfully wrecked one hunt after another'. Lee's overtly mild manner and tiny stature were turned to his advantage on the hunting field. Another member of the Luton group remembers Ronnie deliberately going up to the biggest, ugliest looking huntsman and equally deliberately provoking him; and when the man turned nasty, playing the innocent and claiming the immunity of a pacifist. Right from the start, Lee wanted to play the game both ways at once.

In fact Lee and Goodman rapidly tired of the HSA's reluctance to return violence against violence. There were other, more potent examples to be followed. The papers were full of the doings of a shadowy group calling themselves the 'Angry Brigade'; they specialized in firebombing chosen representatives of the hated Establishment, culminating in a raid on the home of Robert Carr, then Home Secretary in the Conservative Government. No one, so far, had actually got hurt, but the effect in terms of publicity had been considerable. Lee and Goodman were impressed. Of the two of them, Lee was the one with initiative, full of confidence about the cause: Goodman worried about the rights and wrongs of violence as a tactic. Rorke Garfield, a fellow HSA supporter who knew the pair well at the time, thought Ronnie 'a likeable chap, but often his language and his thoughts were quite violent'. More than once, Garfield recalled, he had spoken with some relish of the inevitability that 'someday, someone will get a screwdriver in the face'.

The more temperate Goodman did, however, serve a crucial role in the political education of Ronnie Lee. On New Year's Day 1972, the Luton group were demonstrating at a hunt in Burleigh Park near Huntingdon. Things got rough and in the scuffles a huntsman's whip cut Cliff Goodman's eye. It was a gratuitously nasty act that made a big impression on Lee. It also made a lot of space in the local papers. Later, Goodman described the incident as the point at which Lee decided to make a serious and full-time commitment to the movement.

By the following year, Lee, Goodman and three or four others in the HSA were determined to change the rules of the game. Because of its policy of non-violence, the HSA seemed to be taking an awful lot of stick from the huntsmen and their lackeys, the even more deeply loathed 'terriermen'. These were the working-class hunt followers who followed the horses on foot with their large and aggressive dogs: they had no genteel compunction at all about laying into the unkempt and usually hirsute 'sabbing' brigade who descended from the towns to spoil their fun. Something had to be done; people had to fight back for the animals. So in 1972 Ronnie Lee and Cliff Goodman founded the Band of Mercy, the forerunner of what was to become the ALF. It was to be the first of many successive occasions when the animal rights movement was splintered by a growing appetite for violence.

If the name sounded vaguely do-gooderish, those were indeed its origins. Lee and Goodman borrowed the name from a Victorian pressure group organized by young people within the RSPCA and now long defunct. But 'Band of Mercy' had the right kind of ring to it: decent, concerned, a kind of Red Cross for the animals. Its activities were rather less charitable. When it started, the group was only half a dozen strong, and intitial actions were concentrated on their old enemies, the local hunts. In the summer and early autumn of 1973, the Band of Mercy immobilized and damaged vehicles belonging to the kennels of the Whaddon Chase, the Vale of Aylsbury and the Puckeridge and Thurlow foxhunts. As long as this kind of tyre-slashing vandalism remained the group's sole agenda, the tiny group stayed solid. But then Lee and Goodman started talking about arson, which worried less robust figures. One of them in particular had already been alarmed by Lee's enjoyment of blood-curdling threats; he also thought Ronnie was too fond of giving orders and unwilling to take them. But when it came to fire, Lee's behaviour became downright disturbing. He had heard, 'There was one arson raid where he was dancing round the flames with glee, almost recklessly, so that two of his colleagues had to pull him away to prevent him being injured.'

The Band's first raid was on the Hoechst Pharmaceutical research centre being built at Milton Keynes. On 10 November, the site was set on fire, and £26,000 worth of damage done. This was a double watershed for the movement, in the use of arson as a tactic, and for the first time the targeting of an organization involved in vivisection. Lee and Goodman then decided to have another go at Hoechst six days later: this time a further £20,000 worth of damage was done. If the company assumed that this double burn-out was either an accident or mindless vandalism, they were quickly disabused. Ronnie Lee, wearing, he boasted later, a pair of gloves, and writing laboriously on a pad, making sure it had no indentation from previous writing, claimed the 'action' in the name of the Band of Mercy. 'The building was set fire to,' ran the communiqué, 'to prevent the torture and murder of our animal brothers and sisters by evil experiments.' Then the explanatory coda. 'We are a non-violent guerilla organization dedicated to the liberation of animals from all forms of cruelty and persecution at the hands of mankind. Our actions will continue until our aims are achieved.' Ronnie Lee could hardly have dreamed that within ten years of this action, all laboratory complexes like Hoechst's would be surrounded by barbed wire fences and electric alarm systems.

The Band of Mercy now turned its attentions to the seal cullers of the Wash. In June 1974 two boats licensed by the Home Office to cull seals were attacked; one was slightly damaged, the other totally destroyed. As a reporter with Anglia television I was sent to the small Lincolnshire village of Sutton Bridge to film the damage and the local reaction. A business had been destroyed, and no one could understand what had happened; more confused than angry, the destroyed boat's owner was too upset to talk. This time there had been no communiqué, no explanation. It was an early premonition of the puzzlement and uncertainty that became the regular reaction of those targeted by the ALF and their associated groups. In Sutton Bridge that June morning, all people wanted to know was why hadn't these people talked to them before smashing up a man's livelihood? But the Band of Mercy was not concerned with dialogue.

Already, Lee and Goodman were beginning to enjoy considerable notoriety. The Laboratory Animal Breeders Association were now alarmed enough to write to their entire membership, alerting them to 'a fanatical group of so-called "animal lovers"': they were strongly advised to increase security and watch out for possible attacks. But at the same time, some of Ronnie's old comrades in the Luton HSA were getting a little edgy: there were disagreements about the wisdom of firebombing premises and vehicles, acts of criminal violence that might not go down too well with the sort of person who otherwise might support the cause. Later Lee, in his account of those early years, wrote that 'the step from destroying hunting equipment to burning laboratories and property owned by the animal abusers was indeed a large one. It was the most logical one also.' Not one, however, that the HSA wanted anything to do with. In July a local HSA figure, offered a reward of £250 for information leading to the indentification of the Band of Mercy. The 'area commander' told the press, 'we approve of their ideals, but are opposed to their methods'.

This tone was to become familiar over the next ten years. Every time a new group upped the ante with a fresh outrage, hitherto 'extremist' organizations would issue disclaimers, thereby managing to assume the mantle of moderation.

Meanwhile, the Band of Mercy rapidly expanded its field of action. Later in July a vehicle belonging to Harris Biological Supplies in Weston-super-Mare was firebombed; a gun shop in Marlborough was attacked and damaged; and four more vans from an animal breeding centre at Elstree were vandalized. For a group of just half a dozen activists, they were causing a fair amount of havoc in an arc stretching right across the south of England. Targets now included not just the hunting fraternity and the vivisection industry, but the firearm lobby, chicken breeders, and, most hated of all, the firms that specifically bred animals for the laboratory. In August, another of these establishments, OLAC, was attacked.

At this point Lee and Goodman's rather Bonnie and Clyde-like run of good luck came to an end. Once again, they made the mistake of returning to the scene of a previous crime. This time, they decided to have second go at the animal breeding firm in Bicester they had attacked just two days earlier: but the company, OLAC, were prepared, and, spotted by a security guard, the pair of them were promptly arrested and bundled off to Oxford prison. The Crown Court trial that followed gave the Band of Mercy a fresh burst of publicity. Lee and Goodman were given the status of martyrs: just as the Angry Brigade had been transformed into the heroic sounding 'Stoke Newington Eight', so Ronnie and Cliff were canonized as the 'Bicester Two'.

This was the first big animal rights trial: its significance to the movement lay in the broad measure of sympathy that the two defendants managed to attract. There were daily demonstrations outside the Court, with Ronnie Lee's MP, the Free Church minister Ivor Clemitson taking a prominent part. Support came from even more unusual quarters. 'Many would sympathize with their action,' read a letter to the *Daily Telegraph*, 'against the utterly diabolical and very largely unnecessary form of cruelty involved in animal experimentation.' Lee and Goodman were close to heroes. 'These young men, while defying the law, showed great courage, and the sentences of three years' imprisonment seems unrealistic and harsh. Had they beaten up a policeman they would doubtless have received suspended sentences . . .' Though kindly meant, this was something of a back-handed remark for a convinced anarchist like Lee.

But if the case gave the cause a large dose of the much needed oxygen of publicity, it also revealed the absurd clumsiness behind the Band of Mercy's operations. Quite apart from returning to the scenes of earlier crimes, the activists lacked the most basic level of criminal cunning. When they were caught on the premises at OLAC, Lee and Goodman had left their car parked openly just round the corner: in the back were more of the materials they were using to start fires, bundles of sticks wraped up in old newspaper. The sticks had been chopped from Lee's back garden fence, which now boasted a line of fresh stumps: not the toughest forensic case the local police had had to construct. Nonetheless, as the *Telegraph* reader had noted with disgust, the affair was viewed by the Judge as very far from a laughing matter. Indeed he talked solemnly about the 'breakdown of law and order as we know it', and sent the pair down for three years each.

When the sentences were announced in court, the Band of Mercy's pacifist image suffered something of a set-back, as scuffles, jeering and shouting broke out in the public gallery. Someone tried to set off a smoke bomb and in the mêlée Cliff Goodman gave one of the prison officers a sharp kick on the shin. Soon afterwards, Lee and Goodman were split up, Lee being sent to Winchester prison, Goodman staying in Oxford. Both, after that initial burst of ill-will, seem to have got on well with both the prison staff and their fellow cons, who were somewhat bemused by them since they clearly fitted no hitherto recognizable criminal type. 'The prisoners overall,' said Ronnie later, 'were either vaguely or very sympathetic to what the Band of Mercy had done.' Lee himself, keen to keep the publicity bandwagon rolling, soon went on a hunger strike to demand a vegan diet and clothing not derived from animals. These issues later broadened to include ill-defined demands about Porton Down, the government's chemical and biological warfare research station. The hunger strike came to an end when Lee realized, he told friends, that his own actions were getting more publicity than Porton Down itself. So for the next twelve months he settled down to the rather less glamorous occupation of sewing mailbags, while the authorities acceded to his demands for a vegan diet.

Cliff Goodman and Ronnie Lee served only a third of their respective sentences, being released on parole in spring 1976. The experience had affected them both deeply but in profoundly different ways. Lee's determination, his sense of mission and his conviction that there was wide public support for his methods had all been strengthened. He talked rather dramatically about the need to suffer as the animals suffered; it was a form of solidarity. More than anything else, he had seen the value of widespread national publicity: a year inside had been a small price to pay, but now the movement was going to have to sharpen up, become more professional. It had to become a liberation movement, a revolutionary organization that would learn from the experiences of others.

Cliff Goodman came out with just one thought in mind: he didn't want to go back. For him it was the effective end of his life as an animal rights revolutionary. From now on it was going to be picketing, letter writing, and demonstrations, staying strictly on the right side of the law. He still respected the sincerity of Ronnie's beliefs, but now felt that he was a 'dangerous fanatic', had tunnel vision and was too easily prepared to condone violence. Today he regards the Animal Liberation Front as a dangerous and tactically self-defeating organization: 'quite frankly, it's terrorism now'. When he was released from Oxford prison, Goodman decided to turn informer; he passed on information to the police about the use of radios and wavelengths by fellow activists, thereby earning the much-despised status of the movement's first 'grass'. Unlike later informers, Goodman was left alone by his former comrades, a fact that Rorke Garfield felt showed the movement in a rather charitable light: 'in any other war but this one, he'd have been blown away. This is the only movement that doesn't neutralize its informers.'

Cliff Goodman's serious second thoughts were not shared by the vast majority of those who had got involved in animal rights. The trial of the 'Bicester Two' had two important long-term consequences for the movement. It legitimized violence as a tactic for a large number of activists, and it began to elicit ideological support for law-breaking from all sorts of hitherto respectable sources. Young activists who now wanted to take up the cause of animals came equipped with all the semi-digested revolutionary baggage of the late sixties; for them, unlike their elders, there seemed to be little argument about means and ends. But their elders, too, looked at what the Band of Mercy had done in a few short months, and were forced to compare and contrast the results with the long and hitherto ineffective campaign by law-abiding organizations against vivisection and factory farming. The *Anti-Vivisection Times*, the journal of the British Union for the Abolition of Vivisection, voiced these feelings in its issue of April 1975: 'The history of tyranny alone indicates that its downfall is almost inevitably the result of direct action. The history of the anti-vivisection movement is in itself an instance of a century-long fight against a tyranny imposed on our fellow creatures. It is a long and miserable history of millions of pounds having been expended on dozens of abortive campaigns to change laws which, it seems, have somehow and paradoxically to be respected because they are laws ...' Readers could draw their own conclusions.

Ronnie Lee emerged from Winchester prison the undisputed leader of the movement. The Band of Mercy no longer existed, most of the handful of activists having turned their energies into something called Stop Cruel Experiments: in effect this was just the Lee/Goodman defence and publicity campaign. By Lee's release in the spring of 1976, there had formed a core of about thirty animal rights activists who were prepared to develop the tactics used by the Band of Mercy, and they looked to Ronnie as their mentor. 'Thirty people,' Lee wrote later, 'that had seen direct action as the spearhead of the campaign and had been motivated by the Band of Mercy – its activities, its philosophy, and success.' And thus the Animal Liberation Front was formed.

The group's new name, devoid of all remnants of sentiment, signalled a self-conscious attempt to shift the issue of animal rights into a state of quasi-revolutionary politics. 'We saw the situation as a guerilla campaign,' wrote Lee, 'and those participating in it were very much in the front line.' Direct action was to be stepped up, and for the first time animals were to be 'liberated' from their cages in the laboratories and factory farms. Within a few weeks, the ALF struck for the first time, wrecking packing cases at a Margate firm supplying laboratory

animals. Shortly afterwards, they broke in to a breeder's premises in Salisbury, and 'rescued' large numbers of guinea pigs in
the back of a car; making their getaway, the ALF commando
were stopped by the police, curious about this strange bunch of
people driving apparently aimlessly in the early hours of the
morning. Failing to spot the mass of writhing rodents in the
back, the forces of law and order let them get on their way. Not
long afterwards the breeder closed down, fed up with the
constant pressure.

Direct action had come a long way since the hunt saboteurs
of the sixties. By summer 1976, the Animal Liberation Front
was fully established. As yet it was the mere embryo of what it
would become over the next ten years, but its ideology and its
tactics were understood by every one of that initial core of
thirty activists. The question that must have worried the fainthearted was whether they had both the persistence and the
public support to make a rather more lasting impression than
the short-lived and all too easily crushed Angry Brigade; after
the trial and conviction of the Stoke Newington Eight, revolutionary anarchism had returned once more to the street corner
sale of unsellable newspapers, and the comfortable plotting of
obscure groupuscles in the upstairs rooms of public houses.
Would the same fate await animal liberation? The answer was
no, thanks to two crucial factors. The first was the warm
groundswell of public sympathy for anyone vaguely involved
in trying to better the lot of animals, a broad spectrum of
opinion taking in old ladies in Hove, as well as highly respectable figures on the national committees of well-established
charities. The success, at the same time, of the field sports
lobby in thwarting the Labour Government's anti-hare coursing
Bill in the House of Lords had disabused many in what had
been disparagingly written off as 'the little old lady lobby' of
any faith in democracy.

The second factor was the highly convenient arrival of a body
of written theory that gave intellectual respectability and
backbone to the movement. So far, this had been a revolution
without its Marx: but in 1976, the year that Ronnie Lee and
Cliff Goodman were returned to the outside world, the animals'
Das Kapital was published in England. *Animal Liberation*,
written by an Australian philosopher named Peter Singer
(1975), was to have a profound effect in spreading and legitim-

izing the ideas that Lee and Goodman had incoherently pursued. And in the book's appendix there was further comfort to be found: among the organizations given the Australian academic's unqualified approval was an organization called the ALF.

CHAPTER THREE

Why should the law refuse its
protection to any sensitive being? The
time will come when humanity will
extend its mantle over everything
which breathes . . .

Jeremy Bentham, *Principles of Penal Law*

Human decency, cynics would say, has made more progress in theory than reality in the course of the twentieth century. We have the notion of human rights, and at the same time their most conspicuously savage and efficient abuse in the service of genocide. Nonetheless, human beings have at least begun to recognize the enormous scope of the moral argument for mutual respect, across differences of class, colour, culture and sex. The idea of 'human rights' is universally understood if not respected. And we have invented a potent terminology to deal with our abuse of each other – 'racism' and 'sexism', even 'ageism'. Now there is 'speciesism'.

Speciesism is – even those who use it regularly agree – an ugly word; it hardly trips off the tongue. But it neatly encapsulates the radical shift in thinking that marks the departure from traditional concepts of animal welfare and the arrival of the idea of animal 'rights'. Speciesism is the exploitation of one species by another, more specifically the use and abuse of the animal kingdom by mankind for pleasure, nourishment and latterly medical advance. I have never heard the term used to describe the cat world's relationship with the rodent, nor the wolf's with the lamb, but we will come to that particular anomaly later. The significance of the theory of 'speciesism' is that it argues that animals have a set of rights parallel and equivalent to those of humans; that those rights cannot be defended by animals themselves, and that therefore human animals, recognizing their clear moral duty, must take on the responsibility. Ultimately, we have here an argument and a moral philosophy that can be deployed in defence of terrorism;

the justification for acts of violence in pursuit of the greater good.

Animal rights activists like to draw parallels between animal abuse and slavery, and it is certainly true that the first stirrings of conscience about our treatment of animals coincided with the movement to abolish slavery. William Wilberforce was a founder member of the RSPCA, itself formed to police the first Parliamentary Act to mitigate the ill-treatment of domestic animals: not cats and dogs, incidentally, but horses and farm animals. Some sixty years earlier, in 1780, the philosopher Jeremy Bentham (no vegetarian in spite of it) had first articulated the humane and logical defence of decency towards animals: 'The question is not "can they reason?" nor "can they talk?" but "can they suffer?"' The advance of animal welfare in nineteenth-century Britain was based on the idea that all unnecessary suffering should be curtailed, and the granting of a Royal Charter to the RSPCA in 1840 set the seal of official approval on a movement that had attracted derision and contempt from politicians and writers. The publication of Darwin's ideas in *The Descent of Man* struck a severe blow at the idea that somehow human beings were totally removed from and superior to the animal kingdom; far from being first cousin to the gods, man was merely an ape with ambition.

In the meantime, the societies set up to defend the animals proliferated at a quite extraordinary rate; the Society for the Protection of Animals Liable to Vivisection, the London Anti-Vivisection Society, the World League Against Vivisection, the Scottish Society for the Total Suppression of Vivisection, the Friends Animal Welfare and Anti-Vivisection Society. And still they spawned; the Society for the Protection of Animals in North Africa, the Dumb Friends League, the Performing and Captive Animals Defence League, the Feline Defence League, and the Society for United Prayer for the Prevention of Cruelty to Animals Especially with Regard to the Practice of Vivisection. They all cared about the animals: the trouble was the humans who ran them didn't much care for each other, so splinter groups constantly broke off and acrimonious feuds were pursued. As we shall see later, inter-society feuding became a perennial pastime in the world of animal welfare.

But whatever their differences (to the outsider often arcane in the extreme) and despite the regular clashes of ego and personality that characterized the movements, the animal welfare societies broadly shared the same view of the animal kingdom. Their founders and volunteer workers were fond of the creatures whose interests they protected, they loved animals and thought that humankind had a simple duty not to be unnecessarily cruel. Often their motivation was an extension of Christian charity to those less fortunate than themselves; for example, one of the earliest societies was the Quaker-run Friends Anti-Vivisection Society, followed later by the Catholic Study Circle for Animal Welfare and the Anglican Society for the Welfare of Animals. The traditional welfarists might admit to preferring their pets to other human beings (who had the awkward capacity to answer back) but theirs was a fundamentally decent crusade, summed up by one eloquently sentimental veteran. 'The road we have trod with the beasts,' wrote Doris Rybot in *It Began Before Noah*, 'is a long road, a bloody road, and the end of vileness is not yet in sight. For all that, it is a road lit always by the few in every generation who have loved, marvelled, cared and made true friendships with the beasts.'

However, love and friendship with the beasts has nothing to do with animal rights. The animal rights activist would regard such language as mere speciesist sentiment; pure altruism has taken the place of cosy affection. What happened, in the space of five or six years – in effect the first half of the 1970s – was an ideological revolution in the way thoughtful, and often non-animal-loving humans viewed the rest of the animal world.

To understand how different the animal rights movement is from what went before, take these introductory remarks from the book that, more than any other, has formed the ideological framework of the new movement. In his preface to *Animal Liberation*, Peter Singer tells us about a tea-time visit to a friend who cared for animals. When he and his wife arrive, they are buttonholed by another guest, someone else who has written about animals. '"I do love animals," she began, "I have a dog and two cats, and do you know they get on together wonderfully well. Do you know Mrs Scott? She runs a little hospital for sick pets . . ."' Dr Singer is not bored, he is not mildly irritated at this chatter. He is morally affronted.

'We told her we didn't own any pets. She looked a little surprised, and took a bite of her sandwich' (already noted with disapproval by Singer as filled with ham). But surely Dr Singer was interested in animals, wasn't he? 'We tried to explain that we were interested in the prevention of suffering and misery; that we were opposed to arbitrary discrimination; that we thought it wrong to inflict needless suffering on another being, even if that being were not a member of our own species; and that we believed animals were ruthlessly and cruelly exploited by humans, and we wanted this changed.' Dr Singer and his wife were 'not especially "interested in" animals'. They didn't 'love' animals. They simply wanted them treated as the independent 'sentient' beings they are.

Dr Singer does not record whether or not the ham sandwich was finished. He is too busy admonishing the reader. 'This book is not about pets. It is not likely to be comfortable reading for those who think that love for animals involves no more than stroking a cat or feeding the birds . . . It is intended rather for people who are concerned about ending oppression and exploitation wherever they occur.'

The concept that animals have a set of 'rights' is a specific development in the twentieth-century search for a range of ethics within which we can decently exist. For Dr Singer and his fellow theoreticians in the movement, animal rights exist as equal and parallel to, say, the rights of blacks and women. What is on the agenda now is a political, economic and social struggle – with, of course, one major difference. Unlike women and blacks, the animals cannot achieve liberation on their own: they are reliant on humankind, or rather that small body of altruistic human animals who are prepared to act upon the clear moral imperative. On this point, Dr Singer waxes quite lyrical: 'Animal Liberation will require greater altruism on the part of human beings than any other liberation movement.' Not least, he says, because most of us are too selfish or lazy to give up our meat-eating, leather-wearing habits.

For the ideologues of animal rights, the language of this most esoteric of liberation struggles is the language of full-blooded revolution. In its sense of moral purity, its elevated positioning of the enlightened few, its appeal is clear. It is constantly echoed in the conversations of those who form the leadership of the ALF. Tim Daley, once referred to by police as the Front's 'commander-in-chief', says 'you don't have to like animals to be in the movement: you have to be angry about the injustice of animals being abused in the laboratories and in the hunting field. You don't actually have to like the individual creatures to be against injustice.' One of his colleagues, John Beggs, a law student, openly dislikes animals: he wouldn't stay at Daley's flat for the weekend if 'that bloody dog' was there. Daley understood that: it was what made the movement different from, and superior to, all the others. He liked to draw comparisons with the Irish Republican movement: but the point about the animal liberationists was that, in the end, when they'd finally won, they would have got nothing out of the struggle for themselves. 'When we get, or when the animals get what we are aiming for them to get, it doesn't benefit us at all, and I think that is the difference. Animal rights is a very unselfish movement.'

These were thoughts heard again down at the anarchists' squat in Brighton. Altruism amongst the squalor. 'I'm not an animal lover,' came the contemptuous retort from lanky Steve to the suggestion that the household didn't quite fit in with most people's ideas of what English animal lovers looked like. That was all sentimental, patronizing rubbish. 'I've got a lot of respect for living creatures and stuff like that, but I don't love animals; in fact I get very pissed off with them when they wake me up early in the morning.' So why were they bothering with the animals' cause, and what kind of world were they fighting for? The truth was, they were looking for a way back to the garden of Eden, or rather, their own semi-digested and imagined view of what the garden of Eden might have felt like. 'I believe that human beings have gone so far that we're, like, well away from the system of nature . . . sort of thing . . . everything's got its place and its space in nature, and we're the only one [species] out of all the animals which is really totally turning that upside down and taking what we can out of it, and not giving a toss about how we achieve it and what the effects of it are.' This was Mick, a lank-haired anarchist, older than the rest, less punky, more die-hard hippy: the language was gentle, monotonous, a litany of naïve, decent received ideas. None of the anarchists had read Singer; but they all had to hand a simplistic precis of his moral view of the world.

It was a curious cocktail of ideas because, in addition, there were elements of millenarian philosophy. Things were now so bad, humanity set on such an evil destructive course, that violence was inevitable: it had a cleansing quality about it. 'We're either going to win the war, or the human race is going to be exterminated in the attempt, because the human race at the moment is on the brink . . . you've got pollution of the air, pollution of the sea, pollution of the land, animals being murdered, people not caring about other people, so how can a world like that carry on going on? It just can't.' Mick's fellow humanity faced a stark choice. 'You either change for the better or you die not changing.' It was entirely understandable that bombs were being placed and scientists' lives threatened. This was a righteous anger, and the struggle for animal liberation no less a cause than the survival of the planet.

It is virtually inconceivable that a person should become involved in the animal rights movement and not be vegetarian. That is the bottom line. It is much more likely that they will be a vegan, or even a fruitarian. This is the most extreme form of vegetarianism, based on the belief that human beings should only consume the fallen fruit of trees and plants, and that less rigorously scrupulous diets are an assault on a vibrant, living universe. It is, by all accounts, a tough régime to adhere to, and potentially damaging unless supplemented by extra doses of vitamins and minerals. For many activists there is an appealing asceticism about such a rigid set of restrictions, further visible evidence of the wholehearted altruism of the movement. In prison, animal rights activists will maintain their vegan and fruitarian diets in conditions of extra discomfort, earning the somewhat bemused respect of their fellow cons. At the same time, one of the more endearing characteristics of many 'foot-soldiers' in the movement is the habitual confession of mortal weakness over the ideologically unsound wearing of leather shoes and jackets.

For ideologues like Peter Singer, becoming a vegetarian is much more than taking a personal decision to abandon the cruelty inherent in using animals for food. It involves the dismissal of the factory farmers and 'agribusiness' conglomorates as people beyond the moral pale. Farmers, Singer tells us, 'do not need our approval. They need our money.' In order, that is, to carry on their disgusting business. 'The purchase of the corpses of the animals they rear is the only support the factory farmers ask from the public.' These are cynical, manipulative, corporate giants trading shamelessly on human ignorance and weakness. Singer works himself into a frenzy of disgust over the 'flesh' that 'taints our meals'. 'Disguise it as we may, the fact remains that the centrepiece of our dinner has come to us from the slaughterhouse, dripping blood. Untreated and unrefrigerated, it soon begins to putrefy and stink.' Not unlike, less rigorous souls might argue, three-week-old courgettes, or the strange consistency of tomatoes lurking half-forgotten in the salad drawer.

The idea of 'speciesism' informs every area taken on by the animal rights movement. To use animals for food, for clothing, for sport, or for medical research is morally indefensible. Retaliation, in forms both violent and non-violent, is required from those human animals who clearly perceive the injustices perpetrated by their own species. Critics of the movement, like Bernard Williams, formerly Professor of Philosophy at Cambridge, find this theoretical base seriously flawed. Human suffering is qualitatively more important than animal suffering, he argues. This is not to say that we should treat lesser species without any consideration at all. 'Are there any moral limits to how we should treat animals? The answer to that is yes, of course, you can't just, say, light the fire with an animal, and in that sense animals have rights not to be mistreated.' But there are limits to the impartiality of the human perspective on the world. 'The ugly word "speciesism" is supposed to make this attitude sound like racism – but the important point is this. The question that we are all trying to answer – the animal liberationists and myself – is how other animals should be treated; but that isn't the question with regard to race. Anybody, a white person for instance, who thought that the only question was how black people should be treated is already a racist.' For Dr Williams, it is clear that racism and sexism are prejudices against other, equal members of our own species, fellow human beings. The analogy with other animals of different and lesser species is therefore manifestly false.

But what angers opponents of the movement more than anything else is the introduction of comparisons with human genocide. Speaking with disgust of a prominent scientist who experiments on primates, one leading figure in the ALF told me that he was 'a very cruel, heartless man'. It was unfortunate that a bomb placed underneath his car had failed to go off. It was irrelevant that the man's work with animals was directed towards a cure for human epilepsy. In the opinion of the ALF, vivisectors were no better than the Nazis who ran the death camps. 'I can find no difference at all,' I was informed, in the measured tone of one instructing a child in the absurdly obvious, 'between monkeys being tortured in laboratories, and a Jew in Dachau or Auschwitz being tortured in the Second World War. One is human, and one is a monkey, but they both feel the same amount of pain, and they both shouldn't be there, being exploited by a more powerful being.'

For Bernard Williams, the remark is both absurd, and in some ways obscene. 'That is, to compare these practices [vivisection] to the greatest and most hideous crime of modern, and perhaps any times.' The facile comparison tells us more about the liberationist than the object of his struggle. 'One of the things shown by some – though not all – of the people who take the most extreme views on animals is that the only animal they appear really to loathe is humanity. And I think that it is partly a form of self-hate, to which humanity is indeed disposed.' More cynically, Dr Williams throws in the fact that, in the case of animal rights, the beneficiaries can't answer back, unlike the objects of previous generations of do-goodery. 'People who've been nice to the poor suddenly find that the poor aren't as grateful as they should be; people who've been helping the blacks suddenly find that the blacks actually prefer to help themselves, thank you very much. Animals have a wonderful advantage for do-gooding causes: they can't protest about the help they're being given.'

More than food, fur or sport, vivisection is the issue where both the ethical and the real, petrol bomb, war has become most explosive. Confronted by not just threats of violence but 'viable' devices planted under their cars and round-the-clock police protection, scientists have either been frightened off, or been compelled to defend vigorously the moral basis of their work. Their argument is not just that the human species is more important than other species, and that therefore human suffering more serious; it is that, by any sound utilitarian yardstick, vivisection has lessened both human and animal suffering far more than it has caused suffering to its immediate victims. 'You balance your profits against your losses, and you set any disadvantages which have been suffered by animals used in the experiments against the increase in human welfare that results,' is the way Dr Brian Meldrum puts it. As someone whose research involves the use of primates, Dr Meldrum has become one of the most celebrated hate-figures in the activists' pantheon of animal abuse. Their attentions have merely served to concentrate Dr Meldrum's mind on the argument. 'Take the case of polio, where up to the mid 1950s there were in North America and Europe at least thirty thousand patients a year, paralysed or dying from the disease; and then, from experiments on primates, a polio vaccine was developed, and as a result of that, one can say that there are a million people alive and well today who would otherwise have been dead or paralysed.' Put at its bluntest, the lives of some thirty thousand monkeys were justifiably sacrificed for the healthy survival of those million human beings.

This is territory as much governed by personal experience as simple logic. Anyone who has a friend or relative, or more potently a child, struck down by polio is going to see the argument in fairly stark terms. But emotion is as much the fuel of the activists as any of the coldly detached ideology of philosophers like Peter Singer. Tim Daley was haunted by the idea of animals suffering. Not just cuddly or anthropomorphic creatures like dogs or monkeys, but less obviously appealing species like rats and other members of the rodent family. Daley's flat was stacked with cages full of these beasts, rescued (stolen, the scientists would argue) from laboratories all over the country. He had nightmares about vivisection, and woke up sweating in a panic about the mass murder he sensed was being allowed to continue unabated. He would spend his lunch hours away from the office where he sold advertising space in a local newspaper, just walking round laboratories surveying the horror, and planning future actions. In his neat three-piece suit, he had no problem getting access: Daley was no one's cartoon image of the fanatical animal liberationist. Yet his conversion to the cause had been as profound an emotional experience as any religious rite of passage.

One evening he had watched a BBC documentary called 'Rabbits Don't Cry'. It was a straightforwardly anti-vivisection film, full of upsetting images. From being a rather lukewarm and utterly conventional English dog-lover, Tim Daley became a warrior on the side of the weak, the helpless and the violated. 'I remember sitting there for the forty minutes, dumbstruck. I was watching these dreadful scenes of rabbits with shampoo in their eyes, dogs with weeping sores in tiny cages, and I just couldn't believe it. I was just flabbergasted that that was going on in British laboratories, and I realized then that I would really have to do something about it for the rest of my life.' In forty minutes, everything had changed. A career as a commercial pilot went out of the window; money, job, status, all seemed irrelevant. 'It's like you suddenly find a meaning as to why you're here. When you get up in the morning you think "right, I've got to do as much as I can today in the time available to help animals".' All his old friends had to go – he no longer had time for them; even the work he took up on the local paper seemed like a barely supportable distraction from the real task at hand, the liberation of all oppressed species everywhere.

Breaking the law became inevitable but it didn't really matter because it wasn't the real law. 'It might sound corny, but I don't believe I am actually breaking the moral law. It's purely a legal law, and I'm sure in years to come people will realize that what we are doing is right . . . you have to break the law to change the law.' There were the precedents of slavery, and, inevitably, the concentration camps. There was the example of the Republican cause in Ireland, with which Daley sympathized. 'I can see people in the animal rights movement noting what they've achieved, and going the same way: they haven't got anywhere through legal peaceful means, and I can see an increasing number of people becoming so frustrated and angry that they will go into the armed struggle. At the moment, millions are dying on one side, and no one is dying on the other side. I mean, if an animal is lying on a laboratory table about to have shampoo or weedkiller rammed down its throat and electrodes placed into its head, it's not going to hand out a leaflet, it's not going to go on a demo or a march, it's not even going to smash the place up. If it could, it would kill the vivisector, because it's kill or be killed.'

For Tim Daley and comrades in the movement the rationale behind the experimentation on animals was barely worth discussing. Vivisectors were torturers, motivated by a combination of sadism and material greed. Examples like the polio vaccine were spurious: scientists had come up with alternative methods of research, but they had either been suppressed by the drug companies because they were too expensive, or had been ignored because they didn't appeal to the bloodthirsty instincts of the vivisectors. The issue was simple: this was war and the final outcome inevitable. 'Once the shooting and the bombings actually start,' Daley said, 'they'll be leaving animal research in droves.'

These comments are the common currency of the extreme end of the animal rights movement; they are to be heard in the rank and file chanting on ostensibly peaceful demonstrations, and inform the heated discussions of local animal rights groups and alliances. They are not the preserve of the young and the anarchist, either. Down in Brighton, Kenneth and Christine Harrold sat on neat chintzy sofas and talked calmly about a final solution for vivisecting scientists. They should all die, said Mrs Harrold, in the same way the animals died that were at their mercy: 'They should have the same treatment.' Earlier, the Harrolds had voiced their support for a National Front march against Jewish and Muslim ritual slaughter: the cause was right, the politics irrelevant.

Most activists will use the terminology invented by the theoreticians of animal liberation, without necessarily having read the books. I met many leading lights in the ALF who, like Tim Daley, were capable of weaving passionate and eloquent arguments on behalf of the oppressed species, yet who had hardly bothered with the many texts that had been published from the early 1970s onwards. Writers like Peter Singer have had a profound effect on determining the path taken by the animal rights movement, and yet – in contrast, say, to revolutionary socialism – there has been a marked preference for action as opposed to boning up on correct theory. The ideas behind the notion of 'speciesism' could, after all, be summarized on the back of an envelope. The theoreticians themselves came from a variety of backgrounds, though usually their roots lay either in academic philosophy or in the fringe politics that blossomed in the years after 1968. Some, like Richard Ryder, a respected clinical psychologist, wrote up their ideas on the basis of first-hand experience. He had seen for himself what went on in the laboratory, and found no excuses in the fact that humanity was 'different' from the rest of the animal kingdom. 'When did "difference" justify a moral prejudice?' he asked, as co-formulator (with Singer) of the new sin of speciesism. Besides, Ryder argued, vivisection was only justified in the pursuit of knowledge and 'who can believe today that knowledge is invariably a good thing?' Suspicion of material 'progress' was built into the theoretical dogma of the movement, and with it a harking back to a simpler, more congenial golden age when man had been at one with the rest of creation.

This distinctly unscientific and touchingly romantic theme emerged most obviously when the question of the natural savagery of other species was raised, usually by voices hostile to the movement. If humanity had a pretty poor track record, the rest of nature seemed a great deal worse: big insects ate little insects (indeed, couldn't survive without eating them), foxes ate chickens, cats tortured mice before murdering them for sport as cheerfully as any human hunt, and if the wolf lay down with the sheep, it was only with the latter safely digested inside his stomach. None of this bothered the liberationists too much. Peter Singer simply asserted that the savagery of the animal kingdom had been exaggerated over the years. 'The notorious wolf, for instance, villain of so many folk tales, has been shown by the careful investigation of zoologists in the wild to be a highly social animal, a faithful and affectionate spouse, a devoted parent and a loyal member of the pack.' At which point it may well be useful to point out that Hitler was pretty well devoted to Eva Braun, fond of children, and, of course, a strict vegetarian. Singer goes on to argue that, even if they do go in for killing, other animals have some kind of moral entitlement: because it is the only way they can find food. Human beings are far worse, not just because we know there are viable alternatives to meat but because we alone as a species kill for sport. This is a wonderfully positive view of nature, curiously innocent of rat-hunting terriers and mouse-chasing felines. And only man is vile.

Time and again, both the movement's ideologues and its footsoldiers confess the entirely human desire to return to a Garden of Eden, where man can live in a state of grace with the animals. A world in which nature is uncontained, and human society de-industrialized. It is a vision that is never quite precisely defined, conjuring up both images of a William Morris-style pseudomedievalism, and seventeenth-century radical rural collectives. A kind of sentimental pastoralism informs a great deal of liberationist literature, from the ALF's various publications to the National Front's new 'green' campaign, targeted at the idealistic young. England's green and pleasant land, runs the common theme, is polluted by self-seeking big business; its animals tortured by big (and usually foreign owned) agribusiness; and if not by the factory farmers, then by callous scientists in the pay of unscrupulous drug companies. As Bernard Williams noted, if liberationists have a low view of any species, it is always their own.

That, certainly, was the view of Ronnie Lee. The cause was too important to bother with democracy: indeed, the ALF's founder and guiding force was openly contemptuous of popular opinion. 'My main aim isn't to toady to the public. What we're trying to do is to actually sabotage the industries of animal abuse.' What happened to the people, the individuals, who got in the way of the ALF's 'actions' was no concern of his. 'I'm not bothered about people being unemployed when animals are being tortured all over the place ... I don't care how many people I put out of work if I can save animals from suffering.' The same low view of the rest of humanity is to be found in the ALF Supporter's Group bulletins, and in the bitter expressions of the Front's rank and file membership. 'The "public", slurping down their roasted chicken,' warns Bulletin Number Seven, 'are not going to give up their pleasures without a struggle.' It wasn't just the factory farmer who was the enemy, it was the craven, greedy and callous customer as well. 'Ben', the ALF cell member who had helped to plan the notorious Mars Bar poison hoax, had no sympathy for innocent members of the public, terrified at the thought that they might have eaten contaminated bars. 'We may have frightened a few people – but how many of those people live utterly selfish lives ... they buy their meat in packaged little pieces, they don't want to know where it comes from.'

And so, just as certain white zealots for anti-racism awareness had begun to assume inherent racial guilt in people of their own colour, so the animal rights activists took a dim view of their own species. Yet the theoretical basis of animal rights (as opposed to welfare) rapidly gained ground with organizations beyond the ALF and the radical new animal rights alliances that were springing up by the late 1970s. Animal liberation became a serious issue for both the far left and right, featuring in both *National Front News* and *Marxism Today*. Its appeal to the young was clear; like other 'green' issues, it had the sort of emotional strength to pull in people who were otherwise indifferent to or disenchanted by conventional politics. It was an issue that lent weight and respectability to otherwise questionable causes. When *National Front News* asked the celebrated Swiss author and anti-vivisectionist Hans Ruesch (author of *The Naked Empress* and *Slaughter of the Innocent*) for an interview, he was happy to oblige. When the British Union for the Abolition of Vivisection wrote to him, alerting him to the nature of the publication, he had no regrets: the issue of animals was too important to worry about the conventional political spectrum. For the left, too, animal rights joined issues of race and gender as part of the rainbow of right-on causes. It didn't seem too difficult to develop a Marxist critique of speciesism: true, the animals couldn't develop class consciousness and organize against the boss species, but the human proletariat could do that for them. As Tim Daley said, this was just about the most altruistic movement ever. What's more, its attraction to both left and right was the breadth of its appeal. As Jolyon Jenkins wrote in the *New Statesman*, 'animal liberation is arguably *the* youth movement of the eighties. Magazines as diverse as *Just Seventeen* and *Class War* discuss it, and a host of rock stars and youth cult figures have announced that they have become vegetarians for moral reasons.' It was a large and inviting market.

By the mid 1980s, the theory of animal rights had become so well established as part of the right-on view of the world, that local councils in London, like Ealing and Hackney, were appointing 'animal rights officers', who, funded by the often confused ratepayers, would develop appropriate and relevant animal rights policies. At the same time, the number of different organizations and committees established to defend animal rights proliferated at a rate unmatched since the Victorian explosion of societies devoted to animal welfare; by mid decade there were more than six hundred in existence – divided inevitably and bitterly on every conceivable issue: the question of violence against humans, the question of violence against property, the question of relations and alliances with fascists, communists, and anarchists; the question of diet – vegetarian, vegan, or fruitarian. The question of what to wear, what to sit on, what transport to use. Most human of all – in the non-speciesist sense – there was the burning question of pets. The ideologues argued that to have a pet was to treat a lesser species with patronizing contempt; the more ascetic breed of activists referred to domestic animals as 'political prisoners'. This was not said as a joke. The trouble was, it wasn't very easy being ideologically correct if you actually rather liked animals, indeed enjoyed having them around and looking after them.

Being soppy about your pet, however, was a serious lapse in commitment. When the *Guardian*'s Polly Toynbee wanted to find out more about the movement in 1985, the ALF set up a meeting with one of their press officers, Vivian Smith, on this occasion taking 'Emma Peel' as her glamorous *nom de guerre*.

She had grown up in prosperous, suburban Surrey, she told the *Guardian*, her family had been 'animal-loving', her father a dog breeder. 'Emma' had been a kennel maid, she'd joined the local pony club and mucked out stables; but such sentimental affection for dumb friends was now a thing of the past. Converted to the cause by a film about the horrors of fox hunting, 'Emma' had become firstly a freelance terrorist, paint-strippering the local branch of Woolworths, and then joined the ALF. She was now, wrote Polly Toynbee, part of 'probably the most revolutionary movement the world has ever known – absolutist, impossibilist, bizarre'. The former kennel maid leant forward urgently: 'something has to stop the torture and the horror. We're growing and growing, and our demands will have to be met.' Two years later, Vivian Smith was convicted of criminal damage. She was gaoled for four years.

CHAPTER FOUR

Animal rights people find it very
difficult to keep their mouths shut.
John Beggs addressing the
Bournemouth branch of Animal Aid

The Brighton Animal Rights Group (BARG) met in the back
room of a rather grimy pub well off the seafront. A stranger
wandering into the bar by mistake would have had considerable
problems working out who these people were and what they
were up to. There was no obvious pattern of age, class or dress,
and they certainly weren't there for the booze: hands hesitantly
nurturing halves of bitter and lukewarm lemonade. Michael,
Steve and Felix were the most dramatic – black clad anarchists
from a local squat, with spiky mohicans and all the sub-
masonic symbolism of their inclination. They were to be seen
down on the promenade selling publications like *Black Flag*,
Crowbar and the local anarchist broadsheet *Brighton Bomber*.
Looking deliberately fearsome and anti-social, they actually
spoke in quiet monotones, dealing with more conventional
members of the group with an almost exaggerated politeness.
These included Dorothy Brooke, a retired civil servant and
moving force behind BARG, and a small group of RSPCA
supporters of varying degrees of cord and tweed respectability.
In a corner sat a woman of about sixty with faded, untidy
blonde hair and a distant expression on her face. This was Rena
Collins, once (she told everyone) a 'dolly girl' of the sixties,
now wholly devoted to a personal crusade for the Christian
salvation of the animal kingdom. Rena was Brighton's own
local version of Brigitte Bardot.

Animal rights groups up and down the country looked much
like this gathering, meeting, as it happened, in the spring of
1986. It was impossible to keep a proper count of the number
of groups in existence at any one time: they flourished and
dissolved according to the enthusiasm and efforts of individuals. Today, there are probably more than six hundred in

existence, most formed around a regional centre or large sized town, but some also created to give expression to particular or esoteric developments in the movement. There were groups for Pagan Animal Rights as well as Christian Animal Rights, for students, socialists, libertarians, and, inevitably, anarchists ('RATS – an anarchist animal rights collective'); and, of course, there was 'Youth for Animal Rights', as well. The local groups were mainly loose federations of people who shared a concern for animals but who no longer felt that rattling collecting tins on behalf of the RSPCA or the PDSA was enough.

The groups had begun to form in the latter half of the seventies, largely as a result of the arrival of the theory that animals had 'rights' parallel and equal to those of humans; the implications of the new philosophy were rather more urgent than traditional and rather cosy notions of welfare. These were groups that were going to get things done, groups for activists who wanted more out of membership than demonstrations of de-infestation techniques and the annual charity social. This didn't mean they were necessarily going to break the law but they would mount vigils outside the local fur store; they would demonstrate and embarrass the circus when it came to town; and they would leaflet and petition the Saturday shopping crowds against the farm up the road that kept twenty thousand chickens in sinister 'concentration camp'-style battery sheds.

The new animal rights groups were like the earnest, whole-hearted discussion circles that formed around ideas of socialism at the beginning of the century. Ad hoc, loosely organized, they attracted a broad church, with punks and anarchists sitting with apparent ease alongside local bulwarks of the RSPCA. 'Really good boys' was how one middle-aged stalwart in BARG described the three rainbow-haired lads in black. She could hardly have been ignorant of the 'boys'' involvement in the local exploits of the ALF. For the movement, the arrival of these new groups played a crucial role: in the jargon of the right-on, they raised the consciousness of thousands of people who would never otherwise have contemplated lending their approval to the breaking of the law. Animal rights has not yet achieved the status of a genuine mass movement, but what the groups achieved was the transformation of Ronnie Lee and Cliff Goodman's esoteric and pitifully small band of liberation-ists from a marginal eccentricity to the driving force of the cause. To the new groups, Lee and Goodman were overnight heroes.

A group like BARG served as both umbrella and clearing house for the movement. Concern for animals over-rode differences of class and politics. Long-term members of the RSPCA found themselves almost subliminally radicalized by the experience of sharing a picket line at the local abattoir with a bunch of ALF activists and hunt saboteurs. Animal rights was a hard, confident and uncompromising issue and suddenly old-style animal lovers felt a new surge of adrenalin. Kenneth and Christine Harrold, back in England after years abroad, were delighted at the new hard edge; the no-nonsense talk they heard as they first tentatively went along to the BARG meetings seemed to suggest that at long last the cause of the animals was being taken seriously. 'What appeals to me,' said Mr Harrold, 'is that they are determined that things are going to change. They're doing something which stands out a mile as fighting for the animals, and against cruelty in a way that attracts public attention and gets in the press.' In their day, back in the thirties and forties, it had just been a matter of mending broken bones and rescuing stray cats; now people, especially this rather odd breed of young people, really seemed to be doing something positive.

It was through the Brighton Animal Rights Group that respectable and hitherto utterly law abiding people like the Harrolds for the first time began to question the legitimacy of the law; began to accept the need to support those who broke it. When, in 1985, two activists associated with the group were sent to jail for a total of four years at Winchester Crown Court, the BARG told the local press that the punishments were 'a disgrace'. Michael Nunn, an ex-butcher who had undergone a Damascan conversion to the cause, and Gordon Briant, an unemployed animal rights militant, had been caught breaking into an animal research centre in Hampshire; in the course of this raid the Director had been badly beaten up. It was a nasty incident that had seriously damaged the movement's reputation for avoiding violence against people (rather than property, which was always fair game). But to the BARG spokesperson Nunn and Briant were simply 'being used as scapegoats, and if society and the legal system think lengthy prison sentences are going to put us off, they are very much mistaken'. Rena Collins reserved her Christian goodwill for her former colleagues rather than their victims. The people who should be behind bars, she told the local paper, were the vivisectionists. The stiff sentences would only make the movement stronger still.

And certainly, six months later, sitting in on the meeting in the pub back room, it felt more like a session of a local Sinn Fein ward committee than anything as innocent as a bunch of people who all happened to care about animals. Gordon Briant and Mike Nunn had now been designated 'political' prisoners: BARG had arranged a visiting rota; their cases had been taken up by the national Animal Rights Prisoners' Campaign; visitors reported back to the meeting about the physical and mental well-being of the pair and the other members of the gang who had been gaoled. As long as they were given decent vegan fare, there was no problem; they had earned the respect of their fellow cons, it turned out, because they were seen to be paying a heavy personal price for the unselfish acts their consciences had forced them to carry out. A sense of reverence hung over the meeting: it would take more than gaol walls and prison bars to break their spirit.

These local groups also demonstrated how shared basic beliefs in the ideology of the movement mattered more than individual organizations. You would come across ALF activists who would also belong to radical campaigning groups like the British Union for the Abolition of Vivisection, and probably the RSPCA as well; hunt saboteurs, out at the weekends getting muddy and bloody in defence of the fox, would join the new national campaigning bodies like Animal Aid. Multi-organization membership was common. The most astute national campaigns made use of the huge and growing network of animal rights groups to build up their own recruitment. At BUAV headquarters in Islington there was a large chart listing groups all over the country, which was constantly updated; the Union kept in touch with the regions with its local 'contacts' and these more often than not were involved with or ran a group. The ALF, through the organizers of its local cells, kept a watch on the activities and membership of animal rights groups, campaigns and alliances. Impressionable young people who wrote to the paper about the horrors of hunting or vivisection (usually as the result of television coverage) were contacted and, if suitable, recruited.

This was a new kind of phenomenon, partly recognizable as a political movement, partly a kind of pressure group (with amoeboid tendencies to multiply) and partly a kind of religion as well. Its coherence should not be exaggerated. What had happened was that in a relatively short space of time a new and radically different way of looking at man's relationship with the animal kingdom had gained wide acceptance. Thousands, probably hundreds of thousands of people, a majority of them young and female, had a cause: they would join up to half a dozen different organizations to give it expression. And it tied in with so much else that was happening: the ecology movement, the new vegetarianism and the growing popularity of alternative medicine, with its atavistically anti-drug, anti-high tech view of the world. It also, of course, found a responsive echo in the hearts and minds of those who had turned to the various esoteric cults that came from the East. Semi-digested Buddhist theory was to be heard at meetings, along with anarchist rants and more or less unreconstructed hippy expressions of universal benevolence. The animal rights movement almost from the very beginning became an exotic cocktail of cultures distilled from two decades, topped by that most traditional of British elements, a concern for dumb animals.

When Ronnie Lee's original Band of Mercy metamorphosed into Animal Liberation Front, animal rights was still an issue in its infancy; few of those who didn't already come from a background in anarchism were prepared to countenance law breaking. Within the burgeoning animal rights groups such scruples rapidly became blurred. Yesterday's outrage became today's defensible tactic, in much the same way that the broad Republican movement would come to the rescue of the Provisional IRA. What was being done was not very nice, but what the opposition was doing was even less nice. Addressing the Bournemouth branch of the radical, but ostensibly law abiding pressure group Animal Aid, John Beggs, a charismatic activist well known on the circuit as a rousing speaker, raised the issue of the Animal Rights Militia – the group that had claimed responsibility for most of the bomb attacks on individuals. It was they who had placed the device under Peter Savage's car just a few miles down the coast. Had the ARM damaged the credibility of the movement, Beggs asked himself. His answer would have done credit to a Gerry Adams, because, of course, he wearily explained, the question was the wrong way round. The wrong people were in the dock (Beggs, remember, was training to be a solicitor). 'We really shouldn't be talking about the violence the Animal Rights Militia allegedly have caused, we should be talking about the violence that has been perpetrated against the animals!' This goes down well with another oddly assorted audience: no one stands up and even tentatively begins to question the idea of violence against fellow humans on behalf of animals. Sensing their approval, Beggs warms to his theme. 'The media like to say these vicious people (the ARM) are out attacking our good scientists . . . but what we're saying is that millions of animals are dying in the most terrible cruelty!'

Politicians (Thatcher especially) were shamefully hypocritical about violence anyway. 'All they ever talk about is the violence of the subversive or the radical group – they never talk about the violence being perpetrated by the state. Thatcher was willing to use violence in the Falklands, now Reagan's willing to use violence against the Nicaraguans . . . in Northern Ireland, when they shoot plastic bullets and kill children, that's violence!' All this has been delivered in a tone of rising, emphatic shrillness. The confession that rounds it off is carefully modulated, reasonable even. Owlish, gold-rimmed specs glinting in the dull church hall lights, Beggs admits that if and when a scientist is shot dead on his doorstep, he personally won't lose a lot of sleep. 'I'm not saying it's the right thing, but I couldn't really weep about it because I think it's almost inevitable.'

Within the movement there is an almost absurd degree of cross-referencing between individuals and organizations, partly a consequence of the sheer number of different bodies in existence. In Bournemouth, John Beggs was talking to the Animal Aid supporters as a national committee member of the British Union for the Abolition of Vivisection; but he was also one of the founders of the South East Animal Liberation League, the group responsible for the damage and violence which had led to nineteen people – including Mike Nunn and Gordon Briant – ending up in gaol; Beggs was also involved with Ronnie Lee and other leading activists like his close friend Tim Daley. The only difference between them was that, as he honestly admitted, Beggs didn't actually like animals. Cold logic had dragged him unwillingly into the cause; now he enjoyed his reputation as one of its most daredevil and inspiring leaders. He even had a glamorous girlfriend, Sally Miller, an ex-model, who was also doing time for the Hampshire raid.

Just how extensive cross-referencing could become, and how influential a small group of energetic and dedicated individuals could seem, was illustrated by taking a look at one local group, Oxford Animal Rights. OAR was probably best known to shoppers and students in the university town by its leafleting and petitioning campaigns. Its cheaply produced, mimeographed magazine featured appealing photographs of small monkeys in cages, and inside readers were asked to write to their MP to protest about the new Bill on vivisection that was slowly making its way through Parliament. There were to be demonstrations, a national week of action, leafleting of the town centre. All very legal, decent and unexceptionable. An appeal for Animal Aid featured on page three, and the only vague hint of stronger stuff came in an advert for a local group of hunt saboteurs, and they went out of their way to emphasize that they were strictly non-violent.

The magazine was largely the work of the two leading lights of OAR, Tim Phillips and Mandy Journeaux, both of whom devoted all their free time to animal rights. It was an occupation that involved them in activities far beyond the genteel decencies advertised by OAR. Phillips, a former bank clerk, also went under the name of Johnston, a double existence the point of which he never seemed quite able to explain. Much of his time was taken up as 'press officer' for a group calling itself the Central Animal Liberation League, a group of balaclava'd activists who regularly broke into university laboratories, and local farms to rescue animals. Phillips/Johnston took pride in the group's SAS-style precision. He enjoyed walking about clutching a walkie-talkie close to his mouth, eyes darting hither and thither in search of the unwelcome attentions of the law. He was proud that the CALL had never been caught, and he put it down to his strict, even punctilious attention to detail.

Phillips shared a dungeon-like basement in a Victorian Oxford suburb with Mandy Journeaux. Shared, that is, in that it was their common address. Most of the time he moved restlessly between the homes of fellow activists in London and the Midlands, organizing, talking, developing tactics. One week he would be down in Sussex taking part in one of the regular demonstrations outside Peter Savage's farm, the next he'd be taking rookie CALL members out on manoeuvres in the wilds of Leicestershire. Oxford Animal Rights existed as a highly respectable front for all this: animal loving shoppers out on a Saturday in the town centre would have been churlish indeed to have denied a mere ten pence for the purchase of a few cyclostyled sheets produced in such a worthy cause.

Mandy Journeaux would talk of Tim in admiring, even reverential terms. He was clearly something of a local hero. Mandy was a bit older, early thirties perhaps, with a tendency to dress in long flowing skirts and Indian prints. If Tim looked and talked in a way that only emphasized his erstwhile career behind the counter of a local bank, Mandy had difficulty in restraining deeply felt emotions about the fate of her fellow creatures. Her eyes would fill with tears as she talked about what was going on in the university laboratories, the crimes committed, the savagery of mankind in general. She worked at an electronics factory, putting together components on an assembly line; even though it was just a way of raising cash for the cause (the basement flat was devoid of any hint of extravagence or self-indulgence) it was hard to imagine her making the daily trek on the bus route to spend eight hours of unrelieved tedium. But Mandy was dedicated and, like Tim, her contacts and responsibilities within the movement went beyond Oxford Animal Rights. She acted as liaison between local activists and CALL, whose 'actions' she helpd to publicize; on a more elevated level, she also sat on the national committee of the British Union for the Abolition of Vivisection, alongside John Beggs. Founded at the beginning of the century, BUAV was, with the National Anti-vivisection Society, one of two venerable and highly respectable campaigning organizations that had fallen prey to the zealots of the new activism. Like some rotten constituency Labour party on Merseyside, ripe for Militant entryism, BUAV had been helplessly overwhelmed by Beggs, Daley and their allies. Because, like the 'supporters' of Militant, it was they who had the energy and commitment. And it was BUAV that had what they desperately needed – large reserves of cash, the fruit of generations of legacies left to the society by the animal lovers of England.

There were people like Mandy and Tim at the core of most of the animal rights groups springing up all over the country. It was an informal and often chaotic network, but it spread with extraordinary speed and enthusiasm. It was easy to see why politicos of both left and right looked at the phenomenon and were keen to harness its wildfire spontaneity to their own ends.

What cannot be denied is the strong element of idealism that informed it, naïve and often sanctimonious though it could seem. The ideas of Peter Singer and Richard Ryder, combined with a more general sense that the western world was heading towards self-induced, indeed selfish oblivion, had rapidly found fertile ground within which to grow.

On the big demonstrations, like the National Day of Action against the 1986 White Paper on vivisection, this could be measured in the sheer numbers of banners that were paraded through Cambridge, Manchester, Swansea and Edinburgh. Animal rights groups, campaigns and alliances from Chingford to Dundee marched through the streets in displays strongly reminiscent of the wide spectrum of revolutionary socialist groups that were a common feature during major labour disputes. But these new idealists were more inventive. They didn't just hawk big red banners round town: they carried coffins, they dressed up as skeletons, as giant cuddly rabbits or as blood-stained scientists. And while, by the mid eighties, most demonstrations of the left seemed to be peopled exclusively by drab, anoraked, badge-wearing clones, the animal rights people all looked very different. Middle-aged ladies in Hush Puppies and sensible coats marched next to kids in tattered black jackets and jeans with holes the size of pancakes. In Cambridge, Richard Ryder marched in neat blue suit and posh Crombie overcoat; behind him waved a nest of black flags, each of which carried the anarchist symbol of the white encircled 'A'.

At these major events, Mandy and Tim would be especially active. They would bring the OAR magazine to sell; but more attractive to the harder elements would be Tim's other publication, the ominously entitled *Black Beast*. This was a glossy and professionally produced effort, twenty-four pages long with high quality photography. The movement had always been particularly aware of the power of the picture: a livestock market could become a death camp, a laboratory a torture chamber with hardly any need for text. The magazine was packed with racy articles about the latest illicit activities of the ALF, the Southern Animal Liberation League and a piece by the UK representative of Hans Ruesch who had been also happy to feature in *National Front News*. The ALF and assorted Liberation Leagues were thanked for their help. But, interestingly, *Black Beast* was also full of material from legitimate, law-abiding groups as well – 'Lynx', the anti-fur campaign, and the anti-whaling lobby. Straddling the line between the two was a piece by the scientific adviser to BUAV, still, no doubt, the pinnacle of respectability and moderation to those unaware of the positions held by John Beggs, Tim Daley and friends.

As in the hundreds of animal rights groups and campaigns up and down the land, the borderline between legitimate, legal pressure and the overt commitment to selective acts of criminal behaviour was blurred. The unspoken logic was that if you cared about the animals, concern about the nice details of human (and therefore speciesist) law, particularly the law of property, was secondary. Young people in particular, drawn into local animal rights groups, would find themselves urged on from leafletting to paint-strippering the vehicles of local farmers or Supergluing the locks of shops that advertised the circus. For many, this was no more sinister than following their own conscience, much in the way that CND supporters would trespass and damage fencing at US airbases, or Greenpeace activists would harass whaling fleets on the open sea. There was, as Tim Daley had so confidently put it, a higher moral law.

But it was this very blurring of lines that made the local groups such fertile recruiting ground for the ALF, and those more violent individuals who were prepared to plant bombs or use firearms in the name of animals. At the Animal Aid meeting addressed by John Beggs, a rather blowsy, middle-aged woman had arrived half an hour early and had used the time to distribute a single photocopied newsheet on to every chair in the hall. This was Sylvia Bolt, 'press officer' of the local cell of the ALF. The sheet was a montage of news and recruitment propaganda. 'Broken windows delivered by our fast and efficient bricking service' boasted the slogan, over press cuttings about several butchers' shops smashed up in the Bournemouth area. One cell member wrote rather breathlesly about his 'first window'. 'Heart pounding like mad, I walk past the butchers shop . . . no one around . . . now's the time to do it. The brick takes an eternity to reach the window, then . . . CRACK!' Other rousing tales are followed by the injunction to all interested parties to join in. 'What are you waiting for??? You *are* the Bournemouth ALF!!!' This could not be dismissed simply as the childish and barely literate piece of propaganda it seemed: the Bournemouth ALF had been responsible for the costly 1984 Mars Bar hoax.

Animal rights people all knew each other; they formed a vast and informal network within which you would find a mass of personal and ideological differences, not to mention endemic personality clashes. But to the casual outsider it was never easily clear who was prepared to go outside the law and who wasn't. Down in Bournemouth, Mike Meeks, a local activist who believed in 'direct action', made plain his contempt for Sylvia Bolt and her band of brickers. Lean, muscular and macho, Meeks thought the ALF was unprofessional. Personality played as large a part as any disagreement on tactics. Yet the movement could contain them all and many more besides.

Oxford Animal Rights was also a broad church, in fact more so than most. Mandy Journeaux wasn't just involved in the Central Animal Liberation League, BUAV and *Black Beast*: she was also the Oxford contact for something called Pagan Animal Rights. This had been formed in 1983 because, said one of PAR's founders, Tina Pye, 'many people were looking for a spiritual dimension to the Animal Rights movement'. Like the ALF, the PAR was cellular in structure, with some two hundred members belonging to groups in the Wirral, Oxford, Devon and Sheffield. The organization featured a silhouette of the god Pan dancing with a group of goats on the cover of its quarterly magazine, which came out at the four 'fire festivals' of Imbolc, Beltane, Lammas and Samhain. At a mere £2.00 subscription a year, this was one of the better value rights groups, though preoccupations seemed more to do with a curiously sanitized version of paganism than the mundane issues of animal well-being.

'Pagan Animal Rights', announced their publication, 'starts with the premise that our treatment of the earth and its creatures deeply offends both the Goddess/God within and without (for we all contain an element of the divine). Resulting from this, PAR advocates the treatment of the earth entity, Gaia, (or whatever name you choose) with respect.' Respecting Gaia turned out to be the usual menu of animal rights – no fur or leather clothes, no meat or factory farming, no laboratory use of animals etc, with the additional insistence on 'promoting sustainable, non-polluting, energy patterns, wind, sun, water'. To this end, PAR had a two-pronged attack on the inert and uncaring forces of the status quo: the 'physical', which involved all the boring business of writing letters, drawing up petitions, demonstrating and so on; and the 'psychic', which, rather dramatically, was supposed to use 'ritual magic' for the cause wherever it was deemed appropriate.

Potential initiates into this fellowship were disappointed if they held furtive hopes of wild sexual excesses and 'starclad' encounters with Gaia under the moonlight. The group's literature was full of opaque pieces about 'The Staves of Orlog' and 'Unicorns – a Personal View'. Readers are asked to conjure up apparitions of shrieking fish to terrify and turn insensitive fishermen from the wickedness of their ways.

Tina Pye, a local government officer in her late thirties, welcomed all those interested in this kind of thing to her Victorian terrace on Merseyside. She was a lapsed Catholic, and Paganism, she admitted, was a satisfying outlet for her appetite for ceremony. But what about the magic? What exactly did PAR people get up to? Tina was not keen to divulge secrets: recitations, rituals and incantations seemed to feature large. For instance, in the hunting season they would gather to act out rituals that would make the weather unsuitable for hunting. They also went in for something called 'pathworking'. This was a kind of organized meditation where, say, every Sunday at seven in the evening for three months PAR members, wherever they were at the time, would sit down and meditate on the agreed theme for that quarter. It could be to do with saving foxes, hares or whales – or even pike, as the magazine's screaming fish apparition seemed to suggest.

Measurement of the success of these methods seemed unclear but Tina pointed out that the groups 'pathworks' on the pilot whale just happened to coincide with a BBC TV programme on the same subject. This was more than just coincidence; it was the result of PAR and 'higher forces' working together. Exactly what these were was hard to pin down, but an evening at Tina's home ended with a kind of pagan communion service in which water and wine were passed round, while everyone repeated a kind of homespun blessing.

Pagan Animal Rights seemed in many ways a distillation of some of the central themes that had had such a dramatic effect in recruiting thousands of adherents to the cause of animal rights: a sense that somehow man was dangerously 'out of tune' with the natural world, that science was blind and irresponsible, that an older, better and more harmonious way had been lost. PAR people seemed touchingly credulous about

48

the power of imagination, and politically they were both muddled and naïve. They seemed harmless enough, yet the network of which they were but a small part was to provide comfort and support to those who were certainly not. If this could all too easily be made to sound like some well-organized conspiracy, it was nothing so ordered: the point about the animal rights movement was that it spread very fast, and in its path it swept up huge numbers of people from very different backgrounds. The network of groups, campaigns and specialist interests rapidly provided a kind of animal rights 'underground'. Above board, it had its own lecture circuit, with its recognized elite group of speakers (like John Beggs); below that constantly blurred line of legality, it could provide a comfortably warm bath within which the law-breaker could safely swim. When Roger Yates, one of the ALF 'Sheffield Twelve' arrested along with Ronnie Lee for the concerted firebombing of department stores, jumped bail at the end of 1986, he disappeared into this underground. Yates, northern 'press officer' of the ALF, remains at large today.

The sheer fecundity of the movement in churning out organizations and campaigns, each with its own set of initials, made conventional, human liberation movements look like models of simplicity. But the crucial difference was that while, say, in Ireland the initials did represent serious splits and differences: the groups were more important than any individuals, in the animal rights movement it was precisely the opposite. At the cutting edge, there existed a group of people who would use a whole series of acronyms to claim responsibility for their actions. Throughout the rest of this book there will be ever more frequent, and possibly confusing reference to the ALF, the ARM, the HRS, BUAV, NAVS and so on: organizations of varying degrees of respectability and overt legality. It is important to remember that the core of activists who were seen as the movement's unofficial leadership moved effortlessly between them all.

They were able to do so because in the end their shared set of beliefs on the rights of other species was more important than any differences over acts of trespass, burglary and violence. And because if there was any one recognizable strand of political thought in the movement, it was anarchy: 'don't ask who are the Bournemouth ALF!' ran the newssheet, 'YOU are the Bournemouth ALF!' If you cared about animals, you knew what to do.

CHAPTER FIVE

It is time for us to destroy the old world
and build the new.

ALF Supporters Group Bulletin No. 17

When Ronnie Lee founded the embryonic ALF on his release from prison in 1976, the animal rights movement had barely got started. For the next ten years, as the Front developed its cellular structure, so the number of groups, campaigns and esoteric organizations proliferated, fed by the theories of Singer, Ryder and the growing number of ideologues exercised by the sin of 'speciesism'. The broad church of the animal rights movement, incoherent, disorganized and passionate, gave comfort and support to the ALF. Sympathizers would often talk about it as the 'Alf', as if it were a rather friendly if eccentric cousin; Ronnie Lee's own public persona fitted this image of slightly dotty but essentially well-meaning Englishness. In fact, as we shall see, Lee had never abandoned either the anarchist sentiments that had attracted him in the late sixties, nor the violence of language that had upset the less sturdy souls in the heyday of the Band of Mercy.

Ronnie's year in Winchester prison had given him plenty of time to think about tactics and organization. He was already an admirer of the IRA and its political wing Sinn Fein: he had also got involved in the pro-Republican 'Troops Out' movement as a sideline to his animal rights activities. What was admirable about the Provisionals was their structure, the series of cells connected by only the thinnest line of communication. Above all, after the fiasco that had led to his arrest, Lee was obsessed with the need for security. Combining this with his anarchist convictions, what he came up with was a system that allowed for minimal co-ordination and maximum freelance action by ALF units up and down the country. There was to be no central high command or 'army council', or in fact any precisely defined hierarchy. At the centre Ronnie Lee remained simply the Front's 'press officer': he was the contact who dealt with press and television, supplying information, explaining actions and managing to distance himself from any direct responsibility. Over the years, as the ALF's numbers grew, Lee acted as central co-ordinator helped by a small band of trusted intimates: most of these like Vivian Smith, shared his anarchist anti-politics.

Meeting Lee in one of the seedy coffee bars near Hammersmith tube station where he would arrange rendezvous with journalists, it was hard to credit that here was the undisputed and charismatic leader of the movement. Ronnie's dress sense never improved: no one would ever accuse him of petty vanity. Like his acolytes, he would usually wear black, though not the vaguely trendy post-punk 'gothic' look taken up by his lieutenant Vivian Smith and the younger activists who dominated demonstrations in the eighties. Sipping an ideologically acceptable orange juice through his wispy beard, Lee would talk at the visiting reporter in a high monotone about the struggle, quoting reams of statistics about 'actions' carried out, rodents rescued and economic damage done. He would then offer to put the reporter in touch with his troops.

The cellular structure that Lee developed was simple. Every ALF group was more or less independent: after all, everyone knew who the targets were, so there seemed little point in having all operations directed from headquarters. If a group on Merseyside wanted to set fire to an abattoir, fine: they knew how to do it. All Ronnie wanted was the information. So each cell had its own 'press officer' whose double task was to spread news of all the good deeds through the local media, and secondly to liaise with Lee. The ALF office was always a moveable feast, settling at one time in the head office of the BUAV, and then above an Italian restaurant in a down-at-heel block of offices in Hammersmith. But the trouble was that, as in so many of their operations, the organization lurched between a deadly seriousness and an almost hopeless naïveté. When they were based in their west London office, attempts of almost comic incompetence were made to keep the address secret. When you rang up to speak to Lee, Vivian Smith or any of the part-timers, you were given instructons that sounded like the poorly digested remnants of a le Carré spy novel: 'in thirty minutes, X, dressed in black, will meet you at the third phone box along on the opposite side of the main entrance to the tube station ... the second café along from the Lyric

Theatre . . .' or 'the fourth pub on the left down Hammersmith Broadway'. And yet it was absurdly easy to follow your inform-ant back down the street and into the building where the ALF was housed, masquerading unconvincingly under the trading name 'Independent Tax Advisory Services'.

There were virtually no rules to govern the ALF's cellular structure, barring, of course, the one central commandant 'thou shalt not grass'. A local group would usually be about six or seven strong, and if they grew larger then they would split, amoeba-like. You didn't 'join' the ALF in any strict sense of the word: there were no membership forms or blood-rituals, or oaths of allegiance sworn on the collected works of such luminaries as Peter Singer and Hans Ruesch. What normally happened was that activists followed a pattern of involvement in the animal rights movement that would find its logical conclusion inside the Front. Young idealists, like the Animal Aid supporters down in Bournemouth, would get involved in their local animal rights alliance or protection campaign: the ones that got angry enough would start doing things on their own – bricking butchers' windows on their way home late at night, or undertaking a little freelance 'rescue' operation at the farm down the road. Sooner or later, at meetings, they would come across the press officer of the local ALF cell, and that would be that. Most recruits would be young, a majority (60% according to ALF accounts) of them women. The 'press officer' would be older, something of an authority figure. Recruits talked of men and women in their late thirties and early forties, teachers and social workers with good jobs in local government persuasively co-ordinating much younger activists full of a frustrated and passionate idealism. Recruitment soared every time the BBC or Channel 4 broadcast a documentary like 'Rabbits Don't Cry' or the equally upsetting *Animals' Film*.

This was a loose structure and it worked. From its meagre beginnings in 1976 with a total membership of thirty support-ers, the ALF expanded in ten years into a network that claimed at least fifteen hundred activists, with two thousand supporters providing cash back up. Actually no one, least of all Ronnie Lee's office, knew how many cells, never mind actual activists were out there: but police opinion was (and is) that estimates underrated the real numbers involved. By the mid eighties, at least six million pounds' worth of damage was being done per annum to the industries and individuals marked out by the

Front as animal abusers. What was undeniably impressive, reading the ALF's Bulletins, was the wide spread of this cellular structure: Hereford, Herts and Humberside; Berkshire, Bucks and Bristol; Northants, Notts and Norfolk; Cork, Dublin and Glasgow – not to mention reports from comrades in Sweden, France and Germany.

The troops out in the field were kept up to date with regular 'Action Reports' detailing reported activities from cells up and down the country. The bulletin for February to May 1986, a period of just three months, gives some idea of what had become a nationwide pattern of animal rights terrorism. Bedfordshire, 3 April: 'the windows of several halal [muslim] butchers' shops were smashed, and the tyres of a lorry belonging to one of them slashed'. Cheshire, 27 March: 'about £15,000 damage was caused in an attack on an abattoir in Macclesfield. Two lorries were set on fire, and the tyres slashed of a Mercedes car.' Cumbria, 16 April: 'nearly two thousand fish (trout, salmon and char) were released into Lake Windermere from the premises of the Freshwater Biological Association, where they were being kept in tanks and subjected to cruel experiments for the benefits of factory fish farming. Thirty-five ALF activists took part.' Dorset: 'one of the most active areas of the country with about forty attacks on animal abuse targets in the period February to May; the first of these was on 6 February, when two posh cars belonging to the Adams family, who run a battery farm, were damaged with paintstripper and etching fluid (acid) at Canford Magna. Over the period butchers' shops were damaged in Poole, Bournemouth, Winton, Burnley-Willis, Moordown, Southbourne and West Parley . . .'

So the litany continued, the bare facts of criminal damage interspersed with occasional adjectives by way of derision or explanation: 'posh', 'bloodthirsty' and 'disgusting'. The activists seemed to have a low view of the fellow humans they had targeted. Sometimes actions required lengthier explanations: six shops in Banbury had their windows smashed on 13 March because they were 'displaying circus posters'. In Leicester, two months later, 'a car belonging to a barrister prosecuting animal rights activists at Leicester Crown Court was damaged'. The range of targets seemed endless, even on this (incomplete) three-month scoresheet: and to qualify for the ALF's hit list it seemed that you no longer had to actively abuse animals.

Anyone, however, unwittingly, who got in the way of the movement was a legitimate target.

Nor were some of the chosen representatives of the animal abuse industries quite as obvious as the activists seemed to think. Hampshire: 'the night before the Grand National many betting shops in the county had their locks glued'. Middlesex: 'on 17 April, twenty Co-op and Unigate milk floats were daubed in Hillingdon, where the windscreen of an egg van was smashed on 24 April. The windows of a Cancer Research shop in Burnt Oak were smashed the following week.' Cancer Research, when you thought about it, meant vivisection: shortly afterwards, a veterinary surgeon involved in this work found a bomb under his car. Other less obvious but frequent targets included the fast food trade. West Yorkshire, late March: 'five windows of McDonalds were damaged with etching fluid and damage was done to a door and storeroom in a fire attack on a Kentucky Fried Chicken drive-in'.

Taken individually, most of these attacks seemed petty enough – a few column inches and a photo in the local paper. Taken together, they presented a national picture of high volume and virtually indiscriminate violence. The ALF claimed that they carried out five or six actions a night, every night. With all the 'freelance' anti-animal abuse acts taken into account, the police thought this estimate to be unrealistically low. In just the first two and a half months of 1986, Dewhursts the butchers admitted that they had suffered eighty-seven attacks on branches all over the country. It was an impressive measure of how far things had changed since Ronnie Lee and his initial band of thirty acolytes had dreamt up the idea of the ALF.

In their first year of operation, 1976–7, the Front estimated that they had inflicted over a quarter of a million pounds worth of damage. The targets were all fairly predictable – breeding facilities, fur farms, hunts, abattoirs, circuses and laboratories. But in November, in a burst of considerable initiative, the central London offices of the Research Defence Society were burgled. This was rather like a bunch of convinced atheists making a swift smash and grab raid on Lambeth Palace; the RDS is the public voice of the pro-vivisection lobby and already it had Mr Lee and his comrades marked down on its files. These were removed by the ALF raiding party, as were lists of vivisectors, their addresses and ex-directory phone numbers.

Just a few months later, Ronnie Lee got his second taste of prison life when mice taken from a breeding establishment in Surrey were found in his home. This time he served eight months. It was to be the last time for many years he was to have any direct involvement in ALF actions, either as a raider or 'fence' for stolen animals; Lee's police profile was already too high to indulge in unnecessary risks. From now on he would run the show purely in his public role as 'press officer', keeping his hands clean. Besides, the real power in any movement lay in controlling its ideological direction, and to this Lee now gave his fullest attention.

What was important was to make ALF activists realize that this was not some passing phase; that, like the long march of Chairman Mao and the Chinese Communists, the struggle would be long and hard, the price heavy. The decision to live outside the law had not been taken lightly, and those who cared about the animals should remind themselves that the public at large was all too often selfish and apathetic. 'The fallacious and arrogant belief that the human species is somehow "superior" to the other animals,' wrote Lee in the ALF Supporters Bulletin, 'has been held by the majority of the population for many thousands of years, and has thus become deeply entrenched in the human psyche.' Those who knew better, who rejected 'speciesism' in all its forms and were prepared to fight for their voiceless fellow creatures, had to accept that there would be much to endure along the way. Animal abuse was 'a huge and ugly edifice which can only be sent tumbling if widespread, frequent and hard-hitting direct action is employed. But those who believe in the use of direct action have got to accept that imprisonment is often the price that will have to be paid.' As usual, Lee found it hard to resist a conclusion of ringing self-righteousness: people should not be surprised that muggers and baby batterers were treated more lightly in the courts than animal rights activists – they were only a threat to ordinary people, 'whereas the ALF is a threat to the status quo'.

With at least three hundred prosecutions in the history of the movement, most of them successful, no one could accuse the rank and file of the ALF of failing to heed their leader's words; dozens of activists have served time in prison, and for most of them it has been a deeply unpleasant experience. Nothing in their lives had prepared them for the grim and sordid realities of 'slopping out', the over-crowded cells and the harsh informal hierarchy run by the hardened criminal fraternity. But their set of beliefs exemplified in the purity of their diet and their sense of exclusivity gave them – like the paramilitaries in the Maze – the necessary equipment for survival.

Ronnie Lee's written account of the long-term implications of the ALF struggle are punctuated by constant references to this subtext of exclusivity. Animal liberation as a creed bears a stronger resemblance to a mutant form of religion than anything to be found in conventional politics; liberationists were the 'enlightened ones', puritanical, self-denying and selfless in their struggle for other species. But Lee's language often lurches into violence. He had always been shrewd enough to realize that he was working with many who would take a rather more charitable and certainly less anarchistic view of the rest of human society; but then sometimes he couldn't help himself. Appealing for cash on one occasion, he lashes out at 'the vicious human tyrant' and announces that the only reason the ALF haven't so far killed any of the enemy is only a matter of tactics, 'not because we love the scum who brutally exploit animals, nor because we believe the emotive [sic] unbalanced statement that violence against them would "make us as bad as they are". It is a war without killing, but a war nonetheless. To advocate anything less than a war when faced with the brutal tyranny of the human race against all other creatures is a form of treachery against the animals.' Liberationists might love animals, but they weren't too keen on their own kind. 'Scum' was a word to be found increasingly in the literature of the movement.

How deeply this disenchantment went was to be shown in a series of 'actions' that, right from the first years of the Front's operational activity, were designed to shock the public out of their apathy. The idea was to target their own species; not just to attack fellow human beings and their property, but to strike at the common decencies and basic taboos that human society simply took for granted. In January 1977 three activists broke into the graveyard of St Kentigern's Church in the small Lake District village of Caldbeck. It is a remote and peaceful place, high in the fells, with the croaking of rooks who nest in the churchyard's few trees the only disturbance to the generations of local farmers who lie buried beneath a collection of ornate gravestones. In the dead of night, the three intruders made straight for the grave of a man who had lain there for a hundred and twenty-three years, which turned out to be no protection at all for an arch enemy of the animal rights movement. The target was John Peel, the legendary huntsman and most English of folk heroes. The three men set about smashing the headstone and then desecrated the grave. When they rang the Press Association to deliver their 'communiqué', they boasted that they had thrown Peel's remains into a cesspit. The police later found no evidence of this, but a stuffed fox's head was found in the dug-up grave, together with a note urging John Peel to 'go blow on your horn till your face turns blue'.

Though not specifically claimed as an ALF action, the desecration of Peel's grave had been carefully planned by a friend and colleague of Ronnie Lee, a twenty-four-year-old student called Mike Huskisson. Huskisson was already a veteran anti-blood sports campaigner who had built up a reputation in the movement for bravery that amounted to foolhardiness on occasions. The Peel outrage, for which he and his two co-conspirators were sentenced to nine months in jail, turned Huskisson into one of the earliest folk heroes of the animal rights movement. Over the next decade, this was enhanced by a two year spell working 'undercover' as a phoney huntsman in order to expose some of the nastier elements in the otter hunting fraternity. The son of a professional army officer, the public school educated Huskisson was the prototype of a new kind of activist: fond of paramilitary clothing, a meticulous planner, he saw the future of the animal rights movement as a military campaign. On one occasion, taking part in a raid on laboratories, a shot gun was found in the back of his car.

The desecration of John Peel's grave was to be the first in a series of violent attacks on the liberationists' own species. On most subsequent occasions, when bombs had been targeted on individiuals rather than premises, the ALF would do its best to distance itself from complicity. But the suggestion that there were a large number of different groups out there in the field, with separate sets of initials (Hunt Retribution Squad, Animal Rights Militia and so on) was false. At the heart of the movement there were always a core of hard activists who knew and liaised with each other. Writing in the ALF's bulletin, Ronnie Lee actively encouraged the setting up of new 'groups' with separate identities to cause maximum confusion and to allow the ALF to gain, by contrast, a degree of respectability. 'For tactical reasons I feel that it is best that the ALF retains its current policy on these matters . . . however there is nothing to stop fresh groups being set up under new names whose policies do not preclude the use of violence towards animal abusers.' Some fainthearted comrades might find this all a bit distressing but, Lee goes on confidently, 'it's about time someone did some straight talking on the subject of violence. Only an all out war, fought with intelligent tactics, can offer the animals any hope of freedom.' By 1984 Ronnie no longer felt the need to obfuscate his views on violence. 'If you want to play games then try Monopoly or Snakes and Ladders; animal persecution will not be defeated by petitions, peaceful posturing or the holding of hands round slaughterhouses.' For Lee, violence could be seen as a purifying force. He ended by quoting the anarchist poet Raoul Vaneigem: 'Let ten people meet who are resolved on the lightening of violence rather than the agony of survival: from this moment, despair ends and tactics begin.'

Within a year, the ALF Supporters' bulletin was publishing the 'communiqués' of the self-styled 'Animal Rights Militia' – the first 'fresh group' to openly admit to planting bombs for the deliberate purpose of killing or maiming other human beings.

The anti-personnel bombing campaign had begun in 1982, when four letter bombs were sent to the leaders of the main political parties. A civil servant at Number 10 Downing Street hurt his hand when the package addressed to Margaret Thatcher exploded on being opened. Shortly afterwards, a letter bomb was sent to Professor Roy Calne, the pioneer of kidney transplants, at Addenbrooke's Hospital in Cambridge. As letter bombs were succeeded by Molotov cocktails and devices planted under cars, the ALF kept a judicious distance; though curiously the organization did claim responsibility for the petrol bombing of two scientists' homes in Kent in 1985, adding for good measure a fresh set of threats to the Home Office minister David Mellor, who was responsible at the time for piloting a new and more stringent bill on vivisection through Parliament. 'His time will come' warned the ALF's statement: 'he can expect drastic personal attention.'

Throughout the eighties, the movement continued to punctuate its by now mundane practices of animal 'rescue', property damage and personal threats with large-scale events designed to gain maximum publicity. Imitating the desecration of John

Peel's grave, they also dug up the grave of the Duke of Beaufort. This time they called themselves the 'Hunt Retribution Squad' although those involved were all veterans of ALF actions: they had simply borrowed the name from a publicity stunt dreamed up by John Beggs, who had persuaded a London listings magazine to photograph a bunch of hooded comrades bearing an assortment of weapons including a chain saw.

Because of its cellular structure, autonomous local groups tended to set their own agenda, even when it came to the big, publicity seeking actions and events. When the Bournemouth cell of the ALF organized the Mars Bar rat poison hoax in 1984, it was entirely their own idea. The massive sales loss inflicted on Mars UK was the kind of economic warfare that warmed the cockles of Ronnie Lee's heart, but when he talked to journalists in strangely tentative terms after actions like this he was not being disingenuous; yes, it sounded like 'one of our actions' he would vaguely surmise: 'it's in line with our policy'. The point was that Lee's permission was neither asked or sought. Everyone in the movement knew what they had to do. The police would find one of the most constantly irritating factors in their pursuit of activist networks was the deliberate lack of hierarchy within the movement.

By 1982 when the first letter bombs were sent, the *Observer*, in a lengthy run down on the individuals and groups involved in the animal rights issue, was talking of a new 'culture of violence' to be found among the rank and file. It was an ingredient that had been in evidence since the early days of the Band of Mercy, but, as the ALF grew in numbers and reputation, it became more overt, both in the movement's literature and its actions. 'Devastate to liberate!' and 'learn to burn!' were two of the slogans regularly trotted out to encourage the morale of the troops. And in dozens of cells all over the country, hundreds of balaclava'd idealists were more than willing to oblige.

CHAPTER SIX

I've done it! I've conquered my fear!
And it was so easy . . .

Anonymous contributor to
Bournemouth ALF news

The ALF had always been very keen on public relations. This was partly because they assumed broad public support in the 'rescue' of animals, but mainly because they knew perfectly well that journalists were always game for a quick burst of cloak and dagger excitement. 'Communiqués' were always issued to the local press after large-scale raids on farms and laboratories: the activists knew that local programmes, desperate for lively material, would be happy to transmit dramatic accounts of balaclava'd figures sledgehammering their way into enemy territory.

So making contact with a local cell was not terribly difficult. A meeting with Ronnie Lee in London was followed a few days later by a call from the south coast; it was from the 'press officer' of the ALF's Bournemouth cell, specially selected by Ronnie, apparently, because they happened to be particularly active at the time. Cells waxed and waned according to the bottle and bravado of their leading spirits, not to mention the efforts of the local police. The 'press officer' said she was called Sylvia Bolt: we would have to have a preliminary meeting at her home before actually getting to see any of the activists in the field.

Ms Bolt was well known to local radio and newspaper newsrooms along the Hampshire coast: an indefatigable contributor to phone-ins and constant provider of instant comment in the wake of break-ins and burn-outs, Sylvia trod a dangerously narrow line between the law and those who lived outside it. Nothing in her life seemed remotely exciting or unconventional. Fortyish, blonde, of borderline blowsiness and married to a long-distance truck driver, she lived in a smartish detached house on a new private estate; dogs were everywhere, much indulged. This was clearly one ALF supporter who actually liked animals as well as deriving moral sustenance from asserting their rights. Over coffee, Sylvia explained that it would be possible to meet members of her cell, but not on her premises; she would have to find someone in the ALF Supporters' Group who would be happy to lend their house for the afternoon.

A couple of days later, the meeting was fixed. The rendezvous was at Sylvia's, followed by what seemed an unnecessarily long and twisting drive through endless stretches of south coast suburbia. Our eventual destination was not quite what had been expected. The cars were parked up outside a large red-brick detached house in one of the best parts of Poole: Sylvia had mentioned that several of the 'older' local supporters were well-to-do. The place could have belonged to a doctor or a well-heeled solicitor. But we were ushered past the house and round into the back garden, where a rather dilapidated and weather-beaten caravan sat, grimy with rust. Inside were three figures, identically dressed: brand new army surplus fatigues were topped by a trio of equally pristine balaclavas. For no readily understood reason, all three had stuffed pieces of dishcloth into their mouths: if this was intended to disguise their voices, it turned out to be a dismal failure.

The trio called themselves 'Ben', 'Bob' and 'Jean'. 'Bob' was shy about disclosing what he did for a living, but the other two said they had clerical jobs in local government. They all lived perfectly normal humdrum nine to five lives, except for the once a week when they would dress up in this rather dramatic gear and hit their chosen target for the night. Why the para-military outfits? 'Ben', speaking through his dishcloth in a flat Yorkshire accent, was clearly going to do most of the talking. He didn't think they looked ridiculous at all. 'We buy khaki combat gear because it happens to be cheap and durable. We wear balaclavas because we cannot afford to show who we are.' 'Jean' said she thought it did make them look a bit funny, but security was the important thing, not looking pretty and feminine. She was younger than the men, mid to late twenties; the others were well into their thirties. They had all clearly thought carefully about what they were doing and why. A slight hint of martyrdom hung around them: they would all, they said, much rather be normal husbands, fathers and wives with two kids and a mortgage, no more having to face the terror that every time the door bell went it would be the 'bloody law'.

They had come into the movement either, as in 'Bob's' case, through membership of a conventional animal welfare society, or, like 'Ben', through exposure to literature and television documentaries on vivisection. 'Bob' had joined the ALF when he moved from London down to the south coast. 'I found that people were a little bit different from the group that I was involved in. I saw that I'd sort of been writing to MPs and things, and going on peaceful demonstrations, but that was getting me nowhere – and I didn't want to have to wait around for another hundred years for something to be done. If you want to achieve animal liberation, you've got to do it yourself.' The cell was convinced that time was short and democracy a luxury of no relevance to the animals' cause. 'Working through Parliament,' 'Ben' said with assurance, 'would achieve absolutely nothing!' Yes, but what about the new Bill then passing through the House of Commons, which would tighten up restrictions on vivisection? An irrelevant sop, said 'Ben'. Parliament was full of vested interests, farmers, people on the boards of drug companies. 'They don't want to see animal rights being established: the animals are dying now, and we have to do something for them now!' They didn't like a lot of things they had to do, but they were not living in an ideal society, so sometimes they had to use non-ideal methods. And if they succeeded, said 'Ben', then they were justified.

The Bournemouth cell usually carried out one action a week. Their weaponry was standard ALF gear: an assortment of red paint, Molotov cocktails, bolt cutters and etching fluid. This stuff was in fact hydrofluoric acid, used to etch slogans on the windows of butchers' and fur shops: if it gets on to the skin it causes nasty blisters and can penetrate to the bone. 'Ben' said that the need for security kept organization to a minimum. 'We're not organized in the sense that most people would understand it . . . there's a small group of us and we trust each other implicitly. We don't discuss things on the telephone and we no longer get involved in local animal rights groups': these nonetheless remained Sylvia's territory as fertile ground for recruitment. 'We get together, we have "safe" houses where we can store our equipment; we have "safe" vehicles; we carefully "sus" out our targets before we do anything to them. We get our facts right and then we perform the operation: it's as simple as that.'

The account of recent 'actions' was familiar enough. Butchers' shops bricked and etched with acid, council property disfigured (to discourage the renewal of a zoo licence), the homes of farmers daubed and vandalized. 'Ben' and his colleagues had also attacked local meat trucks, using a combination of tyre-slashing, paintstrippering and Molotov cocktails. Arson was a pretty serious crime, surely? 'Ben's' flat Yorkshire tone assumed an injured air. 'With respect, you seem to be totally committed to using words like "crime", "terrorism" and so on.' But wasn't burning a meat truck just that? 'In my book it is a much more serious crime to abuse animals . . . and I think that by concentrating on laws that are totally obscene and amoral anyway, we're getting away from the issue. All right, the society that you accept says that the burning of a meat vehicle is a serious crime: I say it's a means to an end.'

'Ben' and his two companions seemed to exist on a higher moral plane than the rest of their species. 'We don't want to. We're not judgemental. We just know what we believe. It's as simple as that.' He and the other two were genuinely distressed by the fate of innocent animals; and yet it seemed that they had almost given up on their own species. 'We've spent hours and hours trying to persuade people not to eat meat, not to buy cruelty based cosmetics or to use the drugs that are tested on animals . . . but for most people it doesn't matter: they don't care enough, and that's the main worry.'

So they had to be made to care. That was the thinking behind the Mars Bar hoax, 'Ben's' most ambitious campaign of all. And this had been all 'Ben's' idea, suggesting, among other things, that Ronnie Lee didn't have a monopoly on strategy. The plan was to cripple Mars UK so badly that they would pull out of funding a project at Guy's Hospital in London, which had been designed to develop a vaccine to prevent tooth decay: this involved feeding monkeys a sugar-rich diet that deliberately brought on decay. Mars had become a number one target for the ALF: economic sabotage was to be the weapon. But first, the cell went for a dry run, just to see how the operation would work in practice. Apart from anything else, it meant co-ordinating with other cells in different parts of the country, a sophisticated level of planning foreign to the Bournemouth group.

They chose Boots as the target for their prototype hoax. The nationwide chain had long been on the Front's hit list for just about everything from selling medicines tested on animals to displaying posters for circuses. They were always fair game. And so were Elida Gibbs, the people who made Sunsilk shampoo, because they had admitted testing their products on animals to meet government regulations: it was a perfect double target. In July, bottles of Sunsilk shampoo laced with a corrosive bleach were placed on shelves in shops in Southampton, London and Leeds. A warning was sent by the cell to a national newspaper, with satisfying results. A Boots spokesman said that they were having to remove every single bottle of Sunsilk from their shelves and check them individually; 'it's a mammoth task, but it has to be done'. The bleach, hypochlorite, could cause ulcerations and extreme irritation to the eyes. Customers were urged to return recently purchased shampoo so that checks could be made. It was an expensive operation, especially when it had to be repeated a month later when further 'poisoned' shampoo turned up in Hull.

Three months later the Mars hoax went ahead. 'It was incredibly successful,' said 'Ben' modestly. 'We managed to get approximately fifty bars into shops in ten different regions, which I think shows that people have got to realize that we are more co-ordinated than we're given credit for. The point of it fundamentally was to create a shock wave . . .' This it did, though not perhaps entirely in the way the Bournemouth group would have wanted. More than the letter bombs, the Mars Bar hoax left many potential sympathizers with the animal rights movement perplexed and angry: it seemed to be worrying evidence of callousness towards innocent members of the public. Publicity focused on the outrage, not the monkeys allegedly suffering in the laboratories at Guys.

As an operation, however, it all went very smoothly. Over one weekend, suspect bars were planted in shops across most of the country: they turned up in Plymouth, Manchester, Leeds, Coventry, Blandford, Salisbury and several other towns. Each bar was clearly marked with a ballpoint 'X' on the wrapper, and inside there was a note which read: 'this confection has been adulterated. We have no desire in [sic] endangering life, but those who persist in buying cruelty based products must accept full responsibility for their actions.' It wasn't just Mars that was to blame, it was the entire sweet-chewing apathetic public. In the rusty caravan in Poole, 'Ben' brought out the originals of both the warning note to purchasers, and the messages he had personally delivered to the BBC and the *Daily Mirror* wrapped around two poisoned bars. These did indeed contain the rat poison Alphakill – everything else was a hoax. This did not prevent reports reaching the press of members of the public falling ill after eating 'contaminated' bars, nor, more seriously, of causing a great deal of panic and alarm before the hoax was revealed. This did not appear to bother 'Ben' a great deal. 'There are an awful lot of animals that are caused an awful lot of anxiety as well. We have to weigh one against the other.' The more he talked in his flat northern voice, full of unshakeable moral certainty, the more he began to assume the obsessiveness of a character in an Alan Bennett monologue. 'Nobody died of it,' said 'Ben', 'but there are rhesus monkeys dying in agony from unrelieved toothache!'

This was denied by the company. They accepted that they had donated £25,000 to research into decay: but monkeys were not being force fed, nor were they getting anything other than a normal human diet. 'I would have thought research into tooth decay would have been welcomed' was the sensible if slightly naïve response from the Mars UK spokesman. Financially, the cost to the company was enormous. For the first couple of days, sales of Mars fell to almost zero; it took about ten weeks for sales of single bars to return to the pre-hoax level and about three to four months for sales of the multi-pack to recover. Mars employed a thousand people to check out stocks. If there was any one point at which the animal liberation movement assumed a genuine threat to the economic life of the country, this was it. David Mellor, then junior minister at the Home Office, and himself the target of threats and paint daubing raids at his home, said the ALF could now no longer be regarded as 'loonies who are best ignored'. He was emphatic: 'they are dangerous, and they must be stopped before someone is severely injured, or even killed'. But the Bournemouth ALF group were not stopped: the police never tracked them down, and even if they had done no one was quite sure what they would be charged with. 'Conspiring to cause a public mischief' was the best that newspaper speculation could come up with, but the issue remained academic while 'Ben' and his companions in crime were still at large.

But what, regardless of the consequences, gave these people the right to take such devastating action outside the law? Quite apart from the three million pound loss sustained by Mars, it had caused a lot of people a lot of distress; in the short term it also severely discouraged the confectionary industry from financing research that was aimed at reducing the suffering of millions of children with dental problems. 'Ben' again assumed the role of chief spokesman on matters of morality. 'We're not some sort of group that's saying you should go to church on Sunday, or should do this or that with your life. All we're saying is, leave the animals alone.' Again, a hint of martyrdom crept in. 'We don't do it for fun, we don't do it for an ego trip: we have to stand up and be counted.' It just wasn't fair that millions of creatures were dying simply because they had the bad luck to be born into the wrong species. As for those members of their own species who had suffered anxiety after consuming 'poisoned' bars, 'Ben' had little but contempt. They lived utterly selfish lives, careless of how living creatures were reduced to chunks of flesh.

These three hooded representatives of the Bournemouth ALF spoke in a language that seemed again a curious synthesis of the hard certainty of the convinced Marxist and the high moral tone of the religious convert. On more than one occasion, the cell seemed more like some throwback to an exclusive dissenting sect of the seventeenth century than any modern political cadre. It was not unthinkable that they might welcome martyrdom at the stake rather than recant. But this was nothing unusual. The movement attracted individuals from every part of the conventional political spectrum, from fascists to anarchists, often, in the process providing graphic examples of the circular nature of that spectrum. What they all held in common was an experience not far removed from religious conversion.

Tim Daley – described only half-jokingly by the police as the ALF's commander-in-chief – recalls watching 'Rabbits Don't Cry' as the point at which he realized there was 'a meaning as to why you're here', that is to say a reason for living that would take him beyond a life that suddenly seemed in the face of animal suffering empty and self-centred.

This may not quite be the language of St Augustine, but the same principle seemed to apply: what for others had been provided by revolutionary politics or charismatic religious experience was provided for Tim Daley and thousands of other activists by the cause of animal rights. Within a few months, the Tory stalwart was active in the South London ALF, his phone tapped, and his movements under police surveillance. It was, said Daley, all very odd and confusing for somone from a conventional, law-abiding background. 'My parents, I think, also find it rather sad because they have always been very law-abiding, and have always taught me to respect the law; and, really, up until the time I got involved in animal rights, I had never broken the law, apart from speeding.' He had crossed the threshold into serious illegality because, morally, there was simply no alternative. Like 'Ben', Daley could appear priggish, a sanctimonious though secular version of some Victorian church elder. Everything was absolutely clear, there was no room for argument or discussion. Tim Daley still looked the picture of Sutton and Cheam respectability; he held a perfectly normal job and it is easy to believe that he was good at it. The charm still came naturally, occasional smiles interrupting the bleak and clearly heartfelt speeches; a distinctly unrevolutionary and rather prim moustache decorated his upper lip. In a movement with a preponderance of girls in their late teens and twenties, Daley cut a glamorous figure. Although he never appeared to sully his commitment to the cause with sexual boasting, he did on several occasions remark shyly that one of the bonuses you picked up in the animal rights movement was the chance to meet and get off with women unhampered by conventional moral attitudes.

It was no good looking for a common pattern among activists, either in class or background. There were many of whom it was tempting to suggest that the cause had filled a void in their lives, made them feel useful or wanted for the first time. There was the shabby glamour of belonging to a covert brother(or sister)hood as well. Sitting in the pub in Hammersmith, clutching a half of cider, Vivian Smith talked of the ALF as an organization that could be compared with the IRA. She loved the secrecy, the dressing in black, the sense of being apart and somehow more 'alive' than the rest of humanity. In the manner of Doris Lessing's 'good terrorist', Vivian had found a kind of chilling purity in the cause of the animals: yet it was hard to reconcile her apparently genuine fondness for four-legged creatures with her transparent loathing of humanity. She would be overjoyed, she said, without any visible trace of embarrassment, when the first scientist was killed by animal rights activists.

The Bournemouth cell was ambivalent about violence. They

knew it was bad form for the ALF to be publicly associated with attacks on people rather than property: yet the attitudes that emerged seemed closer to those of Ronnie Lee and Tim Daley than the movement's pacifist tendency. Daley had claimed, having spoken to activists on marches and in the field, that some three quarters of those involved in the ALF would support violence against animal abusers; Lee had already suggested setting up splinter groups to carry out such acts. Inside the increasingly sweaty confines of the caravan in Poole, 'Ben' and his colleagues talked of bombs under cars and shootings on doorsteps as an historical inevitability. 'I think it's inevitable. The frustration that is prevalent within our movement is due to the disinterest of the vast majority of politicians, and that frustration has caused all of us to take some kind of action.' But did frustration with the political process give them the right to put bombs under cars? 'I am certainly not going to judge,' said 'Ben' through his wedge of dishcloth. 'It's not something I'm prepared to be involved in personally, but I can't say that I would cry if a vivisector died tomorrow.' A fairly hard thing to say, surely? 'Well, I'm being honest with you. I couldn't cry if a vivisector was to die ... I just couldn't.' Five minutes earlier, 'Ben' had been genuinely close to tears over the plight of the sweet-toothed monkeys.

At the anarchist squat in Brighton, just down the coast, the ALF contingent shared this ambiguously neutral view on personal violence. 'Mike', the lank-haired ex-comrade of the 'hippy convoy', said that, personally speaking, he didn't like bombs and 'things like that. But I'm not willing to condemn the people that do it, because I know how they feel, and to be honest I think that people involved in vivisection have got to expect more of this.' Violence was inevitable, so highly charged were emotions within the movement; there was the lad in Exeter who had doused himself in petrol because he was 'mentally depressed' at the amount of abuse that was going on. There was a sense of desperate frustration – animals were dying in the laboratories by the million – a bombing campaign was inevitable. As for Peter Savage, the local target for the bombers, it was all his responsibility in the first place. It was his fault for being a vivisector. Savage, it should be remembered, was not doing anything of the kind, but supplying scientists with animals he imported from abroad.

If the Bournemouth cell seemed largely composed of low level clerical officers in local government, the ALF supporters at the Brighton squat came from a widely differing set of backgrounds. Uniformly filthy, to the point where it was hard to tell where jeans ended and grubby flesh began, they sported a cheerful variety of mohican haircuts and black anarchist threads (maintaining a persistent effort to avoid stereotyping by the 'media', one of them denied he was an anarchist, but said grudgingly, yes, he did believe in anarchism). One was the son of a highly-paid senior technician at Thames Television; others came from equally salubrious backgrounds. 'Steve', big, clad entirely in black and with an impressively stiff three inch high Mohican haircut, was refreshingly honest about his views on the movement. It was, once again, all down to basic morality, giving other species a decent break, a kind of ultimate extension of the principle of live and let live. Steve didn't actually 'like' animals at all: he 'respected' them – but animal 'lovers' were oppressively sentimental. Unlike the Bourne-mouth trio, these young punk anarchists, most of them only in their teens, could laugh at the contradictions thrown up by their chaotic way of life.

As for the kind of society they wanted to build on the ruins of the old, corrupt, animal abusing one they inhabited, ideas were vague. Mike said that humans had gone so far that they were 'well away from the system of nature, sort of thing'. All species could live together harmoniously and separately; humans could continue to live in towns if they wished, but not at the expense of the animal world; 'towns' generally seemed like a bad idea to Mike. 'I mean, out there [in the country], we've got sort of all we need to live on ... but as it goes into this system, this concrete jungle that we've made, we're always very dissatisfied ... it doesn't last and it sort of crumbles and decays.' The earth was full of good things if only man were not so selfish and materialistic. Appearances had been deceptive: the squat was a hotbed of sentimental pastoralism.

On one of the walls, next to a large black ALF flag, was the poster urging the reader to 'bash the rich!'. This slogan was primarily associated with a group calling itself 'Class War', which had gained considerable notoriety in organizing disrup-tive riots in the City and at such provocatively well-heeled events as Henley Regatta and assorted Hunt Balls. (They had also started punch-ups with startled members of CND, who were regarded contemptuously by the anarchist sect as 'middle-class wankers'; chairperson Joan Ruddock had had mud shoved into her mouth by one enthusiastic class warrior). The Brighton group liked 'bash the rich' as a rallying cry: only the 'media', they said, were hysterical enough to think that violent language meant they actually went and bashed up people. Anyway, said Mike, the slogan was dreamt up as the rallying cry for a demonstration; some people, he grudgingly admitted might have gone along with the intention of bashing the rich, others (like himself, he hastened to add), simply went 'with the intention of making their views felt'. Why should Mike, Steve and their ilk 'live in shitty little squatty-type buildings, which have no electricity or water or gas, when people live in massive houses, with say three or four people or whatever living in them'? But wasn't there that same old contradiction between violence, if only in words, and concern for animals? 'Animals aren't human are they? And its humans that are causing all the misery on the earth.' This was beginning to sound like reverse speciesism.

On the big marches and demonstrations, the anarchists were always the most dramatic presence. Tall clusters of black flags inscribed with a large white 'A' within a circle, or the ALF symbol, or sometimes a combination of both, were carried by the equally black-clad representatives of sects and tendencies like Class War, Crowbar and Black Flag. The chanting from this section of the procession generally featured words like 'scum' and threatened all kinds of unpleasant ends to vivisectors, fur traders and farming folk. Obscenities borrowed from the football terraces were creatively transformed into a new wave hymnal for the cause of animal rights. This often went down badly with more 'respectable' elements on a demo: these might well be ALF supporters as well, but there were appearances to be kept up. Within the bewilderingly broad 'rainbow' coalition that the movement had become, there were many tensions, more often than not to do with style and personality rather than any political or tactical disagreement. In any case, as one 'respectable' demonstrator indulgently remarked of a particularly noisy bunch of anarchists, 'they've got their hearts in the right places, they swell the numbers, and they believe what I believe basically'.

Violence against people in the name of animals did occur,

despite the official disavowal of the ALF. If a human happened to be on the premises in the middle of a raid, then the chances were they would get thumped. Farmers woke up to find themsevles covered in broken glass after a 'bricking'. A huntmaster in Surrey was thrown into a ditch by hooded raiders, who then broke his arm with blows from a walking stick. And then there were the 'vigilante' actions carried out against known animal abusers, often as a result of press coverage of a particularly nasty court case. In January 1987, gang of five ALF members went round to the home of nineteen-year-old Scott Goodman in Swindon. Goodman had been sent to jail for three weeks the year before for kicking a puppy to death. The vigilante squad turned up at his flat wearing masks and carrying knives, truncheons and rice flails. Clearly they were not out for a piece of quiet remonstrance but unfortunately Goodman happened to be out that evening, leaving two lodgers and a friend on the premises. These innocent parties were nonetheless attacked, two of them being stabbed in the back and the shoulder. The flat was wrecked.

The acrid flavour of the ALF's anarchist tendency was a curious mixture of savage class resentment and a kind of deviant post-hippy romanticism. An anonymous correspondent wrote lovingly of a demonstration designed to break up the Eastbourne Hunt Ball in 1986. The account was printed in *Brighton Bomber*. 'After hearing word of mouth about the local hunters decadent gathering,' wrote this enthusiast, 'groups of people from surrounding towns hit Eastbourne's Grand Hotel. No tactics had been planned, so a disorganized band of balaclavas [sic] and other anti-hunt type dudes surrounded the entrance. One Class War banner showed our anger, as the hunters in smarmy clothes and ballgowns arrived. Echoes of 'scum!' and other anti-hunt slogans were hailed, along with well aimed spit on the animal skin that dripped around some of the shits' necks.' At this point, the tale took a self-pitying and rather contradictory turn. 'The demo originally started out non-violent, until the filth [police] and two plainclothes started picking people out for whatever fascist reasons: three people were completely unreasonably kidnapped. One bloke got nicked for violence to a car.' As in any battle, lessons had been learned: in this case, according to the writer, the merits of 'quick hit and run tactics, using shit smelling and staining substances . . . leading to more humiliation for the decadent!' The piece ended with a rallying cry of superannuated psychedelia. 'Let the colours hidden in your head explode to bring strength to hand, to break the cages that imprison, with the buzz of unity to smash away the grey.' 'Smash' was another buzzword that competed with 'scum' in the lexicography of ALF activism.

Such chaotic 'actions' were popular with rank and file activists, but the Mars Bar hoax showed that by the mid 1980s the ALF could successfully organize a major 'action' demanding considerable co-ordination and planning. Yet most operations continued to be small scale and fairly haphazard. Because local cells tended to operate independently of each other, co-ordination was limited. Sometimes raids would go disastrously wrong, and sometimes the animals undergoing forcible 'liberation' might reasonably have wondered if they weren't better off in the cages they had been taken from. For the ALF, good intentions were often not enough. When things went wrong, it was usually the animals who suffered. On several occasions mink were released from farms and set free into the wild, an environment within which they were simply not equipped to survive; wildlife experts suggested that artificially reared and protected creatures like these faced a much faster and more unpleasant death in the English countryside than within the farms from which they had been freed.

On one occasion in the mid eighties, the ALF organized a night raid on the North East Surrey College of Technology at Ewell. The band of activists broke into the Animal Care department, where fifteen- to eighteen-year-olds were taught to look after mice, gerbils and hamsters. These were youngsters who apparently were interested in working in the field of veterinary medicine, helping in pet shops, or working in zoos. In the course of the raid, several hundred animals were removed from the premises by the ALF, including many babies: according to the head of the college's animal care course, Dr Simon Wallis, 'a lot of those young animals that would have been happy and healthy are almost certainly dead now'. It seemed an odd form of liberation: but in this case, as in a great many, the Front's intelligence failed to match its enthusiasm. The college's principal said that when the students turned up on the Monday morning following the raid they were extremely upset; they had regarded the animals as pets. 'They genuinely care for their animals and would never cause any harm to them. The ALF obviously didn't do their research properly, and all they have succeeded in doing is alienating the very people they draw their support from – animal lovers.'

The raiding party had been convinced that the college classroom was a hotbed of vivisection; later they claimed that they had 'documentary' evidence of cruel experiments on the creatures they had rescued, but all the college found missing was a series of pamphlets on animal welfare published by the RSPCA. As a dismal postscript to a dismal adventure, the college principal said the only disruption achieved by the ALF had been to the students' prospects in their forthcoming exams, a mere two months away. The students were said to be 'deeply upset' about the raid: the ALF were invited to come and explain their actions – an invitation that was not taken up.

The efficiency of an ALF cell depended on the right mixture of idealism and intelligence gathering. Most groups consisted of 'planners' and 'followers', the former usually older activists, in their thirties or even forties, often holding down respectable jobs; 'followers', the huge majority in any group, would be young, and, according to the ALF's own surveys, preponderantly female. By the beginning of the eighties there was an enormous reservoir of sympathetic opinion among young people who were deeply affected by what they saw happening to animals in news footage of events like the controversial Canadian seal culls and the annual whale butchery in the Faroes; television made these issues much more vivid. When you watched some of the documentaries you wanted to get up and do something: for many that meant joining the ALF. But what the Front's youthful and naïve recruits had overlooked was that, like any covert organization operating outside the law, the ALF had its own strict unwritten code: above all, the dictum that anyone who grassed on their mates would not be forgiven. It was a lesson that Karen Wedley learned the hard way.

Karen was seventeen when she got involved. A college student living in Wrexham in North Wales with her parents and sister, she had been fond of animals since childhood. What changed this vague concern into a sense of desperate and passionate outrage was the sight one evening on the local news of a seal culling operation off the Welsh coast. Karen was upset enough to write a letter to the local paper, which they duly published. This brought an immediate reaction in the form of a letter from a man who wondered if Karen might be interested in joining the Clwyd Animal Rights Alliance, the local animal rights group. The Alliance held regular meetings in Wrexham Public Library, where videos of animal abuse were shown and demonstrations organized against local targets. The man who had contacted Karen was a leading light in the Alliance: he was about forty, a finance officer, he told her, who seemed both a respectable and authoritative figure to the mainly teenage acolytes who gathered at the Library. By this time, Karen had got Shane Wilcox, and another couple of friends involved.

Within a couple of months, this informal group was heavily engaged in a round of anti-fur trade petitions, leafleting, and demonstrations, the typical animal rights group agenda. The older man kept phoning Karen, keeping track of what the group was up to, encouraging their activities. Then, one day he invited them over to Liverpool to take part in an ALF organized demo. Afterwards they all sat and talked about the movement, and that was the point, Karen ruefully accepted later, 'when things got out of hand'. The man now came to the point: he wanted to turn the Wrexham group into an active cell of the ALF. 'He got talking to us about direct action and how that was the only way to achieve animal liberation or rights for animals.' The first lesson was on the art of Supergluing a butcher's shop. 'He told us what sort of solvents to buy and how to do it. He said that once the glue had set there was no way the butcher could get into his shop without changing the lock, and that would cost about seventy pounds. Over the next few weeks we Superglued a fair number of butchers' shops in Wrexham.' There was another – and totally unsuspecting – target as well, Karen's own mother. Chris Wedley ran a clothes shop in the town, an innocent enough occupation, but not when a circus poster was boldly displayed in the window. It was enough to earn the wrath (and Superglue) of the ALF.

After a few weeks of this comparatively gentle activity, the group was moved on to a more violent agenda. Again, the older 'planner' decided tactics and weaponry. 'He gave us a very strong catapult and ballbearings and told us how it was the most effective way of damaging a plate glass window. We smashed several windows in the town centre . . . he said many of them would cost up to a thousand pounds to replace. By this time, things were really getting out of hand – we were Supergluing locks and smashing windows every week. The "planner" also gave us the car numbers of people he said were involved in animal abuse, and we slapped paint stripper over some of their vehicles.'

This litany of vandalism, you have to remind yourself, is coming not from the mouth of some loudmouth yob with a capacity for lager-fuelled violence, but a rather plump, homely and reticent girl still in her teens; sitting in the cosy sitting room of her mother's house on a middle-class housing estate, it was rather hard to take this rapid descent into a life of crime seriously. But matters got genuinely serious for Karen when in the autumn of the same year she came back from an ALF demonstration in Birmingham and found the police waiting for her at home. 'As soon as I was arrested, I was interviewed all day and refused to give any information on the "planner"; then I got bail, as did the others [her three friends had also been rounded up], so I phoned him up – but he didn't want to know us anymore; he wouldn't give us any help . . . and, well, he kicked us in the teeth really.'

Two days later, Karen and her friend Shane Wilcox went back to the police and told them everything. And not long after that, the trouble started. First the letters began to arrive at the Wedley family home. They were scrawled in deliberately shaky capital letters. 'If you become a prosecution witness in the trial,' read the first letter, 'you will be the first animals [sic] rights person to volunteer to condemn another AR's person. Are you proud of this fact?' And then the rather nasty coda: 'we don't forget TRAITORS!' The next one was even more direct. 'You fucking bastard. You are worse than the vivisectors and hunters. Keep looking behind you, never leave your house or go out alone. We will be watching you and we'll get you – no matter how long it takes, we'll get you. Your friend Shane is included as well.' The anonymous writer lurched between sinister threats and a kind of childish petulance. 'You are sick, so bloody sick. I bet your friends – perhaps you haven't got any, you don't deserve any – are ashamed of you. Don't forget, we'll get you, cunt. I won't wish you a happy new year. You won't have one.'

Karen suspected, on the basis of strong circumstantial evidence, that this last missive came from the 'planner' himself. He was up for trial at Mold Crown Court on charges of threatening to destroy and damage property, as well as conspiracy to commit criminal damage. Karen and Shane were to be witnesses for the prosecution. As they waited for the trial to come to court, there were other incidents. Windows were smashed at Karen's home: first the kitchen window, and then her bedroom window a few weeks later. Nastiest of all was an attack in the ladies' room of a local discotheque in Wrexham: out of the blue four women set on her, punching her in the face and trying to shove a broken glass at her. There was no hard evidence that these were ALF activists but Karen and Shane were convinced: they had been outlawed by the movement. They knew this because the national ALF Supporters bulletin had singled them out by name: 'local animal liberation campaigners no longer want anything to do with Karen Wedley or Shane Wilcox, but many ALF supporters will no doubt feel that strong action needs to be taken as a punishment'. The Front had learned more than esprit de corps from the paramilitaries of Ulster.

When the Wrexham animal rights trials finally came to court, the 'planner' was found guilty on the charges of threatening to destroy and damage property, and was given a hundred and twenty hours community service; he was acquitted on the conspiracy charge. Karen and Shane were both given reduced sentences of community service, after pleading guilty and turning Queen's evidence.

A year after the trial, Karen was still being treated as a pariah by local animal rights activists. 'There's some people who will go to extremes, and I was worried about it, but I've given up worrying now. You can't run away from them: sooner or later you've got to stand up to them and get on with your life.' Karen had no illusions left about her former comrades: 'You've got people now who are sending letter bombs, throwing petrol bombs through windows ... they'll poison food, so they certainly don't care about human beings or feelings at all.' Hard words, surely, from someone who, after all, had made a considerable commitment to the ALF? 'I was in the ALF, but I never once ever thought about hurting another person. I was more concerned with animal welfare ... I'd never hurt human beings for it.' Those who recruited her were clearly less sentimental. 'Someone, one day, will be fatally injured ... it wouldn't surprise me in the least if someone was killed.'

Chris Wedley says her daughter's involvement in the ALF almost destroyed the family. She wasn't going to keep quiet about what had happened, despite the threats. 'People have got to stand up to them now, because if you're quiet, they'll continue doing what they're doing. It is frightening, because if you get hit or your window goes through, you wonder what they'll do next ... but we're not going to run away from the problem.' Apart from anything else, Chris was less than pleased at some of the habits her daughter had picked up in the ALF: she had been introduced to the sniffing of crushed amphetamines ('speed') at a party held in a sanctuary for rescued animals. Front members, she said, used it for work as well as pleasure: it helped to keep you alert when you were out on a raid late at night or just before dawn.

Karen Wedley was ideal fodder for the Front: naïve, passionate about cruelty to animals, and, she has to admit, out for a bit of fun. Looking back, she found it hard to believe how things could have gone so far in the space of just a few months, the months in which her mother says she was 'brainwashed'. Her case provided a sharp snapshot of ALF methods, personnel and recruitment techniques, at once amateurish and seriously threatening. Like so many others, the Wrexham cell was made up of impressionable and unsophisticated kids in their late teens; the 'planners' were professional people (one was a social worker employed by the county council) in their late thirties or early forties. In the police crackdown at the end of a year of destructive violence, only the one 'planner' – thanks to Karen and Shane's evidence – was caught. But, as the police were to find out, those threats in the ALF Supporters Bulletin proved effective: animal rights 'supergrasses' were to be few and far between.

The violent and obscene language used in the threatening letters was a further reminder that animal rights activists now inhabited a territory far removed from the genteel world of animal welfare. But this was the currency of the movement, the kind of aggressive and impatient sloganizing that appeared with increasing frequency in the ALF's literature. Within the broad coalition of opinions, ages and backgrounds that made up the movement's highly informal membership, there would be disagreements about violence of both language and tactics. But the important thing was that at the highest level, within Ronnie Lee's immediate circle of trusted friends and colleagues, there was unanimity. Writing his essay 'On Violence' for the ALF Bulletin, Lee began with a telling quote from the French anti-vivisectionist Marie Dreyfus. 'What is going to be done? We anti-vivisectionists must wake up! There must be violence on our part, even unto death: there seems no other way ...'

CHAPTER SEVEN

> Ours are military operations: they are
> done efficiently, because there's a lot at
> stake – people's liberty is at stake.
>
> Tim Johnston, Press Officer for
> the Central Animal Liberation League

While Ronnie Lee's leadership of the ALF was never seriously questioned, there were many in the movement who felt that his idea of tactics remained clumsy and naïve. Quite apart from an endless series of personality clashes, there were genuine differences of opinion about how raids should be organized and how maximum damage could be inflicted. In 1980 this splintering of ideas was expressed in the establishment of an organization called the Northern Animal Liberation League: based in the north west (largely in the Greater Manchester area) this was to be the first in a series of Animal Liberation Leagues that would represent a rather more sophisticated (though not necessarily less violent) development in the move to direct action.

The Leagues were established to carry out large-scale operations against major targets: the multi-national pharmaceutical companies and the bigger University research laboratories. Many more 'troops' were involved in League raids than the more modest and haphazard efforts of the ALF: up to a hundred and fifty activists would be marshalled together for a single raid, sometimes divided into teams that would perform a whole series of actions according to a preplanned sequence and often in broad daylight. Too many liberationists, said one League spokesman, thought that all you needed in the movement was a balaclava and a 'crowbar mentality': the Leagues were to be an exercise in precise military planning and subtle media manipulation. In the event, they were responsible for a series of spectacular raids that did indeed produce a wealth of publicity, but they were never quite sophisticated enough to dodge the one major flaw inherent in the idea: they were just too big.

Sooner or later, faced with matching police manpower, they were vulnerable to mass arrest: and that is precisely what happened. Two Leagues are still currently in operation, but most folded in the mid eighties after a series of mass trials, resulting in stiff prison sentences. And yet, for a period, the Leagues represented a serious advance in tactics and the use of technology that was not lost on the ALF.

Part of the rationale behind the idea of these new Leagues, separate from the cells of the ALF, was a growing resentment of the rather snotty exclusivity of certain ALF activists. Often in the animal rights movement it was hard to distinguish between genuine differences of opinion and trivial personality clashes, but the editor of 'Target', newsletter of the South East Animal Liberation League (SEALL), was convinced that his rank and file activists were sick and tired of factionalism. 'This band of activists,' he thundered, 'are not interested in the seemingly endless arguments that torment the animal rights movement. Are not interested in personality clashes. Are not interested in the inverted snobbery that some vegans pontificate about – most of us were carnivorous in our eating habits at one time . . .' John Beggs argued that as well these unnecessary and unedifying squabbles, the movement was guilty of a lack of imagination. 'There is an idea,' Beggs told supporters at a meeting on the south coast, 'running through our movement that all you've got to do is pick up a crowbar and go and smash something. Well, that's all very nice and it sounds good. It makes you feel better, you come home thinking "great, I put through five butchers' windows tonight", but you've got to think a little bit further than that, and think about the effect of what you're doing.' For Beggs and his fellow enthusiasts in the Leagues, the effects they were after were serious economic sabotage and damaging exposure in the mass media.

Up until now there had been a general assumption that the media were naturally hostile to what the militant liberationists were up to: they were, after all, in the hallowed canon of the anarchist, both tools of and at the same time inherently a part of the 'establishment'. People like John Beggs knew better. They realized two crucial things: firstly, that there was a constant demand for dramatic picture material in both press and television, and secondly that few news editors (or the viewers and readers they serviced) could resist touching stories featuring the rescue of animals. Where they were being 'rescued' from was of secondary importance: every story had an inherent appeal to the essential soppiness of the animal loving British public. And so the first major innovation that the Leagues brought to the tactics of raiding was the video camera. Beggs loathed Fleet Street and its 'fascist' proprietors, but he could see that 'even the *Express* wants a good story and the *Sun* wants a good story, and if you've got a photograph of a sheep in a laboratory with a piece of glass in its side so you can look straight in, even those kind of papers will want it. And if you've got a photograph of a monkey screaming because the scientist has got it round its throat, even those right wing papers want it.'

This was a good point. League raids were to include video and photographic equipment as a matter of course: the electronic record of the action often being of more importance than the rescue being filmed. SEALL in particular became highly efficient in servicing the media with what they clearly appreciated. If you took a JVC or Panasonic into the laboratory or factory farm you were guaranteed terrific pictures, as John Beggs had proved. 'If you capture what's going on with those animals, and if you run it up to ITN, as we did three times, because they were by far the most receptive of the channels, they love it; they absolutely love it, because its good action-packed stuff, and each time there was no problem – they just wanted to show it; it was all they could do to get it on fast enough.' The Central Animal Liberation League (CALL) had made it on to regional television with a raid on Oxford University Laboratories in which 'frozen' rabbits had been held up to the camera. It worked every time. 'When it comes to the visual,' said Beggs, 'we can win: the secret is to get the stuff they want.'

The Leagues spent thousands of pounds on expensive video and photographic equipment: cash was raised both by local animal rights groups, or came from donations from well-established and ostensibly respectable organizations like the British Union for the Abolition of Vivisection or the National Anti-vivisection Society. On one occasion, a sum of £5000 was donated by the NAVS to the Central Animal Liberation League alone. Each League, as with the cells of the ALF, would be effectively under the leadership of a small group, sometimes just one individual. The person in authority with CALL was clearly Tim Johnston, notionally the group's 'press officer'.

Johnston was fond of showing off the impressive range of technology at his disposal. It would be possible, he said, to observe members of CALL out on manoeuvres, reccying a future target. We were to meet at a service station half way up the M1.

At the agreed rendezvous, Johnston made himself immediately and rather ridiculously conspicuous by walking through the crowded cafeteria muttering noisily into a walkie-talkie. The impression was of a plane spotter caught up in paramilitary fantasies. This was followed by a lengthy drive through the east Midlands countryside, punctuated by frequent stops in lay-bys during which Johnston would engage in further bouts of muttering with League activists out in the field. Eventually, parking up in a remote country lane, we trudged across sodden fields to what looked like a derelict Bedford van standing on a cart track about a hundred yards away from the banks of a remote stretch of the river Trent. Judging by whistles and audio signals, the van was surrounded by four or five look-outs: inside, the Bedford was anything but derelict.

Three slight, balaclava'd figures were hovering over a mass of complicated looking electronic equipment. A camera pointed out over the fields and the river, recording a sharp picture on a black and white monitor. These people were all new recruits to the League, said Johnston. One was an accountant, another an electrician, the third a student. All of them seemed surprisingly genteel when they opened their mouths: they also seemed to come from a gentler breed than the ALF activists on the south coast. There was a touching amateurishness about their balaclavas, through which prominent features could be clearly identified. It was as though they were embarrassed about having to affect the garb of the terrorist.

Tim Johnston said there were about fifty active members of his League. 'These people', he told us, 'are getting to know the equipment they'd be using in a real situation, so they're familiar with things like videos, radios and so on, so that if things go wrong when they've got real pressure on them they won't panic.' Johnston was proud of the professionalism of CALL, he said. Stealthy, informed, careful operations had meant few arrests: there was no room for macho displays of reckless violence. 'Units like this train very hard. We're not going to raid places every week in order to prove that we exist. The Central Animal Liberation League would perhaps only do one or two raids a year, but they are significant raids that generate so much publicity that the information could be used again and again.' This was considerably more sophisticated thinking than the ALF had come up with. Also it had the merit of containing a genuine element of evangelism: the Leagues wanted the public to see what they saw when they broke into laboratories. Damage and rescue were of secondary importance.

Tim Johnston's finest hour came in 1985, when CALL mounted a much publicized raid on University Park Farm, the holding and breeding centre for animals awaiting vivisection at Oxford University. Thirty-two dogs were removed from the premises, which had been under surveillance for several weeks. The League's press statement detailed the action in clipped military precision. 'At 9 p.m. on 7 July, thirty CALL activists arrived at the perimeter fence of University Park Farm. The fence was quickly taken down and the complex entered. The activists immediately split into separate groups. One group cut the padlocks off a number of gates through which access would be needed; another went to UPF's own van and pushed it into the position where it could be loaded with dogs to be taken away. At the same time another group gained access to the first dog unit by breaking off a corrugated plastic window. By 9.05 p.m. dogs were being passed out of the dog unit and into UPF's van.' Smart work.

The haul included five beagles and a highly personable Old English Sheepdog. Assorted pigeons, guinea pigs and hens were left behind since they lacked, the CALL felt, sufficient publicity appeal. This was a highly efficient operation carried out when there was still plenty of daylight. After the dogs had been bundled into the van and driven off, the League's look-outs gave the all-clear to a second wave of activists to re-enter the complex, this time to steal documents and to film conditions inside. An internal door was sledge-hammered down under the eye of the video camera, and access to the primate unit obtained. Later, CALL rushed copies of their tape to both the BBC and ITN, with photographs made available to the press. The subsequent coverage was enormous, with most attention inevitably lavished on the sheepdog. It was a clever and almost entirely successful enterprise, not least in taking a semi-conciliatory line by way of explanation. 'At all stages of this operation,' said their spokesman, 'CALL had a policy of minimum damage ... doors or windows were only broken when access to a building was needed.' The ALF made no attempt to disguise its contempt for the public: the Leagues were keen to present an image of reluctant and fundamentally decent activism: a kind of animals' SAS with all the cool efficiency and none of the nastiness.

Later, CALL claimed that many of the stolen dogs responded to commands like 'sit' and 'lie down', citing this as evidence that somehow they must once have been people's pets: they also claimed that after the raid and all the subsequent publicity, the Thames Valley Police were inundated with a thousand requests from animal lovers to investigate the source of the University's dogs. Showing further entrepreneurial skills, the League then mounted its own merchandising operation, advertising Park Farm Dog Rescue videos at £14.95 each, with special packs of photographs at £2.50 each. The CALL, like most of the Leagues, was never going to miss a sharp marketing trick. You could buy CALL T-shirts, CALL badges and CALL posters. There was a CALL supporters' group, which was something halfway between a fund raising organization and a fan club: for £5.00 a month local animal rights groups would have access to the growing CALL library of videos, photographs, leaflets and displays; activists would be made available to talk about the League's work in the field.

Tim Johnston talked about the CALL in the quiet, certain, fixed tone that once again seemed to be the orthodox conversational style of the movement. 'All we take on are major targets, where the chances of publicity are very significant. There's nearly always ways of by-passing alarms ... it may not always be the most obvious way – people may have to go through a wall rather than a door.' And how would they do that? 'Using drills and saws. Activists within the Central Animal Liberation League are trained in specific techniques they may need to use: we have training weekends.' It sounded like a curious synthesis of scouting and a revolutionary Marxist weekend summer school.

Johnston managed to make all this sound quite reasonable. But what he was talking about was burglary, surely? 'But I am being very reasonable,' the monotone continued. 'What's going on in these establishments is animals being scalded, poisoned and blinded.' He was unimpressed by existing and planned statutory controls of laboratory practices: they were all guilty, these vivisectors. Utilitarianism was simply a long word to disguise vicious torture. The next refrain was one that was

83

becoming wearyingly familiar: 'there is a law, and there is a higher moral law. Within these laboratories animals are being tortured and dying . . . they have absolutely no say. Their only hope is organizations such as ourselves, and we consider it completely morally wrong to torture these animals.'

This conviction that it was necessary and even ethical to break the law in order to expose wrongdoing of a higher order was given unexpected reinforcement in 1984 – from a court of law. In August, the South East Animal Liberation League had mounted a raid on the Royal College of Surgeons' establishment at Downe in Kent. It was another well-organized effort (Mike Huskisson, the fatigue-clad veteran of the John Peel raid being involved) in which no one got caught, despite a police helicopter arriving on the scene just eleven minutes after the first break in. Local police work was hampered when detectives on board the helicopter mistook a local troop of boy scouts for the SEALL activists. But the real triumph of the raid was the rescue of a macaque called 'Mone', along with a considerable amount of photographic and documentary evidence alleging ill treatment of both her and other primates on the premises. On the basis of material collected in the course of the raid, the British Union for the Abolition of Vivisection brought a series of five summonses under the 1911 Protection of Animals Act against the Royal College, which finally came to court early the following year. To the surprise and dismay of the RCS, the bench found them guilty on one of five charges, the one concerning 'Mone', though this was as much the result of a former employee of the RCS giving evidence that the cages' ventilation system was inadequate.

To win on just one count out of five might not seem the greatest victory in the world but for BUAV and their activist friends in SEALL it was a momentous event. It didn't matter in the end that the verdict was reversed on appeal a few months later, because the publicity had already been won, and it was considerable. 'Mone' became something of a national celebrity, and her picture was used effectively in the emotive logo used by BUAV in its campaign against the government's white paper drawn up to modify vivisection controls.

The RCS raid was the high point of the Leagues' campaign to make direct action a legitimate tactic in the eyes of a sympathetic public. But within a couple of months, perhaps as a result of overconfidence, SEALL fell foul of a police operation that, after the humiliation of Downe, had decided to take these balaclava'd 'fanatics' rather more seriously. The target for the October raid was an organization called Wickham Laboratories, which had long featured on the hate list of both the ALF and less overtly militant animal rights organizations. In the event, both the raid and the subsequent mass trial of those involved turned out to be a significant watershed in the development of the movement. In the rather contemptuously dismissive phrase of one League 'planner' (who in the event managed to avoid arrest) it sorted out the serious activists from the 'weekend cowboys'. For the gentle, herbivorous types who got involved in League actions, imagining them to be a kind of slightly more energetic form of demonstration, Wickham came as a nasty shock.

The Hampshire-based firm carried out a wide range of tests under contract to pharmaceutical and agricultural companies. They used rabbits, rats, mice, dogs, sheep and pigs to test drugs for safety and toxicity. Wickham's managing director had recently further enraged animal rights groups by seeking consent to extend breeding facilities at his local farm to the inclusion of beagles. Deny as it would any sentimentality or anthropomorphism in its view of the animal kingdom, the liberationist movement constantly betrayed a touching partiality towards dogs. When SEALL decided to attack the Wickham premises, it used the same tactics that had worked so well on the RCS labs in Kent. More than a hundred activists were gathered together (no mean feat in itself) and divided up into three hit squads; once again they would strike in broad daylight. On a Sunday in late October, simultaneous raids were launched at the main laboratory headquarters, a local business consultancy run by Wickham's veterinary director David Walker, and on the firm's nearby dog houses (blessed with the somewhat Enid Blyton-style name of Cottagepatch Kennels).

But this time round things did not go quite as expected. SEALL got plenty of publicity but not the kind they were after. It wasn't so much the fact that the police were much quicker off the mark this time (with eight arrests on the premises and eleven more shortly afterwards), but what the details of the raid showed about the liberationists. David Walker was attacked in his own home. 'I was coshed on the head, kicked in the ear, and had my hand trampled on,' he said later, describing something rather more unpleasant and personal than the 'minimum restraining force' that the League had maintained was policy. Despite tight planning (prosecuting counsel later referred to 'generals', 'sergeants' and 'footsoldiers') this time there was panic. Police (and this was before Scotland Yard had set up its specialist animal rights squad) had tracked SEALL activists for the previous twenty-four hours: they caught the Wickham raiders red-handed.

In the mêlée that followed, most of the hundred 'footsoldiers' managed to escape but nineteen raiders were arrested, shortly to be canonized in the movement as the Wickham Nineteen. They included such familiar faces as Mike Huskisson and Michael Nunn, the former butcher. The leading 'planners' of the League had managed to avoid being in the wrong place at the wrong time, leaving a varied and largely untested army of activists to face the consequences. The Nineteen included 'hard' men like John Curtin, who was subsequently found guilty of digging up the Duke of Beaufort's grave in the name of the Hunt Retribution Squad, but also several apparent pillars of the local community, like Sue Baker, a district nurse, and Sally Miller, a successful fashion model. Beyond their common zeal in the cause of the animals there was no obvious social or political coherence to be found among the Wickham Nineteen.

The subsequent trial of the Nineteen at Winchester Crown Court the following year became a rallying point for the entire animal rights movement; encouraged by their previous court victory against the Royal College of Surgeons, the British Union for the Abolition of Vivisection threw their considerable resources behind the SEALL defence fund. SEALL itself set up a thriving marketing division to sell T-shirts, posters, and badges on behalf of the Nineteen. Not for the first time, celebrities from the pop music became more involved in fund raising. Tracie Young from the Style Council made the record 'Can't Leave You Alone' for the campaign, which was based on the slogan 'The Wickham Nineteen are Innocent – Jail the Vivisectors!' The Wickham Defence Fund and associated merchandising operations were organized from the Brunel University Students Union at Uxbridge in Middlesex, where John Beggs, SEALL's 'press officer' was studying for his law degree. For Beggs and his small group of confidants who formed the ideological leadership of SEALL, the outcome of the trial was crucial: for the Nineteen to face conviction and possible prison sentences could well alienate activists from mass actions for the foreseeable future.

In the event, only seven of the accused were found guilty but any rejoicing was cut short by the imposition of a total of nine years and nine months in prison sentences. Far less than the hard core of the ALF did the mass activists of the Leagues expect that what they did would land them in prison? There was a genuine sense that breaking into Wickham was merely the practical application of ideas that anyone of any decency and compassion would approve of; after all, hadn't a magistrates court fined the RCS £250, thanks to a SEALL raid? 'I don't think it can be against the law to save a life,' said Sally Miller from the dock. Surely it was apparent to everyone that establishments like Downe and Wickham were no better than Belsen?

But Sally Miller was found guilty and sentenced to eighteen months in gaol. Of the rest, Mike Nunn was given the stiffest sentence – three years. He had been identified as the 'general' in charge of the whole operation, one that Judge Lewis McCreery QC described as 'meticulously timed and planned'. McCreery's attitude to the case and to SEALL in particular had been rigorous, with occasional bursts of contemptuous humour. Told that SEALL had organized demonstrations against McDonalds, the judge commented 'I'm glad they're not against fish fingers, because what would our children have to eat?' But the central question was the issue of violence. 'Do you think that the suggestion that SEALL is non-violent is a lot of humbug?' McCreery pointedly asked the jury as he reached his summing up.

The trial had lasted ten weeks. The shock waves that permeated the animal rights movement lasted a great deal longer. When Ronnie Lee and Cliff Goodman had gone to prison after the Band of Mercy trial, it had hardened the former and convinced the latter that fighting for the animals was not worth the penalty of a life outside the law: from the trial, the hard core of the ALF had been born. With Wickham, the lessons were tactical and political: this time, on a far larger scale (well over a hundred activists having taken part in the three pronged assault) decisions were being taken in the movement about whether prison was the price individuals were prepared to pay. From this point on, prisoner support schemes, properly and efficiently organized after the model of 'authentic' terrorist groups like the IRA, became an important part of the movement. Visiting Ronnie Lee two years later, on remand at Hull prison, fellow activists were observed dutifully taking their turn on the rota to offer solidarity and to provide vegan supplements to prison food.

John Beggs later admitted that Wickham was 'probably too ambitious, three raids simultaneously in one morning'. But it was also not entirely ineffective as a piece of publicity. Beggs could still have it both ways with SEALL, managing to take credit for paramilitary planning while making fun of the full might of the state descending on a bunch of rather amiable and harmless eccentrics: 'They had about seventy detectives working full time on the case . . . quite an amazing amount of police just to track down some vegetarians, you know, unbelievable really . . .' he told an animal rights meeting. In fact, many of the Nineteen fitted this soft image: bank clerks, local government officials, even a former tax officer. But the hard core, led by Nunn and Curtin, were full-time and deadly serious activists, and on this older, tougher, professional side, there were hard lessons to be learnt from Wickham; and especially about the cardinal sin of grassing on your mates. 'The Wickham trial suffered from that,' Beggs later told a meeting: 'and what's amazing is that big, six foot guys, some of the biggest blokes, very tough superficially, were the first ones to break down and talk to the police. And yet some of the small, quieter women kept absolutely silent for three days.' If every animal rights activist in the past three years had followed this rule, only three or four of them might have been now in prison, said Beggs, instead of thirty. The movement would have to tighten up or many more would suffer. The trouble was that too many of the 'footsoldiers' of the movement were touchingly soft; told by police that 'someone had nearly got killed' on a raid, they would panic and start talking.

If the sentences meted out after the Wickham trial were intended to be deterrents, as the SEALL leadership clearly thought, the tactic seemed to have worked. As John Beggs put it, 'people thought "Jesus, it's just not a picnic anymore these raids".' After Wickham, the Leagues either dissolved or reduced the scale of their operations to the more cautious raids of the kind undertaken by CALL in the Midlands. 1984 had been the *annus mirabilis* of this phase of the movement and, although Wickham had made the biggest impact, there were other raids that had seen similar armies of balaclava'd activists storming major research establishments up and down the country. One hundred and eighty supporters of the Northern Animal Liberation League had broken into the ICI laboratory complex in Cheshire, and later in the same year some kind of record was set by an even more ambitious assault on the Unilever plant in Bedfordshire. No less than three hundred rank and file 'footsoldiers' were carefully assembled to storm the barricades in broad daylight: only 10% were caught and charged and subsequent prison sentences were considerably lighter than at Wickham. In all these raids, video equipment was used and sequences tellingly transmitted on both national and regional television. Later, both the BBC and IBA were to intervene in planned broadcasts involving animal liberation groups; but at this stage the wobbly home-video material was too gripping and emotionally beguiling to be ignored, not least when it featured the more lovable species of sheepdog and beagle.

The series of large-scale daylight raids altered forever the physical appearance of laboratory complexes that were felt, however obscurely, to be under threat. The ICI plant at Alderley Edge in Cheshire, for example, was transformed after the NALL raid into a kind of high tech Colditz, with barbed wire, remote video monitoring units and sophisticated alarm systems. If one aim of the Leagues, with their tactical emphasis on publicity, was to make the vivisectionists look like the latter day proprietors of Belsen and Auschwitz, on this superficial level they certainly succeeded. The pharmaceutical industry and the university laboratory complexes had been seen to be put very much on the defensive. The research at Alderley was mainly into new medicines being developed for the relief of serious and disabling diseases; many human lives had been saved and much suffering alleviated because of the work there, according to an ICI spokesman. But it was hard work convincing the public of your humanitarian intentions when you were busy turning your place of work into something looking horribly like a concentration camp.

The Leagues' clever use of the media achieved something else as well. More than the efforts of the ALF, the mass raids put militant animal rights firmly on the political agenda. Often, League raids would be attributed in the press to the ALF, or just to 'liberationists', who were all assumed to form some kind of homogeneous whole; but their effect on the politicians was marked. When Margaret Thatcher gave a speech to the American Bar Association meeting in London in 1984, the year of the mass raids, she paid the Leagues an oblique compliment. 'A fashionable heresy,' she told the lawyers, 'is that if you feel sufficiently strongly about some particular issue, be it nuclear weapons, racial discrimination, or animal liberation, you are entitled to claim superiority to the law, and are therefore absolved. This is arrogant nonsense and deserves to be treated as such.' Animal rights had now clearly joined the distinguished company of causes to have earned the public disapproval of Number 10.

The big 'show trials' of that year, as the animal rights press like to call Wickham, ICI and Unilever, made the Leagues think rather more carefully about mass action, but there were no second thoughts either about the moral rectitude of their own cause, or the irrelevance of parliamentary democracy. Winding up SEALL in the autumn of 1985, the League's magazine, *Target*, asserted that militant action continued to be 'imperative' for the success of the cause of Animal Liberation. 'Direct action,' it went on, 'is a political pressure, but the effect of increased direct action of various kinds will be that parliament will in many respects become largely irrelevant, a mere rubber stamp for *de facto* change which the animal liberation movement has brought about.' Hunting would only be banned when activists had made the cost of its policing prohibitive; the politicians would only remove the requirement to test products on animals 'when the multi-nationals are on their knees begging the government to do so, such will be the harassment of the vivisection industry'. To abjure direct action now would be 'morally reprehensible . . . and an abdication of our responsibilities to expect that animals should await the whims of politicians'. In the end, the biggest lesson of Wickham was that the state, the Establishment, the despised politicians were running scared: the vigour of police activity was merely a symptom of 'the growing despair which is gripping the opposition'. SEALL might be finished, but this was merely a tactical shift: the struggle would continue in more effective and subtle forms.

CHAPTER EIGHT

I can support petrol bombing, bombs
under cars, and probably shootings at a
later stage. It's a war.

Tim Daley, leading ALF activist

While the Leagues had chosen the brazen tactic of mass raids
in broad daylight, using the media as potential if unwitting
allies, the ALF was moving down the path of pure terrorism:
from the early 1980s, their tactics were largely based on the
use of the bomb. The purposes were twofold – the powerful
economic devastation guaranteed by the planting of incendiary
devices and the personalized terror directed at specific individuals. By 1987, at least seventeen scientists involved in vivisection had been subjected to petrol or car bomb attacks. Most of
these were claimed by an organization calling itself the Animal
Rights Militia, but as we shall see there is little doubt that no
separate grouping existed apart from the hard core of 'planners'
who organized ALF actions. Ronnie Lee had openly called for
the invention of new names to take notional responsibility for
acts too violent to accord with the ALF's public stance of
pacifism. For those who had close contact with Lee and his
confederates, the move towards personal violence was unsur-
prising; from the early eighties, the tone of the movement's
literature and style of management had taken on the curiously
hybrid – and contradictory – character of paramilitary
anarchism.

By 1981, a new generation of much harder, unsentimental
leadership had taken charge of the direction of ALF policy, with
the approval of Ronnie Lee. These included figures whose
political background lay in anarchism and some whose experience lay in the violent confrontationalism of the far right. Dave
Nicholls, the former tax inspector from Beckenham, had been
Essex organizer for the fascist British Movement up until at
least 1981: within a couple of years he had turned his attention
to animal rights. This was not unusual: far right groupings saw

considerable mileage in both the ecological and animal rights movements as a potential source for the recruitment of the idealistic young. And animal rights as an issue had the useful ingredient of ritual slaughter as a means of promoting anti-semitic and anti-Muslim propaganda. Nicholls rapidly became Lee's number one confidant and lieutenant; he was energetic and full of bright ideas. It was his suggestion that led to the establishment of the ALF's Support Group, a sophisticated fund raising operation that milked the softer end of animal rights movement for cash.

In 1982 Nicholls set up a regular bulletin for the Support Group, using it to promote ideas, and to encourage the rank and file to use the language of outright violence. 'Vivisectors are scum!' screamed the front page slogan in issue number four. Inside, a lengthy editorial was devoted to amplifying this: 'The average vivisector suffers from megalomania and a very deep form of schizophrenia.' He was mad, bad and a callous murderer and there was no room for sentimentality in deciding his fate. 'Traditional animal rights organizations' were wasting their time in making excuses: vivisectors weren't 'misguided' or in need of education, they were simply scum.

The older established animal welfare groups, like the RSPCA and the League Against Cruel Sports, now seemed to have become a source of even more virulent loathing than the scientists. Right from the first bulletin, Nicholls put the boot in; these half hearted do-gooders were getting in the way of the serious business. Achieving animal rights was inherently a struggle against the system, that is democracy and the law. 'Animal liberation has to be achieved outside the legal system!' The trouble was that groups like the RSPCA diverted good people who 'would otherwise be doing really useful work'. It was a matter of pride that 'the ALF is now feared by animal abusers'; people who worked in laboratories where vivisection was practised would no longer be named in public, for fear for their personal safety. This was just 'the beginning of justified retaliation.'

In their articles for the ALF Supporters Group Bulletin, Nicholls and Lee were clearly well aware that this sort of line did not necessarily go down well with everyone in the movement; and so there were constant reminders that every piece of unpleasantness was justified by the long term end of animal liberation. To question violence was to question this end. A whole page was devoted to the issue of butchers' windows and why smashing them was absolutely necessary to the cause. No time for second thoughts about the livelihoods of these people, nor indeed for any lingering scruples about whether the public could actually be persuaded rather than terrorized into eating less meat. 'Some idealists,' ran one editorial, 'may hope that the whole of humanity may be "converted" to a vegetarian diet, but unfortunately this is an impossible dream. To suggest that one day there will be enough Animal Rights workers with enough time, enough training, and enough resources to visit everyone to put forward the vegetarian argument and those listening will suddenly see the "light" is a nonsense. The response is usually "I'll think about it" or "you've got a good case, but I can't agree with you etc etc". THIS IS THE OBSCENITY THE ALF IS SUCCESSFULLY FIGHTING AND DAMAGING – The "animals for food trade" will be smashed, destroyed, and finally buried!'

The ALF's dismissive attitude towards democracy was not simply an impatience with the ponderous and imperfect structure of an elected Parliament: the Front by now had more or less given up on the broad mass of its own species. The "public", slurping down their roasted chicken, were not going to give up their pleasures without a struggle, bulletin number seven had warned. Here was the notion of guilt, not by association of class but species. The tactical agenda was one of threat, not persuasion. Under Dave Nicholls, the language of the Front assumed almost manic levels of confidence, owing something perhaps to his years of experience in far right politics. 'If it is necessary to smash and destroy every butcher's shop in the land to stop this foul trade, then the ALF will do it. If this is what it takes to make the population stop to think about whether flesh-eating is right, then it shall be done.' And tough luck, apparently, on anyone who got in the way. After all, 'the butcher's shop with its chatty butcher and blood-stained apron is the high temple of animal suffering and death.' No one who was serious about animal rights could possibly dissent.

Dave Nicholls himself, like so many given to this kind of rhetoric, was as unlikely a figure as the diminutive Lee to take charge of a paramilitary operation. For most of the period in the early to mid eighties when he effectively ran the ALF Supporters Group Bulletin, Nicholls continued to work as a tax inspector in Bromley. Like Ronnie Lee, he wore wire rimmed glasses, and in addition suffered from a fairly serious diabetic condition. Nonetheless, he was full of bright new ideas for formalizing the chaotic ALF structure into something resembling a proper guerilla army; some fellow activists were outraged when he talked of appointing military ranks and insisting on uniforms. For many out in the field, the balaclava held a kind of sub Che Guevara romanticism, softened by the image of the wearer cuddling a rescued rabbit; khaki and stripes seemed a little extreme.

In 1984, the issue of violence against both people and property came to a head. By now, the Supporters Group Bulletin was openly advocating violent actions against targeted individuals, just as long as they weren't actually claimed in the name of the ALF. Articles took a contemptuous view of the traditional pacifism of the vegetarian/animal welfare tradition, with Ronnie Lee pouring scorn on 'this obsession with non-violence, the "worship" of Ghandi . . . some half-baked pacifist ideology . . . the best way to deal with bullies is to give them a damn good hiding'. Only an all out war, concluded this piece, could give the animals any hope. This overt display of aggression had two immediate consequences, driving the ALF apart from the two 'respectable' organizations that had up until then provided consistent support: support that depended on the maintenance of an official position that advocated minimal damage on raids – and absolutely no premeditated violence.

In May, the British Union for the Abolition of Vivisection, who had given the ALF office space in their Highbury headquarters, decided that enough was enough. Flirting with the direct action groups had always been a dangerous game for BUAV, one that had paid off in their support of SEALL, whose evidence obtained by burglary had helped in the prosecution of the Royal College of Surgeons. But when the ALF started talking about targeting individuals, it was time to get rid of their increasingly embarrassing presence. It was not so much that there was any fundamental difference of opinion here (Tim Daley and John Beggs were both elected on to the BUAV committee) but such things should be discussed privately, not trumpeted in the newspapers. There was also, as usual, a strong element of personality clash involved. Ronnie Lee was by far the most charismatic figure in the movement: to many activists, he was the movement. This was not the view of many on the BUAV executive, who had come to animal rights from an assortment of political groupings on the far left, and who distrusted the personality cult surrounding Lee. Dave Nicholls's military posturings had been particularly resented. The ALF had had to go.

Five months later, the Front were dealt a second blow. For four years, they had been allowed to use a postal box number service by the Peace News Collective in Nottingham. The venerable pacifist group had been founded in 1936 as an anti-militarist paper, promoting as a side line the protection of animals and the practice of vegetarianism. Under the banner headline 'Non-violence and the ALF', the Peace News collective explained how, more in sorrow than anger, they could no longer provide the Front with the facility they had used to recruit new members. The paper had been one of the first to publicize the 'horrors of factory farming'; it had happily printed the details of the early beginnings of non-violent direct action. But now, members of the ALF were 'increasingly and publicly showing a willingness to support acts of intimidation and physical violence to animal abusers, which raises difficult questions for pacifists, particularly those who are currently involved with the ALF'.

A long list of complaints followed. No one could claim that the destruction of butchers' shops and acts of arson at animal research laboratories constituted a 'campaign based on principled non-violence'. Peace News was appalled at the random acts committed by the Front's loose network of cells. 'The actions claimed for the ALF by local groups show little sign of strategy and less of an idea of movement building, beyond the problematic concept of "propaganda of the deed".' The piece concluded: 'at root, there's a massive question of principle. You don't have to share the belief – possibly the core belief – of non-violence, that the means used determine the ends arrived at, to see this. The use of violence to liberate animals is itself a contradiction. At its crudest, humans are animals too, even vivisectors are animals.' The Mars Bar hoax had been the final straw. 'The details of the story as it unfolded in the press are irrelevant now. The threat of violence has no more to do with the reverence for life than its execution. Whoever was responsible for it produced the most monumentally counter-productive publicity stunt the animal rights movement has seen this year.'

Deprived in rapid succession of office and box number, the

ALF decamped to Hammersmith and set up home on the second floor of a seedy block opposite the tube station. The name on the plate said 'Independent Tax Advisory Services', no doubt causing considerable confusion to potential clients in search of a decent accountant. As for Peace News, the evidence seemed to suggest that their honourable pacifist notions were now somewhat passé in the movement. Little more than a year later, the paper gave over a whole page to a hunt saboteur who had had his fill of non-violence: all that high principled pacifism had meant that you allowed yourself to get beaten to a bloody pulp by the hunt followers. 'Right now,' he concluded, 'I'd say that effective hunt sabotage and non-violence look about a million miles apart.'

Hunting was the one area where violence was clearly being provoked. The long established League Against Cruel Sports and the more recently formed Hunt Saboteurs Association both assumed that violence against hunstmen was unethical and counter-productive. By the 1980s, the hunting fraternity, and more especially the scavenging 'terriermen' who followed on foot, interpreted this as wimpish behaviour. Beatings were regularly handed out, often while the police stood by and did nothing. In one notorious incident during demonstrations against hare coursing at the Waterloo Cup course in Lancashire, Eddie Coulson, a peaceful saboteur, was severely injured in a violent attack by a courser; Coulson's skull was cracked in the incident, inducing epilepsy in the victim. It was popularly rumoured throughout the animal rights movement that this was the inspiration behind the formation of a group that was to hit the headlines in late 1984 – the Hunt Retribution Squad.

The Squad made its first appearance in a picture feature in a London listings magazine in October. A bunch of about twenty hooded and masked figures were photographed holding a bizarre assortment of weapons, including chain saws, clubs and axes; they were ex-members of the HSA, they said, fed up with its policy of non-violence; the HRS was to be the first anti-blood sport hit squad, offering personal violence to their targets. John Beggs admitted that he had set up the HRS photo call as a stunt. The name was simply a convenience, to be used whenever it seemed appropriate. Beggs had once been out 'sabbing' with a group of fellow students, in the course of which adventure they had all pulled out balaclavas and staves and announced their instant transformation into an HRS hit squad.

Animal rights seemed to lend itself to this kind of ad hoc self-dramatization.

But the HRS ceased to be a private joke and achieved instant notoriety on Boxing Day two months later. In the middle of the night, a small group of masked figures broke into the family graveyard of the Duke of Beaufort at Badminton parish church in Gloucestershire. The tenth Duke, Hugh Arthur Fitzroy Somerset, had been the master of the Beaufort Hunt and a close friend of the Queen: he had died at the age of eighty-three earlier in the year. The HRS managed to dig three feet down into the grave but failed to reach the Duke's coffin. A statement to the Press Association said that 'the intention was to remove the corpse from the grave and to scatter him around Worcester Lodge. We also planned to remove his head and despatch it to Princess Anne, a fellow blood junkie.' Instead, the squad had stolen the cross on the grave and daubed the graveyard with anti-hunt slogans. They had, they told PA, drawn up a lengthy hit list of targets who would shortly be receiving their attentions: these included the Royal Family, Lord Whitelaw, Michael Heseltine (then Defence Secretary), the football manager Jackie Charlton, who presented a television series on country sports, and, somewhat mysteriously, commentator Jimmy Hill.

The same communiqué claimed that the HRS had 'at least a hundred members who are prepared to, and will in fact use violence to achieve their aims – to end bloodsports, including angling of course. It is time the perverted hunters have a taste of their own violent medicine. The men and women of the HRS will be extremely busy in the New Year.' Anyone even remotely connected with blood sports was 'murdering filth' and would be dealt with. The press statement was accompanied by a photograph showing three hooded figures holding the upended cross from the Duke's grave, with the word 'shit' daubed on it.

The Beaufort grave desecration achieved widespread publicity, not least because it was cleverly planned for the otherwise dead news period between Christmas and New Year. Press outrage surpassed the Mars Bar episode, while the League Against Cruel Sports and the Hunt Saboteurs Association roundly condemned the 'ghoulish' adventure. An ex-secretary of the HSA said that if he knew who the people involved were he would turn them in, precisely the kind of 'traitorous' remark that Nicholls and Lee found most contemptible. But within just four days, the police had arrested three men and a woman, all in their early twenties, in connection with the incident. Two of this group, Terry Helsby and John Curtin, were later charged with criminal damage.

The manner of their arrest suggested that the HRS was not quite as devastatingly well organized as the grave robbing expedition might have suggested. Helsby's mother had recognized her son's face behind the hood in the picture on the front page of her paper the day after the raid. She immediately went upstairs and challenged her son, who was still catching up on his sleep after what had clearly been a long night. Terry grinned sheepishly and went back to sleep: his mother went straight to the police. 'The way they were going on, they were going to hurt someone,' she said. 'I think they wanted to be discovered – there's no point in being a secret martyr.' Helsby certainly didn't seem to be the most discreet of activists; while he was on bail awaiting trial he was caught breaking the windows of sports' shops and butchers' shops.

Helsby and Curtin were both found guilty at Southampton Crown Court and sentenced to two years in gaol. What clearly emerged in court was that there was no proper organization based around the Hunt Retribution Squad, who were never heard from again after the Beaufort raid: rather, both defendants were ALF zealots, members of the hard core of full-time activists loyal to Ronnie Lee. Helsby had left home after a rancorous series of rows over animal rights, about which his mother said he had become obsessive. He had moved to a dingy flat in north London and had devoted himself to working for the ALF. John Curtin was a friend of John Beggs (even at one stage sharing the same girlfriend in a spirit of comradely generosity) and was already awaiting trial as one of the Wickham Nineteen.

The short and deliberately shocking life of the Hunt Retribution Squad demonstrated a number of evolving truths about the animal rights movement. By the end of 1984, activists had taken Ronnie Lee at his word in setting up new ad hoc groups who would go further than the ALF in attacking agreed targets; also in evidence was a curious mixture of sound planning and hopeless amateurism in the execution of their actions. As Terry Helsby's mother said, it was almost as if they wanted to get caught, to achieve a kind of brief martyrdom. Like the huge majority of ALF comrades involved in direct action, the pair of them were hardly out of their teens and utterly wrapped up in the cause of animal rights. They saw themselves as romantic idealists, almost desperate to suffer on behalf of oppressed species, and there was indeed a kind of crazy altruism in their behaviour. But like Lee and Nicholls, they had written off their own species: and even within some of the harder elements of the movement, the desecration of a human grave was thought to be somewhat excessive.

In summer 1984, Dave Nicholls was forced to quit the ALF office because of his increasingly serious diabetic condition. He also resigned from the Inland Revenue and went off to live with his mother, together with a large labrador, in Beckenham. The labrador proved useful in dealing with the unwanted attentions of anyone who was interested in talking to Nicholls about his aggregate career as fascist organizer, tax inspector and animal rights activist. But by now, Lee had the additional support of the woman who was later to be described (in crown court) as his 'able lieutenant', the former kennel maid, Vivian Smith. Certainly, after Nicholls's departure there was no sign of any moderation in the language and content of the ALF Supporters Group Bulletin. 'Devastate to liberate!' screamed the headline of number thirteen ('unlucky for some' ran the witty caption), with Ronnie Lee contributing a two-page essay on violence.

The purest vitriol by now seemed reserved for those who the ALF contemptuously referred to as 'the enemy within'. Like the infinitely splintered groupuscles on the Marxist and Trotskyist far left, the liberationists seemed far more obsessed with internecine warfare than any interest in uniting against the supposedly common enemy. Anyone not totally in favour of the Front was against them. A whole page of the Bulletin was devoted to reprints of letters to local papers from people who cared about animals, but who expressed shock and anger at what was being done in their name in their towns and villages: 'more traitors exposed' ran the headline. Prominent among the traitors were, inevitably, the RSPCA and the League Against Cruel Sports; even the national organizer of a comparatively radical (though non-violent) group like Animal Aid was accused of betrayal simply because he had described ALF activists who had sprayed paint over a local abattoir as 'brainless idiots'.

But it was Lee's now open advocacy of violence that clearly

laid out the direction to which the movement was now fully committed. 'Total pacifism' he wrote, 'is an immoral philosophy: violence is the only language some of these people (vivisectors, huntsmen and farmers) understand. This may be a hard home truth for the pacifist ideologues of the movement to understand, but it is a home truth nonetheless.' All the hand-wringing of the Peace News collective had clearly failed to shift Lee's perspective on the issue. In fact, it had appeared to irritate the veteran anarchist (still only in his mid-thirties, but looking ten years older, with his receding hairline, wispy beard and granny glasses). 'To my mind this preoccupation with "non-violence" has a lot to do with the middle-class origins of most of the people in the movement. The middle class traditionally don't like to get personally involved in violence.'

Here Lee, not merely the undisputed leader of the Animal Liberation Front, but by far the most charismatic and respected figure in the movement, the man indeed who had started it all, was making crystal clear his advocacy of personal violence. What he says in the piece is crucial, not just because it gives a logical context to the bombing campaigns, but because it gives absolutely no leeway for ambivalence. The habitual response of liberationists to the charge of personal violence – its deliberate use as a tactic – would be to make dismissive noises about 'one or two individuals' or crazy, fringe elements at the very margins of the movement. And yet, certainly by autumn 1984, straightforward advocacy of violence in the name of animals was absolutely central to it.

'This item may shock many people,' Lee admits, 'but it's about time someone did some straight talking on the subject of violence. Either we do not carry out actions against animal abusers who react violently, or we show them that we can be more violent than they are. To me, the second choice is the only acceptable one.' From now on, only those who were 'resolved on the lightning of violence' could be taken seriously in the movement; everyone else was playing silly and self-deluding games. 'Animal liberation will not be achieved if we treat the struggle for it as a social club or a garden party . . . Animal liberation is not a hobby or a part-time pastime, but a fierce struggle that demands total commitment if the animals are ever to be free. There will be injuries and possibly deaths on both sides before our ultimate victory for animal liberation is achieved. This is sad but certain.' Ultimately, said Lee, the failure to use violence against animal abusers could be seen as the only real immorality. 'If any animal dies in agony because we have failed, through ridiculous ideology, to use adequate force against its torturers, then we are ourselves responsible for the creature's torment.'

Ronnie Lee's anarchism had moved with the times: pacifism and persuasion were now old hat. The brave new world he plotted from the grimy second floor offices of 'Independent Tax Advisory Services' was only going to be achieved through the purging power of wholesale destruction. Writing under the pseudonym 'Captain Kirk', Lee quoted from the anarchist poem 'The Revolution of Everyday Life': 'let the same destructive flame' it cheerfully suggests 'consume all ideologies, and all their lackies to boot'. True freedom, said Lee, for all the earth's creatures demanded a 'decentralized non-hierarchical society', with low level technology, and 'massive cuts' in the human population. 'It is time for us to destroy the old world and to build the new in the only way possible – by our own direct action.' In the bombing campaigns that followed, the ALF did its best to follow the clarion call of its leader.

CHAPTER NINE

Learn to Burn!
ALF Supporters Group, Bulletin No. Fifteen

Arson had been one of the first tactics to which the ALF had resorted in its original incarnation as the Band of Mercy. It was the quickest and easiest way of inflicting maximum economic damage on the enemy, even though the courts took a dim view of such behaviour, as Ronnie Lee had found out all too painfully. But it was not until the Front had been active in the field for eight or nine years that its use of incendiary devices achieved the high level of co-ordination that would earn it *The Times'* somewhat portentous description as 'a highly organized network of urban terrorists'.

From 1983 onwards, the Front waged systematic and extremely damaging warfare against chains of department stores up and down the country who continued to insist on their right to sell furs to the public. In the course of the campaign, sophisticated miniature incendiary bombs proved highly effective, causing in just one single incident a total loss of nine million pounds to one company. The Mars Bar hoax had already shown how vulnerable big business could be to dedicated economic sabotage: with the incendiary campaign, the price of animal warfare became unacceptably high to a government whose leader had already singled out the ALF for its 'arrogance' in breaking the law. Under pressure from the Home Office, at the end of 1984 Scotland Yard established a specialist squad to deal with the animal rights menace: they gave it the rather friendly-sounding acronym 'ARNI' – the Animal Rights National Index. For Ronnie Lee and his coterie it was, in its way, just about the highest tribute they could have earned from the much loathed forces of the 'state'. ARNI was eventually to enjoy spectacular successes in infiltrating the movement: but after every big trial, there were always depressingly spectacular fresh outbursts of arson just to ram home the message that this was indeed a Hydra-headed monster. Fire-bomb attacks on department stores became so familiar a feature of the daily papers that they were soon relegated to one-paragraph status at the bottom of the inside page.

Apart from anything else, arson was exciting. Contributors writing in to the ALF's bulletin to file reports on local actions revelled in pseudonyms like 'Modesty Blaze' and 'Burnadette': accounts of burnings were breathlessly related, the act itself somehow acquiring a significance above and beyond the broad cause of animal rights. ALF Bulletin Number Eleven gave a long personal account of an ALF incendiary raid on a farm at Ampthill in Bedfordshire, back in August 1983, just as the Front's fire-raising adventures were beginning to take a serious toll. The farm had been targeted because it was the site of a poultry processing plant where, allegedly, the production line had been so greedily speeded up that chickens were not being properly stunned before having their throats cut. The despicable profiteers were to be taught a lesson. 'Our group of five met at eleven p.m.,' ran the intimately chatty narrative. 'We spent about fifteen minutes checking our equipment, which consisted of petrol, rags and fuses. Following this check, we spent about twenty minutes going over the plans for the action. We had seen the target beforehand, so discussion didn't take as long as usual . . . we set off about midnight.'

Breaking through the farm's perimeter fence (by the early eighties, battery premises were beginning to take security seriously), the gang of five broke into a vehicle compound, where they found three trucks and a bus used for transporting farm workers. These were busily being splashed with petrol, when a large alsatian suddenly trotted round the corner, giving the gang a nasty shock before thoughtfully plodding off, 'as if it knew what we were doing and approved of it'. Then it was back to business. 'We finished making the fuses and soaked them in petrol. The lookouts ran back to the car to get it started, and, allowing them three minutes, we then lit the fuses. The first vehicle to go was the coach – there was a sound like an explosion as a sheet of flame shot from end to end.' This was better than 5 November. 'The lorries were set on fire and soon ablaze, and the roaring of the flames sounded like something from *The Towering Inferno*. As we ran to the car, the melting wire in one of the lorries set off the air horn and one of the petrol tanks blew up. As we drove away, the whole area of sky behind us was glowing red, and there was a thick cloud of black smoke rising up into the sky.'

The raid got a 'tremendous reaction'. It was all over the local papers, TV and radio and, best of all, the police had said the plant looked 'like something out of World War Two'. Glory indeed. Especially when the local branch secretary of the National Farmers' Union had described them as a bunch of 'bloody dangerous criminals'. No further mention was made about the fate of the hostage poultry. Clearly, this kind of enthusiastic amateurism worried the ALF's leadership; shortly afterwards, guidelines on how to carry out an act of arson without setting fire either to other ALF members or the creatures supposedly under rescue were diplomatically published in the Bulletin. Even 'Burnadette' had admitted that she had inadvertantly set fire to her gloves on one clumsy expedition to destabilize a chicken farm in Kent.

The most adventurous set of fire raisers in the Front at this stage were the two dozen or so cell members on Merseyside, who had managed to get away with a series of spectacular large-scale burnings without getting caught, and at the same time managing to attract a great deal of national publicity. One feature of the ALF's loose structure, with its network of cells operating with virtual autonomy, was that heat was concentrated on the animal abusers according to the waxing and waning of local enthusiasts; and in the early eighties, Merseyside and the Wirral enjoyed a reputation for running the hardest crew of all. Karen Wedley, the 'supergrass' who had turned Queen's evidence on the Clwyd cell, had been to parties on Merseyside organized by local Front activists; it had all seemed terribly glamorous and exciting, with much pleasurable indulgence in the amphetamines that were supposedly on hand to keep the activists alert on late night actions. The cell was divided up into five specialist units, its members sporting army surplus camouflage jackets and trousers; a Belfast journalist who was taken out blindfolded to witness 'E' Group out on manoeuvres was hard pressed to find any difference, beyond a welcome absence of Armalites, between this lot and the paramilitaries across the Irish Sea.

Certainly, when they decided to intensify their local arson campaign, Merseyside ALF did nothing to dispel this impression. Their reputation was based on two factors: the development of a sophisticated new generation of incendiary devices and the choice of high-profile targets. Both factors impressed ALF HQ down in London. The burning down of a hundred thousand pound grandstand at Aintree racecourse – in protest against the Grand National ('the world's cruellest horse race') – was their first major action. It was followed a couple of months later by the planting of incendiaries in a Land-Rover belonging to a well-known local angling champion, on top of which the raiders had the cheek to aerosol the letters 'LACS' all over the front door of the victim's house, to give the appearance that this was the work of the League Against Cruel Sports. This act of black propaganda by the 'maniacs' of the ALF was not appreciated by the highly respectable and eminently law abiding League. Just as the revolutionary left would reserve its deepest vitriol for the 'traitors' within the Labour Party, so the liberationists always made time to fight their own private war against the respectable welfarists they held in similar contempt.

Both these actions were used by the Merseyside cell to test the viability of a new 'device' they had constructed on their own initiative. A week after the Land-Rover incident, the Press Association got a call giving details of the destruction of a meat factory close to the abattoir at Birkenhead on the Wirral. The subsequent explosion had blown the factory's roof off. This had been a well-organized raid involving three vehicles, all of which had been equipped with CB radios: by this stage of its existence, the Front's income, generated by Dave Nicholls's Supporters Group, was able to finance gear costing thousands of pounds per cell, with most active cells boasting several sets of CBs and a lightweight home-video camera. The publicity potential of moving pictures had been readily picked up from the Leagues.

Two cars had been parked at either end of the street as lookouts, while the third had dropped the two bombers off on the factory site. Having broken in, these two rapidly assembled the incendiary mechanism, which was attached to the gas mains. Of Heath Robinson construction, this device was composed of, among other things, a petrol can, four fire lighters, two candles, four table tennis balls and a large plastic container full of water. The explosion that followed not only took off the building's roof, but completely destroyed the factory, doing £200,000 worth of damage. It also destroyed a large number of jobs in an area of devastatingly high unemployment; local protests were dismissed by the ALF as the predictable and self-interested moans of 'local political lobbyists'.

Impressed by these results, Ronnie Lee and his close colleagues in London decided to mount a series of co-ordinated arson campaigns against one specific target: the big department store chains that still sold furs. These outlets represented 50% of the fur trade in Britain. This was a huge target but potentially a soft one, and even, the ALF suggested, a popular one. 'Once these stores become regular ALF targets' the Bulletin announced, 'they will drop the fur trade like a hot potato.' Profits from fur sales were only a small part of the income generated by Debenhams, Lewises and the House of Fraser: if this contentious area could be turned into an expensive headache the companies would just cave in. The point about big modern department stores was that you didn't actually have to burn them to the ground to do serious damage; they were all equipped with sensitive smoke sensors linked to sprinkler systems, so that a bomb only had to smoulder for half an hour under a pile of Y-fronts in order to waterlog the floorspace of an entire department. And there was also the damage to be done in announcing the presence of a bomb during trading hours: in the campaign that followed, hundreds of thousands of pounds were lost as customers were forcibly evacuated in bomb scares, often in the rush before Christmas. The ALF had no intention of attacking the innocent public but they were to make good use of the paranoia already engendered by the less scrupulous IRA.

If the Merseyside ALF had pioneered the new wave of large-scale arson attacks, Sheffield's smaller but equally enterprising cell was to focus attention on the hated department stores owned by the House of Fraser, Lewises and Debenhams. 'Local animal rights campaigners' the cell announced in a public communiqué, 'had tried for many years to persuade Rackhams, a House of Fraser department store, to get rid of its fur department, owned by the infamous Edelson Company. Tactics had included leaflets, sit-ins, pledges and the usual ineffective well-tried procedures.' None of it had worked, it seemed, and to add insult to injury 'still Rackhams had large front page fur ads in the local newspaper at least twice a week, and had considered animal "welfarists" as nothing more than a discomfort'. Well, it was high time that the House of Fraser was taught a lesson.

The campaign began with a comparatively moderate selection of well-tried nuisance tactics. Locks were Superglued and eight large plate glass windows were smashed with a hammer: when this treatment was repeated a few nights later, the store entered into urgent discussions with the Chief Constable of South Yorkshire, who swamped the area with plainclothes officers and police vans. But the next time the ALF struck, it was in a series of co-ordinated attacks on House of Fraser stores all over the north of England, from Altrincham in Cheshire, to Blackpool, Harrogate and Manchester: the only place left alone this time, of course, was Rackhams of Sheffield. The panic and withdrawal of press advertising that followed these raids convinced the ALF that it would be worth sustaining a long campaign against the big stores. Five months later, Rackhams was firebombed, just four weeks before Christmas.

The bomb caused an estimated £200,000 worth of damage. It had been the handiwork of the Sheffield group's expert bomb-maker, Ian Oxley, a twenty-five-year-old modelling expert who had found his skills in balsa and plastic assembly of unexpected use to the movement. Shortly afterwards, the ALF published their own expert guide to the assembly of incendiary devices, with a view to spreading the new sophisticated technology being developed in Sheffield and Liverpool. Strictly for internal consumption, the guide carried the innocent title 'Interviews with Animal Liberation Front Activists', but the so-called interviews amounted to no more than a lengthy illustrated lecture on how to assemble time bombs designed to deal with both stores and parked vehicles. It was a strange mixture of schoolboy enthusiasm for fireworks, and a naïve call to arms: there was a tone of painstaking responsibility about much of the advice.

'Before a device is placed in a vehicle, two things must be done' ran the expert bombers' homily. 'Firstly, we check that there is not a driver sleeping overnight in the vehicles, and secondly we scatter 'Scoot' all around the vehicle. This is a product we get from pet shops that puts off cats and dogs from going under the vehicles . . . If the doors are open we place the device inside on the upholstery. If it's not open, we force a window.' Complicated diagrams featuring nails, batteries (always Duracel for the best effects), cigarette packets (John Player Special, ditto), bin liners, nail varnish, tweezers, mechanical watches, torch bulbs, washing-up liquid and soldering irons, gave the impression of a 'Blue Peter' home-toy-making seminar gone horribly wrong. The devices planted in stores were equipped with twenty-four-hour timing devices, while the car bombs had a simple one-hour timer. Store bombs were packed into a cigarette packet punched with holes: they were placed in the stores between 3 p.m. and closing time, timed to go off shortly after midnight. Each device would produce a small jet of flame for about fifteen seconds when it detonated and, to ensure against failure, bombs were supposed to be planted in batches of three.

'Usually a device is placed under an armchair or settee on the top floor, the result of which is that all the floors underneath are flooded,' explained the pamphlet, giving activists a step-by-step guide on how to trigger off sprinkler systems. And there was a comforting word for innocent furniture-buying members of the public. 'We do not place devices in coat pockets or in a settee – should one fail to ignite, it may do so at a later date when someone has bought it.' In the event, the overwhelming majority of devices did ignite, and continue to ignite: at the time of writing, there was no indication of any pause in the incendiary campaign based on these bombs. Their minute size almost always guaranteed that they would escape detection, sometimes even after they had gone off and failed to ignite clothing or furniture. The car bomb was also packed into a cigarette packet, but was of a much simpler design. It was little more than a variation on the traditional weedkiller (sodium chlorate) and sugar device, harnessed to a mixture of petrol and washing-up liquid via an electrical circuit and a mechanical timer.

Both kinds of device were to be used with conspicuous success in the campaign against the Front's next selected target, the Surrey-based department store, Allders. This was carried out with impressive speed and efficiency, beginning with the usual softening up process of window-smashing and lock-gluing. The first raid was aimed at the store's Sutton High Street branch which did not, as it turned out, actually sell furs: never mind, said the Front, other branches did, so the principle was the same. Allders' initial response to the threat was contemptuous: store director Tony Johnson said the ALF were 'rather pathetic, like all the other yobs who smash our windows'. Mr Johnson, however, had seriously underestimated his enemy.

One of the new generation of cigarette packet incendiary devices was then planted at the Allders branch in Croydon, where there was a fur department. Setting off the sprinkler system, it did extensive damage to stocks, but still the store was adamant that they would continue to run the business the way they and their customers wanted it run, and that included the sale of furs. Two months later, the ALF struck even more damagingly at the store's warehouse at Hackbridge: six delivery lorries were firebombed, using the cigarette packet and washing-up liquid devices. Four vehicles were completely destroyed and the other two severely damaged. Shortly afterwards, another Allders truck was all but destroyed by an attack using the highly corrosive hydrofluoric acid, which was sprayed over the interior and exterior of the van. And two days after that, Allders publicly announced that they had decided to close their fur department.

It had taken just three months from the first broken window to the final acid etching to terrorize the store into abject surrender. Allders, of course, did not put it quite like that: the department was being closed for 'commercial reasons'. They meant that the cost of bomb damage had simply become unacceptably high. Even more remarkable than the sheer speed of the campaign was its remarkably low profile in the media; this had been a vicious and sustained terrorist bombing campaign, thousands of pounds worth of damage had been done and although no one had been hurt it had placed store personnel in jeopardy. And yet events had been reported in the matter of fact manner that characterized, for example, the endless and remote litany of Lebanese car bombs. By the mid eighties, the ALF had become just another part of an already overpopulated terrorist landscape.

Elsewhere, the stores campaign was registering other, less dramatic, successes. Dingles of Exeter were 'persuaded' to close down their fur department after a series of attacks; Debenhams in Guildford decided to sell only 'fake' furs to escape attention; and in a triumph on a scale with the Allders campaign, John Lewis of Oxford Street in central London closed down their fur department because, they admitted, they just couldn't put up any longer with the relentless pressure from the animal rights people. It wasn't just the threat of bombs: once a store was targeted it found itself under pressure from a whole range of tactical directions, some of them legitimate. It would be subjected to continual demonstrations and leafleting, which was both embarrassing and bad for trade. All this was reported by the ALF's pseudonymous correspondent on the anti-fur trade campaign, 'Lady Penelope', with considerable pleasure: one small shop owner, forced into closure by the Front, had lost his temper with demonstrators and screamed they should all be hanged; the feeling had been mutual, 'Lady Penelope' reported with satisfaction.

Meanwhile, the Sheffield gang were still busy. There were eight core members of the cell, mainly in their twenties: in addition, Ronnie Lee, Vivian Smith and Roger Yates, the ALF's 'Northern press officer', based in Liverpool, were frequent visitors to the end-of-terrace house where tactics were planned and targets selected: this was the home of Brendan McNally, the cell's co-ordinator, and his wife Jenny. The Sheffield cell members had little in common beyond their involvement in the movement; Ian Oxley, the cell's bomb maker, was the kind of hobbyist that more sophisticated members of his generation would contemptuously refer to as an 'anorak'. Kevin Baldwin and Julia Rodgers were the romantic interest: later, in court, the judge was to speak forgivingly of Ms Rodgers as a 'tragic' case. She had planted the first bomb at Rackhams that had done a couple of hundred thousand pounds' worth of damage, but she had done it because she was hopelessly infatuated with Baldwin. John Hewson was the 'grandfather' of the cell – a sixty-three-year-old retired school-teacher with a long-standing concern for animal rights, who had gradually found himself – like some Republican sympathizing priest in Northern Ireland – walking on the wrong side of the law. Least impressive as a putative terrorist was nineteen-year-old Isabel Facer, a bright but naïve girl whose genuine love of animals had drawn her, too, into the conspiracy.

This was not a chillingly efficient, uniform team of cold-hearted terrorists, but very much the usual mix of the muddled, the dangerous, the naïve and the vindictive that made up any ALF cell. Because of his expertise in constructing the incendiary devices, Oxley became for a period bomb maker general to the entire movement, and the McNallys' terrace home the ordnance supply depot and factory. Lee, Smith and Yates would act as couriers, transporting the bombs (described later in court by a forensic scientist as 'unique') all over the country. The great strength of the cigarette packet incendiaries was that, once you were in possession of the four pages of instructions and diagrams, they were not that difficult to construct and all components were easily obtainable by legitimate means. The Sheffield cell's activities were brought to an abrupt end, as we shall see, after successful infiltration by the police, but their bomb making technology continued to be used by the Front as the war against the department stores continued unabated. When ARNI finally caught up with Ronnie Lee and his comrades in south Yorkshire, it made little difference to the overall volume of animal rights terrorism.

The most dramatically successful action, and by far the single most damaging act of economic warfare, followed in the summer of 1987. This time the target was Debenhams. In April, the ALF's Cardiff cell had firebombed that city's large branch, but on the night of 12 July all previous actions were dwarfed by a triple arson attack on Debenhams stores in Luton, Harrow and Romford. Small fires were started in Harrow and Romford, before their triggered sprinkler systems flooded the premises. But in Luton things were rather more dramatic: this time, and almost certainly by accident, the liberationists hit the jackpot. Located in the town's huge new Arndale Shopping Centre, the store's sprinkler system had been shut down for maintenance: for the first time ever, the ALF's cigarette packet bombs acted as true incendiaries. Four floors of the department store were gutted and it took five hours for the eighty men of the Luton fire brigade to bring the blaze under control. The cost of the damage was estimated at four million pounds; the cost of subsequent loss of trading came to another four and a half million pounds.

This had been the work of a small north London cell of the Front, led by two young unemployed activists, Geoffrey Shepherd and Andrew Clarke. The ALF's central press office had issued a statement saying that Debenhams were 'a legitimate target' because they continued to be involved in the sale of furs; the spokesman said he was more interested in stopping the slaughter of animals than in winning over public opinion; he didn't think the activists cared too much about what the public would think. Or, for that matter, what the RSPCA might think. They, unsurprisingly, were horrified by the Luton bombing. Over the past three years, the Society press office announced, they had made significant inroads into the fur market by presenting the wearing of fur as a moral issue; this had been highly effective. Now, 'all these attacks do is to provide further ammunition for the fur industry which has tried to portray all those who oppose them as criminals'.

Certainly, from what was to emerge in the aftermath of the bombings, Debenhams had been unlucky to catch the full wrath of the Front. They had been selected, said the ALF, because back in February they had announced that they would be restocking all their stores with furs for the following winter. This, said Debenhams, was a 'straightforward lie'; they had actually taken a decision some months earlier to cease fur sales altogether, because it was a declining market and no longer justified floor space. There were now only four branches in the sixty strong group that were still selling furs, and these operated through separate companies who simply rented store space. Debenhams actually wanted that floor space, but you couldn't 'kick people out overnight'. None of this seemed to impress the ALF very much. A communiqué issued the week after the Luton, Romford and Harrow bombings announced that Debenhams had until 1 October to close down all fur departments, otherwise the attacks would recommence. Debenhams' response was that they were not going to work to any deadline 'set by criminals'.

The trouble was that, although the police quickly tracked down and arrested Shepherd and Clarke, there seemed no shortage of apprentice arsonists to take their place. The Sheffield cell had been jailed for a total of thirty-seven years; Shepherd and Clarke were given just under four and three and a half years respectively at the Old Bailey, having been caught red-handed in their north London flat surrounded by an array of dismantled alarm clocks, bulbs and electrical equipment. Yet still the bombings continued with grim regularity. Two weeks after the Luton duo were sent down, Selfridges in London's Oxford Street was targeted, although this time the devices failed to detonate. A month later, in the week before Christmas, when the stores were at the height of the critical seasonal rush, further disruption was caused by a network of devices planted all over the country. In Kendals, Manchester's biggest department store, two incendiaries caused damage of over £20,000; at Lewis's in Liverpool, the furniture department was severely damaged by a bomb, and another detonated at a store in Cardiff. Police found a further device early in the new year at Debenhams in Oxford Street, clearly still on the hit list despite all protestations of future intentions.

With further store bombs planted in London, again in Oxford Street, later that spring of 1988, it was equally clear that no amount of arrests and imprisonment was going to stop the campaign. Ronnie Lee had by this time been in prison for over a year: he had been the 'general' behind the campaign, the judge had told Sheffield Crown Court during his trial – and yet out in the field his troops continued to harry the enemy, in many cases doing far greater damage than the Sheffield cell had managed in their comparatively brief career. But as the movement's central ideologist, Lee was as effective working from prison as on the outside; the ALF's diffuse structure of virtually autonomous cells meant that the fire-bombing could continue *ad infinitum*. There was no 'network' in the sense of a tightly controlled organization for the police to crack. 'Don't ask who the Bournemouth ALF are' the leaflet distributed to the local animal rights group enthusiasts had run, 'you are the Bournemouth ALF!' This was functional anarchism and it worked.

By the late eighties, firebombing had been refined into a weapon of economic warfare that the tentative Band of Mercy could only have dreamt of. Quite apart from the multi-million-pound damage to department stores, factory farms and meat processing plants were suffering far more serious damage. An attack on a wholesale meat depot in Sussex destroyed seven lorries in one go, doing a quarter of a million pounds' worth of damage; in a three week campaign, two processing plants and a chicken farm on the Oxfordshire/Buckinghamshire border were crippled by a series of raids using multiple incendiary devices. The local fire chief condemned the lack of any warning from the bombers and said his men could have been seriously injured. The ALF merely claimed responsibility and refused to apologize.

The real cost of what had become an extended guerilla war lay not just in the damage done by the bombs but in meeting the necessary price of protection. Factory farms were beginning to look like fortified campsites, with the installation of security systems costing five and ten thousand pounds becoming the norm. Ten-foot fences were topped with barbed and razor wire; remote video cameras positioned on perimeter towers swept the compounds, searching out the camouflaged invaders. Farmers talked about the new rural 'terrorists' and slept with shotguns next to the bed, just in case. Security in the big stores had been drastically increased, insurance premiums even more so.

The road to animal liberation would be pursued by creating a climate of terror against individual abusers and by sustained economic sabotage. That had been the theory: the latter half at least had now been successfully put into practice. 'My main aim isn't to toady to the public,' Ronnie Lee had said, with disarming or chilling honesty, whichever way you were inclined to take him, speaking to BBC Radio Four in his customary soft tones. 'What we're trying to do is to actually sabotage the industries of animal abuse ... If you show them that being involved in the torture of animals is not going to give them a comfortable living, the fact that their property is going to be damaged and they are going to be subject to constant harassment, all that is going in end to make them think that this is not the way to live comfortably and have a peaceful life.' Allders and Rackhams found that out sure enough, and did indeed opt for a peaceful life; it was an unpalatable fact that animal rights terrorism worked. But what about the social cost of the war? About the fact that, as in the case of the Birkenhead meat processing factory, large numbers of jobs were lost as a direct consequence of a firebombing? Lee said that it honestly didn't bother him. This was a time of 'high animal torture'. He couldn't care less about people being put out of work, as long as the animals were saved from suffering.

The declaration of serious and unrelenting economic warfare by the ALF had led directly to the establishment of the specialist ARNI squad at Scotland Yard. As we shall see, there was no shortage of success in picking up and prosecuting generation after generation of incendiary bombers, including Lee. But the bombs simply continued. Muddled, dangerous and sometimes violent, the activists of the ALF were also seriously committed. If people were prepared to go to prison for the IRA, Lee had written, then animal rights campaigners should be prepared to go to prison in their hundreds 'for the glorious and noble cause of animal liberation'. When the time came, they were.

CHAPTER TEN

After our first petrol bombing we
became scared, like children we got
frightened; but we soon realized that
our panic was minute compared to the
sheer terror of the abused animal.
Animal Rights Militia Communiqué No. Two

Arson is a very nasty crime and it carries appropriately nasty penalties: but in its campaign against the big department stores the ALF could at least claim that big business rather than people were the targets, and, as it turned out, more through luck than planning, nobody was hurt. The public could understand if not approve, of this war of economic sabotage; when it came to bombs aimed specifically at human beings in the name of animals, the sheer craziness of what was going on was met by incomprehension followed by widespread outrage. Every petrol bomb intended for a vivisector, the RSPCA ruefully admitted, knocked thousands of pounds off the incomes of the animal welfare societies. Of all the forms of terrorism to which the British had been subjected since the war, this seemed the most conclusively barmy. The anti-personnel bombing campaign lurched between levels of high professionalism in the construction of what the police called 'viable devices' and a kind of amateur ad hoc gangsterism, with the deployment of crude Molotov cocktails. Curiously, the opening shots were amongst the more sophisticated.

On 30 November 1982, letter bombs were delivered to the offices of the leaders of the four main political parties at Westminster. Three of them were successfully made safe, but the fourth exploded in the hands of civil servants at 10 Downing Street, causing minor injuries. The bombs were claimed in the name of an organization calling itself the Animal Rights Militia, a grouping hitherto unheard of in the movement. This was not in itself peculiar: animal rights had become a movement as prolific in spawning fresh splinter groups as the Shi'ite factions in Beirut. Some in the movement thought the bombs were the work of *agents provocateurs*, a piece of black propaganda designed to discredit the more respectable end of the movement; this was, after all, the first time that violence had been directed with deliberate precision at individuals. There were those who thought that the letter bombs had actually been sent by some other, possibly Irish, terrorist organization, and that the claims of responsibility had been made by some freelance crazy, desperate for a little reflected notoriety. This theory took a knock when a further bomb was sent to Professor Roy Calne, the pioneer of kidney and liver transplant surgery, at Addenbrooke's Hospital in Cambridge. Professor Calne could not conceivably be on the hit list of the IRA: he was, on the other hand, a battle-hardened veteran of a campaign of abuse and vilification from the animal rights movement.

No one has ever been arrested or charged in connection with the letter bombs. Within the movement, there has been much gossip and speculation about the culprits, with certain well-known names receiving particular attention. Most information suggests that it was a one off gesture. Certainly nothing more was heard from the ARM for a full two years, until the announcement of a hoax involving the alleged injection of Christmas turkeys with mercury: this suggested that the original bomber(s) had either remarkable patience or had changed tactics. The intials ARM were not to surface again until after Ronnie Lee's call for new groups to indulge in acts of violence that might discredit the ALF's image if claimed by the Front. And yet ironically, as a measure perhaps of the movement's characteristic lack of any recognizable consistency, the next set of bomb attacks was actually claimed by the Front.

In January 1985, the home of two scientists associated with the Wellcome Foundation's research laboratories at Beckenham in Kent were petrol bombed. Two Molotov cocktails were thrown at the home of Sir John Vane, the Foundation's research development director and a Nobel Prize winner, who was upstairs in bed at the time. The bombs set fire to his garage doors, but the blaze was dealt with before it could get out of hand. The nearby home of laboratory administrator Warwick Dench was given the same treatment, but this time the crudely made devices failed to detonate properly. An anonymous representative of the ALF told the Press Association that 'every vivisector in Britain' would be 'liable to petrol bomb attacks on their homes'.

In retrospect, this looks very much like a prototype for the sequence of raids claimed by the reborn Animal Rights Militia shortly afterwards. Possibly it was the work of an individual ALF cell that had decided to embark on its own maverick campaign. Either way, once again no one was caught or charged. Three months later, the ARM claimed its first bombing since the explosion at Number 10. Shortly after midnight two balaclava'd figures were spotted by a passing motorist running away from the front door of a house in South Cheam in the heart of sprawling south London suburbia. Two smouldering Molotov cocktails had been thrown at the front door, but this time the ARM's research seems to have been less than impressive. Their intended target, Dr David Conning, Director of the British Industrial Biological Research Association (BIBRA) laboratory complex in nearby Carshalton, had separated from his wife some sixteen months before. On the night of the petrol bomb attack he was safely in bed in central London, while his wife and teenage son and daughter had to deal with the attack.

Two months later, the ARM claimed a second petrol bombing raid, this time on another employee of BIBRA, Dr Sharat Gangolli. Like several other senior BIBRA workers, Dr Gangolli had for a long time been the subject of a sustained campaign of harassment by SLAM, the South London Animals Movement, the local animal rights group, which featured several ALF figures of national prominence, including Tim Daley. Daley had himself led mock funerals to Gangolli's home, announcing over a portable tannoy to his neighbours that Sharat Gangolli was a 'mass murderer'. This had not gone down well with the locals, who had on occasions to be restrained by the police from physically intervening in the noisily aggressive demonstrations.

In September of the same year, Dr Gangolli was the subject of a second bomb attack, this time in the company of another colleague at BIBRA, Dr Stuart Walker. The devices used on this occasion were much more effective and of far more sophisticated construction: the bombs were made out of a series of gas cylinders and were placed under their targets' family cars. One vehicle was completely destroyed, the other severely damaged.

A spokesman for the ARM told the local paper, the *Sutton Herald*, 'we will go to any lengths to prevent these animal abusers' murderous activities. If this means killing an individual we will not shy away from such action.' The irony was, said Dr Walker, that most of his work involved computer research; he was actually engaged in looking at ways of reducing the number of animal experiments. Neither he nor Dr Gangolli were going to be terrorized into leaving their work. Both accepted police protection.

Until now, the only public utterances of the shadowy Animal Rights Militia had been terse phoned statements to newspapers and press agencies. But in the next edition of the ALF Supporters Group Bulletin, published just before Christmas, a full page communiqué from the ARM set out the group's aims and expectations. The language was violent, paranoid and boastful. 'Our power is in the two petrol bombings ... and the car bombings, all of which are answers to animal abuse.' The statement claimed that 'the system' had deliberately suppressed publicity about the Walker and Gangolli car bombs, even though stories had, in fact, appeared in both the London *Evening Standard* and the *Daily Star*. The ARM were not 'irresponsible lunatics or madmen', they claimed, but serious activists who no longer saw any point in persuasion. Besides, they had moved on from the simple notion that animal rights could somehow be separated from the wider struggle. 'Animal liberation must be part of a wide spectrum of revolutionary change in the structure of society, for British democracy is based on more blood, terror and exploitation than any other country in history. It has a brutal police force whose crimes against people and animals the media will not report, and whose government blatantly supports repressive systems of governments [sic] around the world.'

The Militia, the communiqué went on, did not want to become like the IRA, feared by ordinary people who might get in the way of the bombs and bullets; all they were going to do was attack specific targets: 'the real animal abusers, the vivisectors, huntsmen and slaughterhouse owners'. No numbers or organizational information were given away; the impression was of a small band of amateurs who were learning on the job. The first petrol bombing had been scary, the communiqué admitted, but 'then it flashed we were unbeatable, for we were everybody in the animal rights movement who really cares

Anarchist Ronnie Lee, founder and leading organizer of the ALF, currently serving a ten-year sentence for conspiracy to cause criminal damage.

Animal rights activists chain themselves to the railings at 10 Downing Street, protesting about treatment of laboratory animals, March 1983.

The ALF's 'Poisoned' Mars Bar hoax of 1984, which cost Mars £3,000,000.

First 'publicity' shot of the self-styled 'Hunt Retribution Squad'
complete with chainsaw and axes. The HRS threatened
celebrities like Jackie Charlton and Jimmy Hill with acts of
vengeance.

The ALF's version of Father Christmas, complete with balaclava and walkie-talkie, 'liberating' turkeys before Christmas.

ALF activists in standard uniform of combat jacket and balaclava, raiding a battery hen run.

Bournemouth cell of the ALF – the Mars Bar hoaxers – interviewed by the author.

'Ben', the ALF organizer of the Mars Bar hoax of 1984, interviewed by the author in 1986.

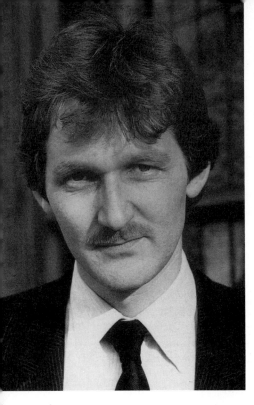

Tim Daley, former trainee commercial pilot, and leading animal rights activist. 'It's a war – and in a war you have to take up arms, and people will get killed.'

John Beggs, press officer of the South East Animal Liberation League and BUAV activist. 'If a scientist died, I wouldn't lose a great deal of sleep.'

Dingles department store
in Plymouth, destroyed
by an ALF firebomb
Christmas 1988, part of a
relentless campaign
against the sale of furs.

The Hunt Retribution
Squad pose for a shot
after the desecration of
the Duke of Beaufort's
grave in 1984. They were
going to send his head
to Princess Anne.

Animal rights groups proliferated in the eighties: demonstrations against vivisection turned out an uneasy alliance of anarchists and animal lovers.

Close-up of 13.

about animals'. The Wickham Nineteen and the Hunt Retribution Squad were specifically singled out as innocent victims of a corrupt society. 'But one thing you can be sure of, every day our comrades and fellow animals stay behind bars, their torment will be avenged, even if this means some of the filth will lose their lives.' A tone of messianic exclusivity ran through the piece, which was printed without any further comment from the ALF, whose publication was being generously made available to the Militia.

Six weeks later, the ARM carried out a far more ambitious operation, which suggested a fairly efficient level of coordination. On the night of the 7 January 1986, four bombs of gas cylinder construction, similar to the ones that destroyed the BIBRA scientists' cars, were placed under vehicles belonging to four human targets; the locations stretched from the Sussex coast, to south London, Staffordshire and Harrogate in Yorkshire. The devices had been timed to go off at hourly intervals: the four targets included Peter Savage and Dr Brian Meldrum.

This time, a phoned warning in the early hours of the morning alerted police to the devices, all of which were found to be 'viable'. In scenes common enough in Belfast and Londonderry, streets were cleared and army bomb disposal teams brought in. The devices were neutralized with controlled explosions triggered by the remote controlled 'wheelbarrow' robot vehicles developed in Northern Ireland. In four quiet, middle-class residential neighbourhoods, people looked at their neighbours and wondered why ordinary and apparently unremarkable families had attracted the baleful attentions of the terrorist. Peter Savage remembers worrying about what people in the street thought of his family hurrying out of the front door, half-dressed and under police escort. He had become used to being called a 'murderer' by demonstrators but it was hard to accept that the 'personal attention' some of them had threatened would come to this. It was even harder to accept that, from now on, looking under his car for explosive devices would simply have to become part of his morning routine.

The four January devices were followed in April by a further ARM operation and once again, according to police sources, there was a marked increase in the skills and equipment used by the bombers; despite early blunders, these people seemed to be learning fast. Curiously, this time their target was a veterinary surgeon, Dr Andor Sebesteny. Dr Sebesteny had been marked out for the Militia's attention because he ran the animal welfare unit of the Imperial Cancer Research Fund, which used vivisection in the course of research into determining the causes and potential cures for various forms of cancer. Dr Sebesteny's job was to ensure the welfare of the animals used for research: and this, visiting members of the local animal rights group admitted after the bombing, he did conscientiously. The vet himself said that he had devoted twenty-four years of his life to the job; he didn't do it because he relished experimenting on animals but because he wanted to see they were properly looked after.

None of this seemed to carry any weight with the ARM, who planted their device under the petrol tank of his car sometime before midnight one evening in early April. This time, no warning was phoned through to the police, who later said that, had it gone off, the device would not just have blown up Dr Sebesteny's car but probably hurled it over the roof of his house. As it turned out, the plot was foiled by a nice piece of irony. Just before midnight, the vet came out to call in the cat which he found lurking under the parked car. Reaching down for the animal, Dr Sebesteny noticed a suspicious-looking package under the car. By now, police had alerted most prominent figures working in branches of medical research involving vivisection that they were potential targets; Dr Sebesteny immediately called his local station and within less than an hour an army bomb disposal squad had dealt with the device.

In their next comminiqué, again published without comment by the ALF, the ARM alluded to this episode. 'In line with our "no more warnings" policy, we planted a powerful bomb at the home of a cancer research vivisector in north London. Unfortunately, shortly before it was due to explode the vivisector saw it and it was defused by the bomb squad. Next time the scum won't be so lucky.' Referring to the January car bombs, the statement said 'we could have killed all four bastards, but we didn't'. But now, said the ARM, it would be no more Mister Nice Guy: 'whatever action the Militia now takes there will be no warnings'. There was more abuse for the weak-kneed 'lefties' in the animal rights movement who still placed some residual trust in MPs and parliamentary democracy: 'the Militia says to these people, either get out of the struggle or knuckle down to the fight ahead, because things will be getting much worse, that the Militia guarantees'. The ARM, it was claimed once more, was no less than the vanguard of a sweeping tide of revolutionary change, further echoes here of the anarchist fantasies of the Angry Brigade fifteen years before. 'The role of the Militia,' the communiqué sententiously concluded, 'is to widen, with actions, the concept of animal liberation, so that Militia-style actions will take root in all areas of the country with nothing short of total revolution as the ultimate goal.' The piece was signed simply with the single word 'Revolution'.

No more communiqués were to follow. Later that year the ALF offices in Hammersmith were raided and shut down and publication of the Supporters Group Bulletin brought to an abrupt halt. With the arrest of Ronnie Lee, Vivian Smith and other core members of the movement, serious activists decided to keep their heads down; out in the field, local actions by ALF cells continued uninterrupted, but the spate of anti-personnel bomb attacks came to an abrupt halt. And then, in March 1987, without any warning, a letter bomb was delivered to Dr Ian Rigley, a retired research scientist in Kent. Dr Rigley escaped injury in the blast but slight damage was caused to some of his furniture. It was a sharp reminder that the bombers were still around and that no one, so far, had been caught or charged in connection with any of the ARM actions.

Throughout the letter, car and petrol campaigns, the ALF press office had maintained an air of informed indifference. They appeared to have remarkably rapid access to press statements prepared by Militia sources but at the same time Ronnie Lee managed to sound suitably vague when it came to identifying these sources, or even speculating on the origins of the extremist group. In fact, the burden of evidence suggested all along that the Animal Rights Militia had no real separate existence, any more than had the Hunt Retribution Squad, from the central core of activists in the ALF. Ronnie Lee had in 1984 openly advocated the establishment of new groups under new names who would be prepared to take more extreme action than that allowed for under the unwritten rules of the ALF: it was not just a matter of preserving a spurious image of moderation for the Front – Lee was clever enough to realize that there were many among the movement's supporters who might baulk at the direction of violence against specific animal abusers. Indeed, after the publication of the first ARM communiqué, there were several dissenting voices to be heard in the Supporters Group Bulletin, accusing the Militia of being 'wankers' who were using the animal rights cause as a vehicle for their own ludicrous fantasies.

There was, of course, a measure of truth in this. The problem was that those who overtly or covertly supported what the Militia was up to included the ALF's top brass. Ronnie Lee had already written at length about the need to take up violence, to use terror as a tactic. Tim Daley, according to the police the 'commander in chief' of the ALF in south London in the mid-eighties, endorsed that wholeheartedly; and he went further, ignoring Lee's instinct for discretion, in openly backing the ARM. 'I would totally defend their tactics,' he told BBC TV's 'Brass Tacks' programme in the midst of car bombing campaign. 'In a war you have to take up arms and people will get killed, and I can support that kind of action by petrol bombing and by bombs under cars, and probably, at a later stage, shooting of vivisectors on their doorsteps ... It's a war, and there is no other way you can stop vivisectors.' But wasn't the ALF's, if not the entire animal liberation movement's claim to any kind of moral high ground fatally undermined by such a brutal analysis? Daley thought not. 'Because, as I say, you've only got to look at Northern Ireland and see how far the Republican movement has got since they took up the armed struggle with such a vengeance in 1969. I mean, we're now in 1986, and you now have the Republic of Ireland actually having a say in a country that is unfortunately still being run by the British government – you wouldn't have had that without the IRA and without the armed struggle. It's unfortunate, it's very, very sad, but it seems to me that that is the only thing that people seem to respond to.'

Such words would not have been surprising had they come from Ronnie Lee, with his past association with the Troops Out movement, but coming from one who until very recently had been a solid, Conservative, *Daily Telegraph*-reading trainee commercial pilot, they were indeed curious. The more violent the sentiments expressed in this movement, the less any obvious pattern in ideological background seemed apparent: it was full of contradictions and populated by characters far more diverse and bizarre than were to be found in the marginal politics of the far right or left. In his epistle on the cleansing properties of violence Ronnie Lee had poured scorn on the wet middle classes who never seemed to have the stomach for a fight when things got tough; and yet the higher echelons of the ALF were crowded with refugees from the professional classes, whose families lived in the more salubrious reaches of the Home Counties. Lee himself had been a trainee solicitor; Vivian Smith came from an upper middle-class family in the Surrey stockbroker belt; Daley would have seemed seriously out of place in any smokey back-room assembly of Trotskyists; and although John Beggs sported a mildly sinister pair of gold rim glasses, he too was heading for the largely unsubversive career of a solicitor.

And yet all of these people either directly or indirectly backed the tactics of the Animal Rights Militia. Talking at the home of his girlfriend's parents in suburban north London, John Beggs said the movement had to 'put the boot in'; fear and instability had to be created in the industries that abused animals; violence against animal abusers was 'inevitable'; 'The ARM', he claimed (wrongly, as it turned out) 'will kill or severely maim an animal abuser by the end of this year.' He was positive about the Militia's existence and its clearly held aims: this was not random but selective terrorism only taking out those targets that were clearly identified as the enemy: 'forget Parliament, we've got to raise public consciousness'. So positive indeed was Beggs about the ARM that he had six months earlier acted as 'intermediary' in putting an ITV team from Television South, based in Southampton, in touch with the Militia. How exactly did he manage to contact the elusive group? 'By passing on messages', simple as that. The animal rights movement was one vast grapevine, said Beggs; everyone knew what everyone else was up to. As one who had talked only half-jokingly of being the 'Gerry Adams' of the movement, this was the kind of knowing vagueness that kept Beggs out of serious trouble. Yet he seemed to know a great deal of what the Militia had been up to: they had raided, he said, a battery chicken farm at Biggin Hill in Kent and poisoned a batch of eggs with mercury – then it had all been 'hushed up by the establishment' who had slapped a 'D' Notice on the story. Certainly it seemed to be true that Scotland Yard was keen to discourage sensational reportage of the activities of animal rights groups, but, as in the case of the car bombings, there was no evidence of 'D' Notices being applied.

In the case of the TVS team, Beggs had told the reporter, John Stapleton, that he had 'heard' that the ARM were about to make serious attempts to kill scientists; he offered to act as liaison in setting up a clandestine meeting. This turned out, according to Stapleton, to be a somewhat overdramtic exercise which began with the telephoned command to be in the bar of a respectable Winchester hotel at a certain time. Turning up with his crew, Stapleton received a second call in the hotel, giving him a map reference in the New Forest. Making their way to this remote point in a deserted part of the Forest, the TVS party were met by two polite but insistent young men wearing masks, who proceeded to blindfold everyone, before driving them for another half hour. Blindfolds removed, the crew found themselves in a clearing, with perhaps half a dozen hooded figures. Three of them gave an interview, during which they duly promised more bombings and alleged that they now had possession of stocks of advanced plastic explosives. John Stapleton said that he thought they believed what they were saying, but seemed ill at ease, almost amateurish. His crew, however, dismissed them derisively. This was the only time people claiming to represent the ARM had surfaced in public; even then, the interview was never broadcast. Two days before the TVS show was due to go out, the four ARM car bombs were planted. In a curious compromise with the management at TVS the IBA reacted by insisting that only a precis of the hooded figures' dialogue be broadcast.

In the wider animal rights movement, John Beggs was a popular and exciting guest speaker at meetings all over the country. At a gathering like the Animal Aid group in Bournemouth, he could double the usual attendance figure and this was the kind of occasion when he would play 'Gerry Adams' to perfection. Inevitably, the question of the ARM would be raised from the floor; equally inevitably, Beggs had to tread a careful line, avoiding close association but at the same time trying to demonstrate the positive aspects of the bombing campaign. The style and logic were bought wholesale from Sinn Fein. 'The first thing to say about the Animal Rights Militia and violence is that we really shouldn't be talking about the violence the ARM has allegedly caused, we should be talking about the violence that has been perpetrated against the animals.' No vivisector or huntsman had had to suffer the violence inflicted on animals; 'none of them have had their eyes blinded, none of them have had stuff forced down their throats, none of them have had electrodes stuck in their heads', none of them, in short, had had to suffer from the long and upsetting list of assaults that Beggs would recite. But then the media didn't care about that; all they cared about was 'these vicious people attacking our good scientists'. It had been the same with the miners' strike: 'it's characteristic of the British system that if anyone uses any violence, all they ever talk about is the violence of the subversive or the radical group, but they never talk about the violence being perpetrated by the state.'

What was curious about this was not that John Beggs, despite his respectable persona as committee member of the BUAV, would come out publicly and say such things, but that a large meeting of some hundred animal rights supporters should accept it without any noticeable dissent. This was, after all, a meeting of Animal Aid, an organization that would not accept the need either for violence or law-breaking in its campaigning. And although there was a smattering of local ALF activists in the hall, most of the audience listening to Beggs seemed like a sober cross section of decent Middle England. And yet no one stood up and questioned or denounced what was being said in defence of the ARM. This suggested that Tim Daley was not exaggerating when he claimed wide support for the ARM within the movement: 75% of people out on a demo the day after one of the petrol bombings had supported it, Daley had remarked; they might not be so forthcoming to those outside the movement, but in their own company there was overwhelming support.

When activists complained that the press and television gave disproportionate publicity to the ARM actions, it brought sharply into focus the gulf between the movement and the speciesist majority. In liberationist terms, what mattered was the volume of numbers of animals being killed, or, as they put it, tortured. For the speciesist mass media and the authorities the assault on one human being was of more consequence than the vivisection of a thousand rodents, cats or dogs: there was an essential and obvious qualitative difference. The fact that those in the centre of the movement had not only removed themselves from this consensus, but were proud to have done so, produced conversation that could be chilling. Sitting in a Hammersmith pub just round the corner from ALF head-quarters, Vivian Smith ('The Witch' in the parlance of the

Animal Rights Squad at Scotland Yard) smiled with genuine pleasure as she said she looked forward to hearing that the first vivisector had been blown up. No regrets about the necessity, no sense of anything being particularly sacred about a human life. The ALF Supporters Group Bulletin later ran a cartoon which showed a circle of animals dancing round a gibbet: 'There, that's the last vivisector hung by the guts of the last huntsman!' went the cheerful caption underneath.

But the links between the ALF and the ARM were clearly practical as well as ideological. As John Beggs had shown in his helpful liaison work for TVS, the terrorist cell seemed remarkably easy to get hold of. Neither Ronnie Lee nor Tim Daley seemed to have much trouble either when the opportunity arose, as Neil Roberts found out when he was working on the *Sutton Herald*. In 1985, the year of the petrol bomb attacks on the BIBRA workers in Surrey, Roberts was the reporter covering what became a major local story. The patch he covered had been for some time the scene of consistent activity from animal rights activists working both within and outside the law; SLAM (the South London Animals Movement) was constantly mounting noisy desmonstrations at the homes of scientists associated either with BIBRA or the Institute of Psychiatry in Dulwich, featuring mock funerals, adults dressed up as vivisected animals and much chanting of 'scum', 'filth' and the by now familiar verse 'one, two, three, four, nail the scientists to the floor!' There was also a highly active operational cell of the ALF working locally, concentrating their incendiary efforts on Allders in Croydon.

When the first ARM petrol bombing happened, Neil Roberts followed normal practice by ringing up Ronnie Lee at the ALF office in Hammersmith; if the action was illegal, Roberts reckoned, the ALF was the best place to start. He was right. After the Gangolli Molotov cocktail incident in June, Ronnie called him back after half an hour to read out a complete prepared statement from the Militia; no explanation was offered as to how this had been obtained with such impressive rapidity. Lee was to be of similar use after future bombing incidents. Certainly, by the end of the year ARM communiqués were being published in the ALF's magazine by Lee, with no explanation as to where they had come from or why they were being printed.

Roberts saw a great deal of Tim Daley that year in his

capacity as a leading campaigner in SLAM. Daley, too, seemed remarkably well and swiftly informed about the doings of the Militia. On the morning after the gas cylinder bombs had exploded under the cars belonging to Gangolli and Walker, Daley dropped into the *Sutton Herald* office claiming that he had just heard on the radio that the ARM had blown up a couple of cars and proceeding to give most of the details. The *Herald* office constantly monitored two local radio stations but had heard none of this: Roberts concluded that Daley's information must have come from direct contact with the Militia. Six months later, after the attempted bombing of Andor Sebesteny's car, Daley was again able to quote details about the event before they were released in the media.

Neil Roberts concluded that all those different sets of intials in the local movement were almost meaningless and that the same bunch were probably connected with most of the actions, claimed under a variety of names. Under pressure from increasing police scrutiny, the movement had become far more sophisticated in evading detection in setting its plans. Tim Daley, for example, took it for granted that his car was under surveillance and his phone tapped; it was a matter of some pride, and the subject of something close to admiration among less daring activists. 'Initially, I thought it was private detectives following me, hired by a lab; but I followed it through, checked the car out through a friend on the police computer, and it turned out it was hired from a company in Thames Ditton ... So I went to the hire company and they told me, thinking I was from a newspaper, that the Metropolitan Police were hiring the cars ... so obviously then I knew I was being followed.' Shortly afterwards, the hire company had its fleet of cars paintstrippered by the ALF for loaning vehicles to Scotland Yard.

Daley also took it for granted that his mail was opened. 'I know that most animal rights people say that, but you get a bit sick to death after a while when things are opened blatantly and then stuck back badly.' He had proved that his phone was tapped, he said, by setting up a phoney raid on BIBRA in Carshalton, pretending to assemble a hundred activists and an assortment of crowbars and sledgehammers. At the time arranged, eight transit vans of police had positioned themselves securely in front of the laboratories: Daley and friends drove past slowly, grinning insolently at the enemy.

Tim Daley, even more than Ronnie Lee, trod a perilous line;

unlike Lee, he got away with it. He was able to go on television and tell the 'Brass Tacks' programme that the sooner Dr Brian Meldrum 'was killed, the better'. It was a great pity that the ARM device planted under his car had not gone off; this was a war and people got killed in wars. Daley had been picked up by the police in connection with ARM actions but he had never been charged. After his outbursts on television there was talk of prosecution for incitement to murder, but in the end nothing happened; the only penalty paid was his instant dismissal from the newspaper whose advertising space he had sold with conspicuous success. And yet, Daley had clearly and unequivocally advocated murder in the cause of animal rights; he regarded this, he said, as 'a very promising prospect'.

In the absence of regular bulletins from the ALF, the continued existence of the ARM, as a sub-grouping within the movement, was not clear. There had been a gap of two years between the first letter bombs and the south London petrol bombings; another year elapsed between Dr Sebesteny's car bomb and the letter bomb to Dr Ian Rigley in Kent. That had been in the spring of 1987; nothing since has been heard from the Militia, at least in Britain, and no one has been charged in connection with any of their actions. But in the latest 'Diary of Actions' published by the ALF's Supporters Group, the ARM surfaced in unusual circumstances: a group using the Militia's name had just burned down a cattle feed barn in San José, California, worth £200,000. By the end of the eighties, it seemed sets of initials had become the interchangeable currency of international animal rights terrorism.

CHAPTER ELEVEN

I am nowhere near to being a violent
person, but I believe that the crimes of
vivisectors against creation are so bad
that they deserve to pay for them with
their lives.

ALF Supporters Group Member 289

Every terrorist organization feeds on two vital elements – a
constant supply of what Mrs Thatcher likes to describe as 'the
oxygen of publicity', and an equally constant supply of cash.
The IRA solved the latter problem by indulging in lucrative
protection rackets and Bonnie and Clyde-style bank raids in
the Republic. The ALF could hardly descend to these desperate
measures: besides, in their muddled, contradictory and hesitantly British approach to these matters they drew the line at
deliberately involving non-animal abusers in acts of violence.
But keeping some thirteen hundred activists in the field sup-
plied with communications gear and surveillance equipment
cost money, as did the increasingly steep roll-call of fines levied
in the courts. In 1982, the arrival of the former British Movement organizer Dave Nicholls meant that for the first time the
Front was put on something approaching a professionally run
financial footing. The ALF Supporters Group that Nicholls set
up guaranteed an annual income of at least £50,000 a year:
peanuts by the standards of more conventional liberation
movements, but undreamt of wealth for a group that had lived
from hand to mouth for six years.

The idea of the Supporters Group was to draw in all those
who basically supported what the ALF was up to, but who did
not want or could not afford to get personally involved in illegal
activities. The ALF SG was perfectly legal and above board. To
become a member you contributed a minimum subscription of
£2.00 a month, £24.00 a year, with cheques and postal orders
made out to the ALF SG; later, standing-order forms were
available to make your contribution directly to the Supporters

Group's account with the Co-operative Bank in the City of London. At the beginning there were complaints about the subscriptions being too steep, especially in comparison to the more moderate £5.00 a year demanded by the national animal welfare groups; the ALF responded tetchily by arguing that to query the cash was to question the right of animals rescued by the Front to be liberated. No cash, no liberation, it was as simple as that. Certainly there was never any suggestion, apart from the occasional illicit booze-up, that funds from the Supporters Group were diverted into personal bank accounts or provided corruptly luxurious life-styles for the movement's leadership. Materialism was never one of the sins that could be laid at the door of the ALF, as anyone who met Ronnie Lee, almost tramp-like in his black threadbare clothes, would accept.

As it was, there were soon many SG members paying four and five times the minimum subscription: there was a high proportion of older and wealthier members whose inability actually to go out on raids was due more to old age than any lack of enthusiasm; even so, the Front liked to boast that local cells often had the odd fifty- or sixty-year-old acting as driver or look-out: Mike Nunn, the ex-butcher who had been gaoled for three years as the 'general' behind the Wickham raid, had been in his mid fifties at the time. What members actually got for their money, apart from the satisfaction of knowing that they were financing the movement's direct action, was a bi-monthly Bulletin, which rapidly became the Front's main arm of internal propaganda. It also became the forum of heated discussion on the direction the movement ought to be taking and the kind of tactics to be employed. Beginning as a rough, cyclostyled series of sheets stapled together, the Bulletin developed into a sharply produced periodical, the covers of which gave a vivid indication of the movement's direction.

Early issues, when the SG, like its parent body, was still using the premises of Peace News in Nottingham, tended to feature touching close-ups of balaclava'd figures cuddling 'liberated' rabbits and beagles; later, the Bulletin resembled far more closely the anarchist papers, like *Class War* and *Crowbar* with which a growing number of activists were associated. 'Vivisectors are Scum!', 'Devastate to Liberate!', and the advice that 'Factories Don't Burn Down by Themselves – They Need You!' were the currency of the slogans gracing increasingly lurid covers; these now featured photos of burnt-out meat wagons and gutted factories. Inside, the language of contributors mirrored this gradual change of emphasis, although Ronnie Lee and David Nicholls were always anxious to counterbalance inflammatory sermons on violence with letters from SG members who would only condone direct action against property. Alienate half the membership and half the income went with it.

From the first issue, the Bulletin went in heavily for merchandising, beginning with postcards, and going on to take advantage of the whole modern rock tour marketing machine, involving T-shirts, sweatshirts, badges and stickers. Souvenirs of prestige raids were an early feature of this trade. 'Can you honestly resist this? A set of three large photos (approx. 9 inches by 7 inches) taken while Operation Valentine was being carried out at the Animal Death/Torture establishment "Life Science Research Centre" at Stock, nr Chelmsford' ran one seductive special offer . . . 'These are actual photos and NOT photocopies!' For £7.00 you could pick up pictures featuring 'the immense damage done inside the centre', 'ALF activists storming the centre, and an activist with a rescued beagle'. The medical laboratory complex had suffered £75,000 worth of damage in the raid; shortly afterwards, forty workers (dismissed as 'pro-vivisection', therefore of no account, by the SG Bulletin) were laid off as a result.

The first issue also saw the introduction of a scheme to involve law-abiding SG members in the ALF's campaign of harassment. Under the heading 'Adopt an Animal Abuser', supporters were urged to take follow-up action against named enemies of animal liberation. 'When an ALF action takes place against an animal abuser, it is usually one hundred per cent successful; but after the action has been completed, the animal abuser breathes a sigh of relief, presuming the ALF has plenty of people on their list, and a repeat action is unlikely.' Which is where the willing supporters came in. What precisely they had to do was not spelled out, but the name, address and personal information about the target was laid out in detail. Anonymous letters, phone calls and unwanted deliveries were the commonest form of petty harassment practised within the movement. Qualms about such behaviour were soothed by the information that the Front's named victim and his wife inhabited their seven-bedroomed, detached home only because it had

131

been 'purchased with the blood of tortured animals'. To be firmly placed outside the pale, every vivisector had to be clearly identified as not merely a sadist, but a greedy materialistic sadist, whose work was purely undertaken for personal gain. It did not matter to the Front that the scientist they had named actually had a good record for his humane concern for animals, and had publicly condemned what he considered unnecessary areas of vivisection, such as the LD 50 test on rabbits' eyes: indeed traditional animal welfarists saw him as an ally. None of this washed with the Front: 'vivisectors often think that apparently "sympathizing" with anti-vivisection will reduce the chances of them being attacked . . . well, the ALF has news for the animal torturers – we haven't even started yet!'

Unfortunately, the Bulletin's intelligence was often erratic. The second issue (without apology) noted that the phone number given for the first abuser to be 'adopted' was incorrect: supporters were given no further information about any innocent parties whose lives had presumably been made confusingly hellish by this mistake. A woman who was a regional secretary of the British Field Sports Society ('Bloody Fiends and Sick Sadists') was named as the next adoptee. 'Why not let her know what YOU think??????' urged the Bulletin, confidently publishing the woman's name and address.

There were other ways that SG members could provide practical back-up to the activists out in the field. With the dozen or so raids a week being organized by the early eighties, the ALF found itself with the problem of having to find homes for the hundreds of rodents, dogs, rabbits and battery chickens 'rescued' from farms and laboratories. Most ALF activists were happy to accommodate large numbers of these creatures in their own homes (Tim Daley's flat smelled like a zoo, thanks to a substantial collection of white rats caged in the kitchen) but clearly there were limits. And so supporters were urged to write in with offers of good homes. 'Even if you can home [sic] just one small animal – a mouse or rat etc, it is one animal that the ALF will not have to worry about.' Supporters were asked to start their own sanctuaries exclusively for the benefit of liberated creatures and many responded. There was, the Bulletin warmly reminded its readers, 'nothing so satisfying as giving a home to an animal rescued from the clutches of sadistic murderers'. Whether or not the courts might construe this as receiving stolen goods was not an issue the Bulletin cared to debate.

Money was a perennial problem. Despite (or perhaps because of) the £24.00 annual subscription, supporters who couldn't or wouldn't sign a standing order were soon being blamed for the potential deaths of innocent creatures. Every forgetful or mean-minded member who forgot his sub, went this logic, was directly letting down activists who had fines to pay in court; and if fines went unpaid, activists went to prison and animals remained unliberated. Ronnie Lee was constantly looking at ways of diverting the vast sums that flowed into the bank accounts of the 'respectable' animal societies into those of the Front. 'It is disgraceful,' he wrote, 'that ALF activists have to exist on the breadline in order to carry out important actions against the animal abuse industry while those who make loud noises but do nothing more take home large wage packets.' This was clearly aimed at the RSPCA, whose leadership had undergone something of a crisis after scandalous revelations about misappropriated funds. Later, as we shall see, the libera-tionists obtained substantial funds from both the BUAV and the NAVS, but never managed to crack the RSPCA. Nonethe-less, individual wealthy members of the RSPCA were prepared to divert their own cash to the ALF Supporters Group.

But who exactly were the two thousand or so anonymous financial backers of the movement? The evidence was that certainly a high proportion of those who joined the SG were very different from the activists they supported. Older, often prosperously middle-class, their profile seemed far closer to that of the traditional animal lover than might have been expected. Richard Course, for many years the Director of the League Against Cruel Sports, saw this as evidence that history had gone full circle. When he first got involved in animal welfare back in the forties, he said, the committees were full of hatchet faced middle-aged women who loved animals but appeared to loathe their fellow human beings: Course saw the same phenomenon now resurfacing with a vengeance.

For many of these older supporters, the arrival of the ALF had seemed positively heroic: a last desperate means of achiev-ing aims that whole lifetimes involved in conventional animal welfare had singularly failed to meet. One elderly supporter told the Bulletin that he always felt a sense of 'happiness' when the ALF mounted a successful action. He didn't consider

133

himself 'extreme' at all, he was involved in most of the mainstream animal charities, but without direct action to sabotage the animal abuse industries nothing would change: the illegality was irrelevant – after all, the selling of ten-year-old girls as prostitutes had once been perfectly legal. 'I know so many people that have campaigned against animal abuse since the nineteen thirties and forties who have expressed deep regret that the ALF didn't exist earlier than 1976.' He had, this older supporter, given a home to five rats liberated by the Front; every time he fed them, he thought admiringly of the brave youngsters who had rescued them.

Here was something to connect that tired old cliché, the English love of animals, with the hard terrorist tactics of the liberationists. As Richard Course had experienced, the corollary of that love had often been a deep dislike of one's own species. Across the country there were many hundreds of perfectly respectable older RSPCA members who welcomed Ronnie Lee and his friends. Reservations might be expressed about the dress, manners and politics (where anarchist) of the troops in the field, but there was full support for what they were up to. When the ALF agreed to an interview with the Bournemouth cell – the originators of the Mars Bar hoax – the meeting was held at the home of a prominent local member of the SG. It was a large detached house, clearly the property of someone extremely well off – a doctor, solicitor or businessman. Some surprising people were prepared to back an organization identified by the Prime Minister herself as a bunch of terrorists.

Kenneth and Christine Harrold, whom we have already met, were two of them. Mr Harrold was a member of the ALF Supporters Group; he and his wife Christine were the kind of members Ronnie Lee would have prayed for, donating five times the regular subscription, plus, as Mrs Harrold put it vaguely, 'some extras' every now and again.

The Harrolds' home was a kind of suburban temple to the animal kingdom. The living room was full of elegant and expensive animal sculptures brought back from abroad, and a mechanical bird in a cage that made remarkably life-like movements and chirping noises when wound up. In the garden there were bird tables and feeding bags and an appreciative flock of local wildlife enjoying the Harrolds' hospitality: there had been two much-loved dogs, one of which had recently died, leaving Christine Harrold distraught for several weeks. Christine was the talker. Bright red hair swept severely backwards, extravagantly-framed glasses glinting with heartfelt conviction, she saw nothing odd about defending the ALF's recent fire-bombing of meat trucks at the local abattoir. Of course, the meat traders would say that someone could have been killed, they always said that didn't they? But as to the bombing, no, she couldn't honestly say she was opposed to it. She was very sorry if people might be surprised by that – but then people had a duty to learn a great deal more about what was going on in this country. 'This government,' chipped in her husband, 'and all the previous governments have demonstrated how futile it is to try to achieve change by peaceful means.' Of course, they didn't like the word 'terrorism' but this wasn't terorism; it was just showing the government you meant business.

There was about both the Harrolds again that weary sense of having exhausted any patience or interest in their own species. Their concern for animals had been the major feature of their adult lives; they had joined animal welfare groups in their youth, when welfare meant little more than 'mending broken bones'. They were both longstanding vegetarians, anti-vivisectionists who had been on all the marches over the years, signed all the petitions. It would be nice to think, said Mrs Harrold, that democracy had some weight, but for her generation of animal lovers it just seemed to be a waste of time. 'For over a hundred years now we've been trying to get things changed by democratic means; we must have had billions of signatures and millions of petitions, and what I would like to know is what has become of them all?' It didn't matter which government was in power; they all just threw the petitions on the bonfire and forgot about them.

The Harrolds seemed to have little politics outside the animals issue; they would line up with anyone who shared their concerns. Anarchists in the local animal rights group had got upset and called them 'fascists' when they had announced that they were prepared to march with the National Front in a demonstration against Jewish and Muslim ritual slaughter. The Harrolds were surprised and hurt; you could be a fascist and still work for the animals, surely. Other ALF supporters, particularly the older ones, who had only their pensions to draw on for their subscriptions, agreed: and Ronnie Lee himself wrote in the Supporters Group Bulletin that differences between fascists and socialists were of little account if they were united in the struggle for animal rights.

What the Harrolds found so invigorating about the ALF was that here, finally, was a bunch of young people who were prepared to go out and do something dramatic on behalf of the animals: 'they're doing what I wanted to do when I was fifteen or sixteen,' said Christine, 'but unfortunately in those days there wasn't the freedom that young people have today'. And if Lee and Nicholls worried that older supporters might be inclined to baulk at the increasingly violent path of the movement, listening to these two sixty-year-olds provided surprising reassurance. Scientists, said Mrs Harrold fiercely, were 'evil sadists', only in it for their own interest and to make money. Vivisectors should all die in the same way that the animals they experimented on were put to death.

The ALF supporters were as curiously varied as the Front's activists. Celebrity support came mainly from the rock music industry, although the film star James Mason had donated several hundred pounds to the movement, along with a message of goodwill, shortly before he died. Within the rock world most of the performers and writers who came out and openly backed the Front were those who had already adopted a set of more conventionally left-wing attitudes. Paul Weller, founder member of the Style Council ('a really good bloke' according to Tim Daley), Beki Bondage and Chrissie Hynde of the Pretenders all gave time and effort to benefits raising funds for the movement. On the back of this wave of public support, the *New Musical Express* even gave an interview to Ronnie Lee. The rock world's most conspicuous effort came from the Manchester band, the Smiths, whose lead singer Morrissey came up with a song that, with its baleful lyrics and doomladen melody, became the movement's unofficial anthem. 'Meat is Murder' gave its name to one of the band's most successful albums, a song full of repellently vivid imagery conjured up by Morrissey in his vision of death in the slaughterhouse. Earlier, the singer had expressed not only a wish to see the Prime Minister dead but also a readiness to execute her himself.

Several of the rock fraternity got together in an organization called 'Artists for Animals', turning out records and appearing in regional concerts in support of the movement; three compilation albums were issued, featuring a mixture of well-known bands, like Madness and Siouxie and the Banshees, alongside fringe anarchist groups like Conflict ('This is the ALF'). By the early eighties there was a potent fund of idealistic goodwill towards any organization that seemed, like the admirable Greenpeace, to be doing something positive about the destruction of the environment. To many young people, the ALF simply seemed to be a natural extension of this, part of a widespread movement of revulsion against high-technology farming and medicine. The Front's bank account thrived on much decent but hopelessly muddled goodwill. From 1984 it also benefited from the efforts of a new group called RATS, an anarchist 'collective' who raised funds for the Front, specializing in financing homes for animals rescued from vivisection. RATS were based at the anarchist bookshop in Brixton's Railton Road, which was popular with the direct action rank and file supporters of the Class War sect.

For all these splinter groups, campaigns and fund raising fraternities, the ALF's Bulletin became a clearing house for information; targets would merely be identified, tactics would be left to groups and individuals. With the increasingly visible involvement of the anarchist groups in ALF activity, there was even less cohesion and central planning of actions: it was chaotic but it made life that much more difficult for the police. When Ronnie Lee told the press that he didn't know whether it was one of his cells that had carried out a raid, he was more often than not probably telling the truth. The Bulletin became all the more important as the movement's central log of actions carried out across the country and latterly across the world.

As early as 1983, a notice announced that the ALF Supporters Group had now gone international, with members in France, Canada and Australia. The month's diary of actions included a line about a raid carried out on a dog pound in Sydney by a group calling themselves the Animal Freedom Fighters ('Australia's ALF'), who had apparently gone on to smash up half a dozen fur shops as well. A group in California called the 'Urban Gorillas' had rescued three cats from a Los Angeles laboratory. Two months later, the Bulletin proudly announced that 'direct action has now started in South Africa'. Several businesses selling ivory from elephants had been severely damaged and a fur shop destroyed. The anonymous group responsible told the press that they were only doing this because 'the animals cannot speak for themselves'.

Later, reports were filed from Germany, Sweden, France and Holland. Raids were sometimes claimed for the 'IALF' (International ALF) but more often local autonomous cells were at work. In some countries, the liberationist organizations grew rapidly and established support groups similar to the ALF SG. By 1984 the Canadians had their own ALF Support Group, with separate bank accounts, defence funds and mailing lists. Even in France, not perhaps the most immediately obvious home of animal causes, the activists had got themselves organized under the banner of the FLA – Le Front pour la Libération des Animaux. With no apparent irony, the Bulletin reported that the FLA had recently liberated fifty-nine frogs from the prospect of untimely deaths in the classrooms of students taking their biology finals. This being France, the FLA were not going to take half measures and when they were interrupted by a laboratory assistant half way through the raid the unfortunate man had tear gas sprayed in his face.

For all these foreign groups the ALF Supporters Group acted as a central clearing house for information and debate. From the very beginning, the ALF had been highly sensitive to damaging publicity in the newspapers, especially when it was suggested that activists were seriously ignorant about animal behaviour, that raids intended to 'liberate' actually did more harm than good to their intended beneficiaries. When, for example, the RSPCA roundly condemned as cruel and irresponsible two raids on mink farms in Scotland and Essex, several worried supporters wrote in to add their condemnation: they were particularly upset at what they had read in the papers about mink tearing innocent kittens to pieces and causing havoc in the countryside. This was all nonsense, said the Bulletin, omitting to print the letters, but clearly worried by the breaking of ranks, and not least on the issue of what amounted to incompetence. These 'so-called' members of the movement were either ignorant of the true facts or simply hypocritical: animal liberation had to include mink liberation or it was meaningless. 'There can be NO EXCEPTIONS' thundered the editorial with all the righteous vigour normally provoked by spineless revisionism. The RSPCA were a bunch of hypocrites, the press liars: the point was that, even in captivity the creatures were fed on fish and meat, so release into the wild, where they had to catch their own food didn't really make much difference. Free mink were better off than captive mink and that was that. Later it was reported that several of them had found life in the wild rather intimidating, and had literally queued up outside the farms to get back in again.

Solidarity among the supporters was important; not just because they were the movement's paymasters but because argument was a debilitating waste of energy: there is nothing so unedifying as the prospect of a liberation movement tearing itself to pieces in public. It was also confusing to the young who were, after all, the future of animal liberation. Since its beginnings, the Supporters Group had attracted mainly older enthusiasts. In January 1987, a 'Young SG' group was set up: membership was open to anyone under sixteen, at a subscription of £2.00 a year. For this, the young supporter received an ALF badge and a quarterly newsletter from 'Uncle Alfie'. This egregious character was soon full of useful suggestions as to how the young supporter could profitably use his or her spare hours. 'Write a story,' 'Uncle Alfie' instructed the children. 'Imagine that you take a trip in a time travelling machine. It takes you into the future, to a time when animal liberation has already been achieved. Models of Bernard Matthews and Professor Meldrum are in the Chamber of Horrors, the milkman only delivers soya milk, and Porton Down has been converted into a leisure centre. Write about your adventures, as funny or as serious as you like.' For Brian Meldrum, the scientist who had already had a bomb under his car and a limitless supply of death threats, there didn't seem to be a great deal of fun in 'Uncle Alfie's' little fantasy.

From the very beginning, a large proportion of the Supporters' Group cash donations had been siphoned off to pay the fines of activists facing prosecution: the knowledge that the Front would pay your way if you got caught was encouraging to cell members who were by and large young, otherwise law abiding and not well off. As the level of activity increased in the eighties, so the ALF devoted more and more funds and organizational time to the setting up of a formal structure to provide solidarity for liberationists 'lifted' by the police. They called it SARP, Support for Animal Rights Prisoners, and it was not simply a tranche of cash to pay off the courts. Through the SG it distributed information about prisoners, acted as a clearing house for letters to and from prison, organized letter writing campaigns to prison governors to urge vegan diets for prisoners, and subsidized travel costs for friends and relatives of those inside.

SARP was yet another pale mirror image of the Sinn Fein/ Republican style so much respected by the ALF leadership. And it appeared to work. Visits to animal rights prisoners were organized strictly by rote, ensuring that there was a constant flow of friends and supporters to keep up morale. Cockatoo plumed hairstyles, black punk anarchist uniforms and Smiths promotional T-shirts were regularly to be seen providing splashes of excitement in the drab and usually rather defeated lines of wives and families queueing under the watchful eyes of the screws. Fines of up to four and five hundred pounds a head were tough, but life on the inside was a great deal tougher. Prisoners found the diet difficult to cope with; you had to provide documentary evidence of membership of the Vegan Society to qualify for a vegan diet – and if you couldn't, you ended up on a régime of boiled onions and unflavoured soya. Animal liberationists were a mystery to both regular prisoners and the prison staff. Mostly, they received a grudging respect or were dismissed as inpenetrable 'loonies', with their fondness for Buddhist texts, unappetizing meals and utter removal from the regular prison culture.

But mostly, it should be said, animal rights prisoners served their time with patience and considerable dignity. Letters from prison suggested that serious activists were prepared to accept their time behind bars as the necessary price of animal liberation. Few had any regrets. Mark Houghton had done £5,000 worth of criminal damage to a total of fifteen meat trucks: writing from Winson Green Prison he told the SG that he still felt good about what he had done. 'I want to let other ALF supporters know,' he wrote, 'that they shouldn't be afraid of breaking the law in their crusade for animal rights . . . We must not be afraid of being sent to prison for our beliefs. Whether one is prepared to undergo the humiliation of imprisonment must surely be the acid-test of one's genuine commitment to animal rights.' Being in prison, harsh though it might seem, was nothing compared to the misery endured by millions of animals.

Sometimes, though, the SG had to act tough. The trouble with too many animal rights activists, as John Beggs had once publicly complained, was that they could be horribly naïve when brought in for questioning. Faced with threats, or exaggerated police suggestions about the kind of charges they were likely to face, many would crumble and make damaging statements incriminating others. Police custody could be grim for young activists with no previous experience of law-breaking; there were letters to the SG detailing acts of petty brutality and humiliation, the kind of rough treatment that clearly brought rewards. Police officers, it was said, would suggest they were gay or deviant, in between bouts of roughing up in the cells. And so people would talk. By 1985 the SG had a new rule. Only those who made no statement whatsoever would get the full sum of their fines and costs met by the ALF; those who admitted their own guilt, but made no mention of anyone else would be entitled to half their expenses being paid. The rest would get nothing.

By the end of the eighties, the ALF SG was still very much a going concern, operating from a London postal box number, and with Account Number 50381708 at the Co-Op Bank's City Office Branch still in receipt of subscriptions. The majority of its finances were directed towards the work for animal rights prisoners, on whose behalf groups like Artists for Animals continued to organize benefits. The survival of the SG had been no mean feat following the successive trials and imprisonment of most of the ALF leadership: the organization's somewhat tenuous claims to a separate, lawful existence beyond the cellular structure of the ALF were emphasized by po-faced announcements. The Supporters Group, who produced the Bulletin, were 'in no way involved with the actions mentioned. These are received anonymously through the post from press cuttings.' But, of course, nothing had changed. The movement was simply a little bit older and a little bit wiser.

CHAPTER TWELVE

If it goes on like this we're going to
need a human liberation front.

Anonymous vivisector,
interviewed by the *Guardian*

It was often hard to imagine that a movement venturing so close to a state of permanent chaos could be responsible for so much damage. And yet if they listened to what their human targets had to say, the liberationists must have been pleasantly surprised by the panic and alarm engendered by their campaign of terror. The ALF, said one senior research scientist, who had himself been the object of multiple death threats, were now a much more serious threat than the IRA. This was rather more than the understandable hyperbole of a potential bomb victim: while it was true that so far the Front had not assassinated anyone, they had materially damaged the health and happiness of more than a million people. That was the research scientist's conservative estimate of the number of patients whose chances of recovery or cure had been severely hampered by the campaign. Whole fields of research were being shunned for fear of personal attacks; bright young academics were deliberately moving into areas free from controversy; worst of all, some of the country's best brains were being silenced.

Roy Calne, Professor of Surgery at Cambridge University, was the exception. One of the leading pioneers in liver and kidney transplant surgery, Professor Calne had had the gall to write to *The Times* to protest about an ALF raid that had temporarily interrupted his kidney graft programme at Addenbrooke's Hospital. He wondered whether the idealism of these 'criminals' would be sufficient for them to refuse treatment with antibiotics or withhold insulin from their children should they become diabetic; he wondered if they would deny open-heart surgery to babies born with congenital heart disease, or forbid a life-saving kidney graft to a child suffering from kidney failure. For these were all the material benefits of experiments on animals. In return for raising these issues, Professor Calne was sent a letter bomb by the Animal Rights Militia. He was worried for himself, his family and his technicians but he would not be silenced because the consequences of bowing to this very real threat of violence were unthinkable. Other scientists, Professor Calne told a meeting of the Research Defence Society, had already been silenced. 'Opposition is not being voiced – for fear of attacks against the individual who has dared to question the anti-vivisectionists.' This was a dangerous precedent, because the terrorization of opposition into silence was the favourite strategy of all tyrannical movements. If the public wished to end vivisection, they would vote for it; in the meantime, for the sake of humanity, the spirit of liberal intellectual enquiry should proceed. But, as Professor Calne had admitted, it was already on the retreat.

The range of those who found themselves under threat from the animal rights movement was extraordinarily broad. If the most serious long-term damage was being done through the campaign against individual vivisectors, the long target list of people under direct threat included some bizarre candidates. The television naturalist David Bellamy, it might have been imagined, was a friend of the animals, a proven advocate of ecological good sense and a respected conservationist. He was all these things, but this was no protection against a series of threats to his life by liberationists. Like Professor Calne, Dr Bellamy had had the effrontery to be honest – in particular about the daftness of the ALF in continuing to 'liberate' mink into the wild and about the regretful necessity of maintaining some animal experimentation if medical research was to progress. He also publicly argued with the idea that if everyone became a vegetarian the world's food crisis would be solved: the opposite was true, he said, thus earning further threatening letters.

Learning to live with the presence of this new and often apparently random form of terrorism could cause confusion. The National Farmers' Union London headquarters was anxious to be as open and helpful as possible in talking about the threat; but some county secretaries would not talk at all about levels of ALF raids, or discuss the kind of precautions being advised to their members. All publicity was bad publicity as far as they were concerned: it merely served to glamorize 'a bunch of dangerous anarchists', as one local spokesman described them while refusing any interview on the subject. Others were more forthcoming. Peter Barton, an official of the NFU in Sussex, said that in his district there had been a serious increase in levels of violence to property, livestock and against individual farmers; such 'rural terrorism' had got out of hand. Farmers were so intimidated that they were no longer prepared to appear on television to talk about the issue. This was said while standing in the compound of a large battery chicken farm in the peaceful heart of the Sussex countryside, some ten miles north of Brighton: the term 'terrorism' was hard to take seriously. Peter Barton agreed that it all sounded unbelievable, but the fact was that it was going on now, and his members were in the firing line. The farmer whose land we were standing on had just spent several thousand pounds on the installation of an electronic surveillance system, with twenty-four-hour video scan. His staff had been threatened personally by the local ALF cell: he couldn't afford to take chances. What was disconcerting about all this was that there had been no point of human contact or debate with these people. He had no idea who the enemy were, or even what they really wanted, beyond the disruption of his business.

Other targets were even more confused and with better reason. Mike Adams was running a network of car dealerships in the Midlands when he began to receive a stream of letters threatening personal violence if he refused to stop selling one particular make of car imported from South Korea. It turned out that, according to the International Fund for Animal Welfare, there was an old South Korean custom that involved the stringing up of cats and dogs and then barbecueing them at family picnics. Selling Korean cars apparently made Mr Adams an accomplice to this crime. The IFAW blamed a few 'bad apples' for the threatening phone calls: the understandably worried Mr Adams rang the South Korean Embassy, who assured him that dog lynching had been outlawed. Equally confused were the secretary and membership of the Fairhaven Golf Club at Lytham St Annes in Lancashire, who woke up one morning to find that every green on their course had been dug up. An ALF spokesman later rang a local press agency to say that the greens had been destroyed because leaders of the poultry industry were due to play a sponsored match at the club while attending their annual conference in the town. Repairing the greens cost the Fairhaven club several thousand

144

pounds; the poultry men simply played their match on temporary greens.

Ignorance of the principles of speciesism was no excuse. Families who called in the pest control experts, Rentokil, to rid their homes of rats, mice and cockroaches by and large were not troubled by the eventual fate of these creatures. But the ALF was: a communiqué in 1987 announced that Rentokil were mass murderers, responsible for 'the horrific deaths of mice and rats they poison when called to homes'. Vans belonging to the firm were now legitimate targets. The same afternoon, a Rentokil driver was driving through north London when he felt his hands burning; it turned out that the steering wheel and most of the van's interior had been sprayed with hydrofluoric acid. The driver and two garage workers who tried to remove the fluid were rushed to hospital with acid burns. Further acid attacks on Rentokil vehicles followed.

In the event, Rentokil went on to a war footing. Confidential plans for dealing with ALF attacks were distributed to staff; vans were repainted to look anonymous, and a proper sense of discretion encouraged in the ranks. It was the same with more obvious targets like the large laboratory complexes. These were quite visibly under siege, with their barbed wire and electric fences, their remote control video monitoring systems and uniformed security guards patrolling the perimeters. Most now had emergency plans for dealing with raids from activists. The Harlow laboratories of Merck, Sharp and Dohme distributed a special sheet of instructions to all staff as they joined, warning them of the danger of an attack from 'animal activists'. Anyone approached outside working hours by a member of the public with an enquiry about life in the labs was to be immediately directed to company headquarters; telephone calls were never to be answered with full name and working area, only an extension number. All suspicious letters and parcels were to be referred to security immediately. If the premises came under attack, staff were not to use force unless to defend themselves or other staff members. 'Sufficient force for that purpose is fully justified.' Careless talk could cost the company: employees should realize that this really was war.

The big companies were not keen to talk about either the level of damage they were sustaining or the measures they were taking to defend themselves. Dewhursts would not discuss their security precautions but admitted that their nationwide chain of shops had suffered a total of eighty-seven attacks in the previous three months. McDonalds, occupying a particularly distinguished place in the demonology of the ALF, would only divulge that they had 'contingency plans' to protect their premises. Boots also took the threat seriously, but they didn't want to make public statements; there was a reluctance, said their director of PR, to raise their corporate head above the parapet.

But the crucial battleground in this war was to be found in both the working and private lives of the vivisectors. The pressure that the liberationists were able to bring to bear on not just those individuals but the authorities responsible for the places where they worked was often greater than they probably realized. Several scientists talked about their shameless betrayal by governing bodies who reneged on research projects out of a combination of embarrassment over lurid publicity and outright cowardice in the face of bomb threats. One researcher whose work involved the use of monkeys and baboons said that even before the bombs and the raids on his laboratories, the governing body of the Institute where he worked had suddenly become chillingly unsympathetic to his project: the mere presence of regular pickets and the painting of slogans had been an embarrassment. They would rather he took his work elsewhere. Such spineless behaviour had depressed the researcher rather more than the attentions of the ALF.

In their propaganda the liberationists suggested that most projects involving animals were neither of first-rank significance nor of any broad benefit except to the inevitably self-seeking careerist in charge. But the fact was that more than half of all animal experiments were required either directly or indirectly by the demands of legislation. And among those whose lives were threatened and who were actively reconsidering their willingness to continue their work were several scientists engaged in vital research. Professor Colin Blakemore, head of the Department of Physiology at Oxford University, used primates in the course of experiments designed to explore the early diagnosis of sight problems in young children. It was important work, but if the campaign against him continued, he admitted, he had doubts about whether he would stay in Oxford. Professor Blakemore's laboratories had been attacked, but far more worrying had been the personal attention. Phone calls had threatened him and his three children with death;

when his wife was pregnant, an anonymous caller had rung up saying 'I hope your baby is born deformed.' Regular death threats arrived at the family home by letter. The three Blakemore children were no longer allowed to leave home unaccompanied. At the time of writing, the campaign continues unabated.

In London, a major research project into potential cures for brain damage had, concurrent to Professor Blakemore's problems in Oxford, been put back a year in order to make the animal house secure from ALF raids. No one could precisely measure the global effect the terror campaign had had in restricting medical research, but Dr Brian Meldrum felt that it was widespread. 'They have certainly stopped important research in certain areas of head injury, and high velocity missile wounds, certain behavioural studies, studies on depression. In all these areas, and more, work has been stopped as a result of pressure from the animal liberationists.' Work, that is, licensed directly by the Home Office under the new and more stringent Animals (Scientific Procedures) Act passed in 1986.

Dr Meldrum was particularly well placed to comment. For more than six years he had come under probably more pressure as an individual than any other vivisector. It had built up slowly, beginning with the petty harassment of showers of red paint thrown over his terraced home in Dulwich. There had been endless nuisance and obscene phone calls, sometimes more than a hundred in one week. Double-glazing salesmen turned up at his door, huge skips were delivered, mini-cabs were ordered to pick him up at two and three in the morning. Gradually it got nastier. Dolls splashed with ketchup were left on the family doorstep; demonstrators with loud hailers announced to his neighbours that they lived next door to an 'animal torturer'. Then, on his birthday, the death threats began. Shortly afterwards, the Animal Rights Militia placed a 'viable device' under his car. Dr Meldrum and his wife were provided with round the clock police protection, with regular half-hour checks at his home; a video camera kept a constant watch on the entrance.

Tim Daley, the ALF leader who supported the use of bombs, had said that Dr Meldrum was 'an evil man'; that he deserved to die, and that the sooner he was killed the better. What ghastly crimes had he committed to be wished so final and certain a punishment? Well, he was a torturer, said Daley; he could name many vivisectors, but Dr Meldrum was particularly cruel, a heartless man. It was a great pity that the bomb hadn't gone off. His experiments were meaningless; all he was after was 'a nice big fat grant' from the Medical Research Council. 'I mean, flashing white strobe lights eighteen centimetres away from the eyes of monkeys that have come from the jungle is just such out and out obscene cruelty.' Dr Meldrum did this, said Daley, without a blink of the eye, with no compassion at all.

And yet Brian Meldrum didn't seem like a man without compassion. Getting to see him wasn't easy; you had to negotiate understandably nervous security staff before gaining admittance to the rather dowdy, besloganed laboratory complex attached to the Institute of Psychiatry in south London. Most vivisectors targeted by the animal rights movement won't talk at all in public: this one would, but only reluctantly, and in the realization that not to defend what he believed in was to surrender the initiative, and, by default, the argument. Sitting behind his desk, Dr Meldrum seemed less than monstrous. He wanted to talk about the people he was working for, the hundred thousand epileptics, about a third of the country's total, who could not be treated by existing drugs and whose condition remained uncontrolled. Walking round the laboratory it was important to remember their misery. Without progress here, their suffering would continue; the qualitatively far less serious suffering that his monkeys endured in the laboratory had already contributed to the discovery and development of more efficient drugs with which to treat epileptics.

Pictures of Brian Meldrum's monkeys distributed by animal rights pickets looked grim. The creatures appeared to be suspended by their necks in painful frames: this was the apparatus of 'torture' described by Tim Daley, the miniature straitjacket in which the primates were constrained as they were bombarded with strobe lights. In the laboratory, it was clear that the frames were rather more humane in construction than had been credited; the monkeys were not suspended at all, but supported on small plastic seats. The particular strain of monkey used by Dr Meldrum was specially imported from Senegal in West Africa; they were the product of generations of inbreeding, as a result of which they were naturally prone to epileptic fits. On a weekly cycle, the monkeys were removed from their cages (rather more salubrious than most zoo premises would have to offer) and placed in the seating frames. They were then injected with drugs and subjected to flashing light from a stroboscope, the idea being to measure the effect of the drug in inhibiting fits. It doesn't sound at all pleasant and undoubtedly it isn't. But the fits induced by the stroboscope last only about a minute and cause no pain. If the subjection of an epileptic monkey to strobe lighting is torture, then it is no more than the treatment that human epileptics are subjected to in the course of diagnosis.

There was no evidence that Dr Meldrum or his laboratory assistants seemed to be getting illicit kicks out of all this. The comparison with Josef Mengele seemed even more offensive, hearing at first hand the purpose of this research and seeing the condition of the creatures involved. The Institute of Psychiatry was part of the Maudsley Hospital, where even a brief walk round the wards would provide upsetting evidence of the human suffering endured by the thousands of epileptics who could only be treated with current drugs at the expense of crippling side-effects. These, said Dr Meldrum, were regarded by his patients as even more unpleasant than the fits themselves. Five million people worldwide stood to gain from his research.

And yet for six years Brian Meldrum's life had been made a misery, and was now actually threatened, by people who condemned him as a cruel, self-seeking torturer. Quite apart from the attentions his home and car had received, he and his patients had to run what was sometimes a daily gauntlet of abuse and shouting from pickets at his laboratory. He could accept that he was himself fair game, but this frightening kind of behaviour did not seem very fair on the psychiatric patients passing in and out. Most of the overt, legal opposition came from an organization called SLAM, the South London Animal Movement, the most militant of the local animal rights groups and one composed largely of prominent ALF activists, including Tim Daley. This was the group that had persecuted Dr Conning and Dr Gangolli in Carshalton, whose cars had been petrol bombed by the Animal Rights Militia. And yet, as Tim Daley had stated quite clearly, Brian Meldrum was the most loathed vivisector of them all.

Occupying this unenviable position, Brian Meldrum had worked out very clearly in his own mind the rights and wrongs of animal experimentation. You had to start any moral argument with some system of evaluation, 'and in practice the only system that's been consistently accepted is that of utilitarianism, which says you balance your profits against your losses'. In other words, you set any disadvantages suffered by the animals used in the experiments against the increase in human welfare. This, of course, was predicated on the assumption that the human species was inherently of greater value and moral worth than lesser species. If you accepted this, there were plenty of clear examples to illustrate the utilitarian line. 'Take the case of polio', said Dr Meldrum, 'where up to the mid 1950s there were in North America and Europe at least thirty thousand patients a year paralysed or dying from the disease; and then, from experiments in primates, a polio vaccine was developed, and as a result of that one can say that there are a million people alive and well today who would otherwise have been dead or paralysed.' For the development of a vaccine, Dr Meldrum estimated, some twenty to thirty thousand animals would need to be used: and, put crudely, the use of those creatures for the benefit of a million human beings was a useful summary of the utilitarian equation.

But if all this about the development of the polio vaccine and its subsequent benefits to mankind were true, why was it that the liberationists appeared to ignore the argument? Dr Meldrum thought they were simply ignorant of the facts. 'They are mostly too young to know about the polio epidemics that paralysed ones' parents when I was a teenager; people then were really very frightened, but this is something no longer remembered.' How many of those who threatened his life or abused his wife, he wondered, had refused vaccination as a matter of principle? This was the kind of question often asked by the Research Defence Society, an organization founded as long ago as 1908 to counter the arguments of the first generation of anti-vivisectionists. The RDS existed to defend necessary, as its members thought, animal experimentation within the scientific community: this was never a popular task in a country agreed to be besotted with animals, but which at the same time happily enjoyed the benefits of vivisection.

Tim Biscoe was the Society's Secretary. He was Professor of Physiology at University College, London, and he was personally involved in the issue: his current work on spasticity had included experiments on mice. So far, those experiments had not led to any definite conclusions, but that did nothing, he argued, to invalidate his methods of enquiry. 'We know from the history of science,' he said, 'that if you do not understand the fundamental processes, there is no way you will get the advance.' Progress in medicine was a slow process of brick building. 'You have to build on what people have done before ... you cannot have Banting and Best discovering insulin in Toronto in the 1920s except in a context of knowledge, some of the knowledge acquired in this institution [University College] in 1896 and subsequently in the early part of the century. Without that previous thirty or forty years' knowledge, the questions could not even have been formulated.' In other words, the fact that some research does not at the time appear to have positive and practical results does not necessarily mean that it is useless.

Speaking at the Anniversary Meeting of the Royal Society in 1983 Sir Andrew Huxley quoted a powerful instance of this. In 1976 two scientists, J. H. Comroe and R. D. Dripps, had published an analysis of the work that had led up to ten of the major advances in treatment of diseases of the heart, lung and circulation that had been made since the Second World War. They found that some 40% of the key publications had contained no indication that the author had any practical objective in view when he began his research. Pure science, science for science's sake, had produced practical long-term benefits for mankind. But Sir Andrew went further. There were philosophical arguments as important as the practical. It was morally better to have correct ideas about the nature of man and his relationship to the world in which we live, and to the whole universe, than to base ourselves on fictions. Pure science was the legitimate and necessary pursuit of these truths.

To the members of the RDS, the notion of 'speciesism' was absurd: it was based on a false analogy with forms of discrimination against other members of the same species – humankind. Animals could not be said to have 'rights', even though mankind, as a higher species, had 'duties' towards the whole of the natural world. In his book *Man and Mouse – Animals in Medical Research*, Sir William Paton, Professor of Pharmacology at Oxford, argued that the 'scale of creation' was a continuum, and that there was no absolute dividing line between different categories. Human beings simply used common sense in making practical, operational distinctions between, say, bacteria and cats, or reptiles and mammals. 'Rights' were the function of human society, as indeed were duties: it was up to humankind to evaluate the moral worth of animal life. There was certainly no 'morality' to be found in the natural world. It was fundamentally amoral, despite the liberationists' rather cosy view, for example, of life in the wolfpack.

Sir William had little time for the view that humans had no right to inflict suffering of any kind on animals. The world was full of suffering, a very large proportion of it to be found within the society of animals. 'It is all the more strange, therefore, that the suffering which carries the hope of reducing future suffering seems to be so bitterly attacked. What "use" is there in the suffering as a cat plays with a bird, or a dog worries a sheep, or in any of nature's predatory activities?' The general assumption amongst the liberationists that the process of vivisection corrupted the vivisector ('torturers' all) angered Sir William: his own experience was that animal work made the investigator more sensitive to animal needs as he learned about their behaviour and physiology. No one called the casualty surgeon heartless as he went about his bloody work in a state of clinical and apparently impersonal detachment.

But above all, when you looked at the balance sheet, it was hard to ignore the benefits of animal experimentation. Not just the recent, more dramatic examples such as the development of successful chemotherapy to combat forms of cancer like leukaemia and Hodgkin's disease, but the wide impact on the way we all lived and worked. 'Even as late as the 1930s,' Sir William argued, 'a schoolboy could have lost a companion from tuberculosis, mastoid infection, diptheria or scarlet fever, and might play with a friend crippled with polio. Deformity, pain and disability were familiar experiences. For the routine pains of sinusitis, colic, peptic ulcer or "rheumatism", laudanum (or alcohol) was available for those who could afford it in the last century, and asprin in this, but a great deal of suffering was simply accepted as part of life. Cruelty for its own sake seems always to have been reprobated; but parents who had lost most of their family in infancy, and learnt to speak coolly of it, could readily be equally cool about the suffering of animals.'

We took for granted, Sir William pointed out, enormous areas of medical advance that had been reached largely as a result of animal experimentation. Quite apart from the vaccines and the antiobiotics, there were the striking improvements in the safety and efficiency of surgical techniques. If you took the case of a soldier suffering from gross injuries to the face from a bomb blast, the consequences of subtracting all the forms of treatment derived from vivisection would be horrific. Thanks to experiments on animals, 'blood loss could be compensated for by blood transfusion, and infection could be combatted by antibiotics. Surgical operation would be under a safe anaesthetic combined with analgesics if necessary. The suture material used would leave the minimum scarring. Skin or bone graft could help in reconstructing the face. If he could not swallow, artificial feeding of a carefully worked out nutrient "cocktail" would be infused into a vein. If shock had produced renal failure, some form of dialysis could be used. The dressing applied would prevent infection, be non-irritant, prevent fluid loss and foster healing.' All these techniques, Sir William reiterated, whether people realized it or not, were the fruits of animal experimentation. It should be very clear in the minds of his opponents what precisely they were prepared to abjure.

It seemed, on closer inspection, a very strange and rather dangerous Garden of Eden to which the liberationists wished to return. But at least in their assault on individual scientists they had produced one noticably useful side-effect: under the twin pressures of personal violence and ideological dissent, some of the more courageous researchers involved in vivisection felt a new obligation to discuss the logic and morality of their work. As a result, the 1980s saw a proliferation of careful and well-argued texts from those eminent enough to have felt previously that there had been no need to explain what they were up to to the broad and largely ill-informed public.

And the most telling contributions came from nationally well-known figures like Professor Calne at Cambridge; thanks to his work on liver and kidney transplants, particularly on very young children, he had become something of a national hero. It was not a status that he had sought, but it gave him a sympathetic audience when he was called on to explain his methodology: it was up to the public to decide whether he was a callous 'torturer' worthy of letter bombs from the ARM, or the pioneer of surgery techniques that would save many young lives.

The trouble was that for every Roy Calne and Brian Meldrum there were rather more researchers who, in Professor Calne's words, had been 'terrorized into silence'. Twenty-four hours after 'going public' on the research programme at Dulwich Hospital in south London designed to transplant pigs' organs into human beings, one of the hospital's leading surgeons, Michael Bewick, was forced to withdraw from the programme. Publication of Sunday newspaper articles had resulted in angry and abusive calls to the hospital from liberationists; carried away by his enthusiasm for the project, Mr Bewick had underestimated the sheer volume of anger that the principle of animal transplants provoked. The rest of his team were horrified: too late, Mr Bewick admitted that he was now seriously worried about attacks on the hospital and on his own property. For scientists engaged in this kind of work, work in which they wholeheartedly believed, the penalty for openness and discussion was sometimes too severe.

Across the wide spectrum of those who supported the concept of animal rights, there were many 'moderates' who disliked the word 'terrorism', who thought it both unfair and derogatory. But the fact was that in every area chosen by the movement as its target, terror had proved a practical and effective means of silencing the enemy. There was a butcher's shop in a quiet, unremarkable suburb of Coventry that looked like a police station in the Falls Road; even during shopping hours, it was solidly shuttered from roof to pavement; customers ducked in through a small hole in the side, as if in search of something illicit, dirty magazines or drugs. The butcher did not know how much longer he could go on like this: even old customers were going elsewhere. They did not like the idea that selling meat could provoke such rage or could make the buying of it so embarrassing. Elsewhere, butchers were giving up and getting out of the business: the insurance premiums had become ridiculous. Laboratory complexes looked like concentration camps; battery farms were equipped with razor wire perimeter fencing; decent scientists engaged in work that they genuinely felt to be of long-term benefit to humanity were being silenced.

It was all the more remarkable, then, that Brian Meldrum should refuse to be terrorized. Sitting in the living room at the back of his Dulwich home, Dr Meldrum talked about the strain of living under constant threat. Things would have been a lot harder without both the support of his wife (also a scientist) and his neighbours; he would not have been surprised if people in his street had turned against him as the focus of so much disruption. The opposite had happened; people had rallied round, expressed disgust that so called 'animal lovers' could behave in such a bestial way.

Tim Daley had talked contemptuously of Dr Meldrum's greed, had suggested that he was only in it for the money, to purchase bigger, better and flashier sports cars to stand outside his luxury home. The 'V' registration MG B did not look like the property of a rampant materialist, nor did the modest terrace home with the pocket-handkerchief garden at the back. It seemed as though it was necessary for the liberationists to distort their human target in order to justify the inhuman treatment they were prepared to mete out. In one particularly gruesome circular, the ALF Supporters Group distributed photocopies of some of Dr Meldrum's experiments together with pictures of experiments carried out by Mengele and his colleagues at Auschwitz and Birkenhau concentration camps. Mengele the Nazi and Meldrum the 'speciesist' were indistinguishable. 'As long as vivisection continues', the circular confidently suggested, 'then the likelihood of a vivisector being killed remains.'

Brian Meldrum had learned to live with this kind of language. He accepted that there were now people in the animal rights movement who really did want to see him dead and were prepared to kill him. His private life had been disrupted, his work made infinitely more difficult. But he had the strong emotional support of his wife, and his elderly mother: he had worried about her reaction when the death threats had started but she was now more robust than her son in her angry contempt for his persecutors. For himself, Brian Meldrum just felt depressed at the thought that he was dealing with people who seemed to have given up on democracy, who regarded public debate and argument as somehow irrelevant. What was certain was that he would not bow to their threats. There were more than a million people in the country whose lives were severely impaired through psychiatric disorders: and we had to do something to help them. 'That's more important than the question of what a few maniacs are prepared to do in terms of damaging or sacrificing human life.'

CHAPTER THIRTEEN

The RSPCA Council consists largely of
individuals who commit crimes of
violence every day by consuming the
carcases of dead animals.

RAG circular

'We were winning until these people came along. We don't
want to be associated with nutcases.' The Director of the
League Against Cruel Sports could be forgiven for these intemperate
remarks. Until the arrival of the Hunt Retribution
Squad, with their Christmas raid on the grave of the Duke of
Beaufort, public sympathy had been moving steadily towards
the anti-blood sports lobby. Some of the more violent scenes
involving the hunt saboteur groups might have worried more
traditionally-minded souls, but the assumption was that the
'sabs' hearts were in the right place. It was difficult to imagine
that the kind of person who would attempt to dig up a rotting
corpse and send its head to a member of the Royal Family had
any heart at all.

But the anti-blood sports campaigners who ran the LACS
were not just concerned about the long-term publicity fall-out
from this kind of stunt; they were busy fighting a vicious
defensive action against the takeover of the League by the very
extremists whose tactics threatened the flow of donations upon
which its income depended. By the mid 1980s, every one of the
major national animal welfare and protection societies, including
the RSPCA, was under threat of subversion by those who
actively supported, and in some cases participated in, the direct
action campaign of the ALF and associated groups. In the case
of two of those societies, the liberationists won significant
victories, enabling them to channel large sums of money into
equipment and prisoners' defence funds. In the battle for the
societies, the ideological conflict between animal rights and
animal welfare reached a bitter climax. In their adoption of

'entryist' tactics, the liberationists were often accused of copying the style of the Militant Tendency: the truth was, they were infinitely more successful.

There was no global, coherent plan behind all this. There was no single conspiracy dictated from ALF headquarters; within the ranks of the new 'entryist' radicals there were differences so arcane as to be incomprehensible to an outsider, yet at the same time these were the cause of extraordinary bitterness. 'The politics of animal rights,' said one war weary veteran, 'make Westminster look like a child's game.' The liberationists' success came first and foremost in the widespread acceptance of the radical notion that animals had rights, as opposed to simply being the recipients of human consideration: in the two main anti-vivisection societies, and to a lesser extent within the rank and file membership of the RSPCA, this philosophical proposition replaced traditional ideas of animal welfare. So now the same ideology that fuelled the direct action groups and the informal network of local animal rights groups also became the orthodoxy of some of the most influential and wealthiest animal protection societies.

Of course, a belief in animal rights didn't necessarily make you a bomb thrower, but it lined you up behind the rationale for bomb throwing. It meant you at least could understand the idea of threatening human life on behalf of the animals. Richard Ryder, the former research psychologist, who had abandoned his work in Oxford on the principle of animal experimentation, and who then developed – with Peter Singer – the coherent theory of animal rights, was certainly no terrorist. Turning out on demonstrations in neat dark suit and sober tweed overcoat, he was the model of respectability, as indeed would be expected of the Alliance parliamentary candidate he was. But Ryder could understand why the ALF had felt driven to take the course they had; there was, he said, 'total frustration' in the animal rights movement after fifteen years of lobbying that had seemingly got nowhere; the government, successive governments, had a lot to answer for; it was not surprising that some in the movement had turned to violence.

Richard Ryder, as it happened, was at the forefront in the first wave of radicals who moved in on the British Union for the Abolition of Vivisection; he was also active in attempting to 'ginger up', as he put it, the RSPCA. The movement of radicals into these established national organizations was haphazard: partly it reflected the growing interest of young people in ideas of animal rights that were in turn part of a broader concern for the environment. It was natural for any eighteen-year-old who had just watched 'Rabbits Don't Cry' to join the BUAV or the NAVS. Others who had become more radical as they had got older didn't simply tear up their RSPCA membership forms; they waited and they planned. The smaller the membership, the more vulnerable the society; the RSPCA alone had both the numbers and the skilful political organization to meet infiltration head on. The problem was that, quite apart from all the plotting and the politics, the fact could not be avoided that animal rights was no longer an odd-ball fringe philosophy: for most people under thirty they were a proper and obvious extension of human rights. The idea that you could care about animals and still eat meat, support vivisection, or even fish seemed absurd and hypocritical.

Founded in 1898, the British Union for the Abolition of Vivisection had been established originally as a breakaway organization from the National Anti-vivisection Society. In one of the more dramatic schisms of the many that rent the animal welfare movement in the Victorian era, the BUAV's founder, Frances Power Cobbe (author of *The Rights of Man and the Claims of Brutes*), had taken violent issue with the weak-kneed gradualism of the NAVS: they were prepared to seek 'lesser measures' on the road to getting rid of vivisection. She wanted total abolition immediately. This had proved to be a rather ambitious programme. By the 1970s, the BUAV had long settled into a state of genteel and, thanks to a generous flow of legacies, wealthy decrepitude. The charity occupied a large house in the upwardly mobile area of Islington in north London, enjoying assets well in excess of half a million pounds. Membership was in decline, down to some ten thousand from a peak of several times that number, campaigning fervour more or less non-existent. It was, in short, as ripe for takeover as any constituency Labour party in the remote reaches of Bootle.

The BUAV was captured by the liberationists in two successive waves of attack. In the late seventies, Richard Ryder and Fay Funnel, the founder of the highly successful Co-ordinating Animal Welfare organization, virtually took over the Union. This was neither as difficult nor as sinister as it sounds. Both figures were eminently respectable middle-class representatives of the decent, moderate wing of the animal rights movement, the kind of people who got involved in the new charity 'Animal Aid', which was starting up at the same time; radical, committed to 'rights' not 'welfare', but kosher, law-abiding and democratic. By 1980, after a spell as president of the BUAV, Ryder himself found that there were younger and more impatiently radical young members ready and willing to argue with him; it was a classic case of a revolution generating its own momentum, he said; and while he had a lot of time for the young Turks, he had decided to take a back seat and let the new blood take over.

During this second period of transition, two distinct types of younger, more active members began to assert their influence. First, there was the inevitable arrival of the new generation of pure animal rights lobbyists; these were almost always from an apolitical background, concerned only with the single issue of animal rights. John Beggs and Tim Daley, both BUAV committee members, were the most prominent of this group, which also included less orthodox figures like Mandy Journeaux, leading light of the Pagan Animal Rights organization. Equally energetic, and viewing this group with more than a little suspicion, were the politicos. By the late seventies, the issue of animal rights had joined gays, women and the disabled as part of the right-on impedimenta of the new left: local Labour councils were beginning to appoint 'animal rights officers' alongside existing agencies dealing with the rights of both sexes as well as all races within the human species. At the BUAV's Crane Grove Headquarters, in the wake of Richard Ryder's departure, a caucus of new left activists seized the high ground, beginning, naturally, with the means of communication.

The 'Liberator', the BUAV's professionally produced bi-monthly broadsheet, was edited by the team of Kim Stallwood and Margaret Manzoni. Stallwood's official title was 'campaigns officer', but by the early eighties his was the commanding voice in the always chaotic Islington set-up. Phone calls about policy always seemed to end up being referred to Stallwood, as were most requests for information. Kim Stallwood, bearded and in his late twenties, was by nature a full-time activist, a creature of the times that had produced a curiously pure and humourless zealotry in the town halls of Haringey and Lambeth. A former catering student, Stallwood had been converted to the cause during a spell working in a chicken processing plant one vacation, as a result of which he had become a strict vegetarian, and busily read up on the theory of animal rights. He didn't like, he said, the idea of domestic 'pets'; if humans looked after animals, these should be regarded as 'refugees'; to call someone an 'animal lover' was like calling them a 'nigger lover'. True to this purist view of the struggle, Stallwood, like John Beggs, was thought personally not actually to like animals very much; there were upsetting stories about him cursing the many stray dogs who seemed to pant around the BUAV offices without any noticeable control. What Stallwood did like was the exercise of political influence: he was happy to go along with 'direct action' as long as it provided tangible results, but the real work lay in lobbying the new left. Animal rights purists complained that he spent all his time hobnobbing with the heroes of the GLC's parliamentary vanguard, the Tony Bankses, Jeremy Corbyns and Ken Livingstones.

The politicos, like Stallwood, believed in the ideology of animal rights, the principle that they were parallel and equivalent to human rights; but when it came to the balaclava'd hit squads of the direct action tendency, there was some embarrassment. After the ALF had lost the co-operation of the Peace News Collective, Ronnie Lee was allowed to use office space at BUAV headquarters, but this arrangement did not last long. Personality as much as ideological differences seem to have been at the root of the Stallwood/Lee relationship: Stallwood was not happy about the consistently chaotic and informal structure of the ALF, nor was he sympathetic to its leader's longstanding fondness for a particularly aggressive form of anarchism; but more important was the fact that the broader movement seemed unable to hold two charismatic leading figures within one set of offices.

Yet, under Stallwood's editorship, the 'Liberator' always gave plenty of sympathetic coverage to the ALF, printing pictures of raids and giving graphic accounts of assaults on farms and laboratories. But the politicos took a more sophisticated view of the struggle: animal rights would be won only by a combination of the kind of direct action that would win public sympathy (producing upsetting pictures of dogs, monkeys and 'evil experiments') and hard political lobbying. It was a kind of animal rights version of 'the Armalite and the ballot box', though of course Stallwood did not condone attacks on people. Ronnie Lee thought it was rubbish. All politicians were corrupt, whatever their complexion. 'There is no way,' he wrote in the ALF Bulletin, 'that animal or human liberation can be achieved through Parliament.' Nonetheless, Lee and the rest of the ALF leadership were more than happy to work from a BUAV office and make use of BUAV donations.

It was hard to find consistent threads running through the seemingly endless disputes that racked the newly radicalized BUAV in the 1980s. There were fights between the animal rights purists and the politicos, but there were more obscure vendettas as well between some of the older, more 'conservative' supporters of direct action and the young firebrands, like John Beggs. 'Menopausal old bitches' he called them, singling out one particular stalwart as an hysterical animal lover of the old school; Beggs, it should be remembered, had always admitted quite happily that he personally couldn't stand animals. Often, ideological differences would be sought in attempting to explain a particular dispute, only to force the conclusion that personalities – as they had been in the splintering of the Victorian animal protection societies – were the problem.

In 1985, the BUAV annual general meeting (held with no apparent sense of irony at the Friends' Meeting House in London) and a subsequent extraordinary general meeting, were riven by scenes that would have made seasoned Mafiosi wince. What actually happened was that, gathered for once under one roof, several of the many diverse strands that made up the animal rights movement found that the powerful strains of contradiction outweighed the common cause of fighting for the animals. Stallwood and Manzoni, editors of the 'Liberator', and leaders of the BUAV's fourteen-strong staff, effectively had every member of the executive committee they disapproved of removed. The scenes at the extraordinary general meeting where this piece of political manoeuvring was carried out were hardly redolent of the genteel traditions of the Union. 'Fuck the rich!' was one cry that upset unsuspecting elderly members, who found that some two hundred black clad young people, of anarchistic aspect, had been bussed in for the occasion.

It was, by all accounts, a lively meeting. A journalist from the *Sunday Telegraph* was threatened with physical violence if he refused to leave; microphones were switched off, four-letter words flew in batteries of targeted abuse; and older anti-vivisectionists of a delicate disposition were reduced to floods of tears. Now part of this was simply the time-honoured tradition of in-fighting and personal vilification, but the character of the conflict had changed: it was more vicious, and the floor was now held by younger people using the language of personal violence. This was a war not between the welfarists and the rightists, but between two factions both of whom publicly supported direct action outside the law. The superficial cause of the dispute was over the issue of whether or not the BUAV should try to modify the Animals (Scientific Procedures) Bill currently before Parliament or, as Stallwood and Manzoni argued, lobby to have the Bill thrown out; but the sub-plot lay in the growing tension between Stallwood and Ronnie Lee, some of whose friends were the people now being thrown off the committee: the irritating, 'hysterical' and 'menopausal' women that John Beggs had complained of, in a burst of what seemed suspiciously close to both sexism and ageism.

So, on the face of it, those who favoured a combination of political lobbying and direct action seemed to have won the day. The point was that the faction around Kim Stallwood was now in charge and wanted to stay in charge. Stallwood himself said that he supported direct action whether it was within or outside the law. He had no real differences with Lee on ideological grounds – he just thought he was a far sharper operator.

Difficult as it is to provide any kind of coherent analysis of this blood letting, the simple truth was that the BUAV had become the public arena for every minor dispute that preoccupied the animal rights movement, for the obvious reason that control of the BUAV meant control of considerable sums of cash. The ALF had done very nicely in terms of resources (office, equipment, phones, etc) but they were not the only direct action movement around: the Leagues wanted their share of the cake as well. The idea that the Leagues were in competition with Lee seemed daft to most activists who participated in a wide range of direct action under a whole range of different banners; most ALF raiders were in the Leagues, and vice versa. But Ronnie Lee himself saw the Front as the only serious means of carrying on the struggle. By far the longest serving veteran of the movement – indeed the man who had virtually invented the idea of direct action – Lee thought he had special claims.

Ever since the first wave of radicals under Ryder had come to power in BUAV, the ALF had lobbied its supporters to join the Union and support the new régime; this had been a sensible tactic. 'The BUAV is the only organization that openly supports the ALF in the media, and in its newspaper "Liberator",' claimed the ALF Supporters Bulletin in 1983, urging all activists and supporters to turn up for that year's AGM to vote for the abolition of the office of President in the BUAV's constitution. This was not just a matter of Ronnie Lee's anarchistic instincts; the ALF had heard that someone who was inimical to both direct action and indeed the very phrase 'animal rights' was being put forward as a 'moderate' candidate. So, rather than risk anything so uncertain as an election, why not abolish the elitist presidency altogether – which is precisely what happened. Encouraged by this success, the following year the ALF was again encouraging its supporters to turn up and vote in a committee suitably sympathetic to the direct action movement. Ronnie Lee apologetically noted that for some activists, turning out at a stuffy AGM in the middle of July might not seem the most dramatic way of helping the animals; but it was 'not an overstatement to say that the 1984 AGM could be one of the most important dates for the Animals, certainly more important than most demonstrations etc'. What he meant, of course, was that it was important for the material survival of the ALF. Again, it worked. The BUAV committee that emerged was more than happy to give Ronnie and friends office space in Islington.

The same year, the BUAV committee was even more generous in its contributions to SEALL – whose 'press officer', John Beggs, conveniently happened to be a member of the committee. In the course of September, donations amounting to £2,750 were made to SEALL; the following month, more than a hundred of the League's activists attacked Wickham Laboratories, injuring the veterinary director. The cash grants were hardly surprising to regular readers of 'Liberator', from whose glowing accounts of SEALL raids it could be deduced that a close and harmonious relationship had developed. When BUAV took out its private prosecution against the Royal College of

Surgeons, it was largely on the basis of evidence provided by the SEALL raid on the College's laboratories.

There was never any attempt made at BUAV Headquarters to fudge this close relationship. Callers were referred to SEALL activists with a minimum of delay; after all, two of them, Tim Daley and John Beggs, now sat on the BUAV committee, along with two prominent members of the ALF Support Group. Within the committee there were differences about the rights and wrongs of premeditated violence against animal abusers, but on the issue of direct action against property there was unanimity. The 'Liberator' carried adverts for other direct action groups as well: the Central Animal Liberation League merchandising operation was busy selling off T-shirts, badges and stickers in return for 'donations'. BUAV's own merchandising was even more impressive, requiring the employment of a full-time official. There was a strong element of naïveté in this policy of openness. In other, perhaps less self-consciously altruistic causes, it would have seemed manifestly absurd to both pursue the path of parliamentary lobbying and at the same time encourage law-breaking. But somehow, because it was all about animals, the idealists of BUAV felt that theirs was a special case. They were, after all, following what Tim Daley had described as 'a higher moral law'.

The very public way in which BUAV was overtaken by the liberationists contrasted with what happened shortly afterwards at Britain's other main anti-vivisection society, the NAVS. The National Anti-vivisection Society had continued in parallel with BUAV down the decades ever since Frances Cobbe had defected in 1898; it had maintained its reputation for being the more gradualist and flexible of the two societies. It had long been the home of little old ladies and eccentric European aristocrats with large bank balances and a genuine, if sentimental, fondness for animals. But in the mid eighties, the NAVS too fell to the supporters of animal rights and direct action. Unlike BUAV, this was a short sharp shock. In the twelve months preceding May 1987, eighteen staff members resigned or were sacked and nine members of the governing council decided to leave. There were allegations of physical threats and Stalinist tactics.

The old guard blamed the NAVS' new general secretary, Jan Creamer. In her mid thirties, Ms Creamer, was a convinced and militant supporter of animal rights. 'She wants to go further than ever before,' complained one self-styled moderate who had been forced into resignation. 'She demands total obedience and ordinary members have been trodden underfoot by her tyranny.' Another former staff member alleged that people working at NAVS headquarters in Harley Street had been threatened by members of the ALF; Terry Helsby, one of the violators of the Duke of Beaufort's grave, was now a NAVS regional contact. This all made the BUAV story sound like a model of politeness and decency. Ms Creamer, unlike her colleagues over in Islington, did not feel obliged to discuss these matters with nosey journalists. In a confidential letter to a society member she wrote: 'we will not discuss our methods with anyone – I don't care who they say they are'.

By summer 1987, the newly radicalized NAVS was already deploying its considerable funds on behalf of the direct action groups. At a meeting of the NAVS Council in late spring, Tim Phillips (aka 'Johnston') of the Central Animal Liberation League presented the Society with a collection of CALL videos, photographs and documents. CALL was paid £5,000 for these favours, with Phillips happily agreeing to join NAVS. It was not difficult to see where the expensive video and walkie-talkie equipment that CALL had proudly displayed in their 'man-oeuvres' by the Trent had come from. Next to benefit from the change of régime at NAVS was the ALF itself. Like the Leagues, the ALF saw its increasing collection of photographic evidence from raids, as well as documents stolen from laboratories, as saleable items. On one occasion, NAVS agreed to pay £4,000 to the ALF SG for a selection of this material.

Because of the secretive nature of NAVS Council delibera-tions ('we will not discuss our constitution, structure or meth-ods with anyone' Jan Creamer asserted) it was not clear whether the full membership understood precisely what was going on. If some traditionalists worried about the Society flirting with Ronnie Lee's balaclava'd activists, many also probably agreed with one member who admitted having voiced disquiet over 'having any connection with these sort of people'. The trouble was that, when it came to what the ALF had to offer, even though it had been obtained illegally, the temp-tations were too great for nice considerations about the ethics of receiving stolen property. 'Some of the material they can provide is very good – they have access to places that we don't, and their photographs are ideal for our leaflets and publicity purposes' the reluctant accessory rather lamely admitted.

By the late eighties, both major anti-vivisection societies were fully incorporated in the sprawling network of animal rights activism. In the regional contact lists of both societies, the same names and the same local animal rights groups repeated themselves. Tim Daley was both a BUAV and a NAVS contact; he ran Croydon Animal Aid (which he had founded), organized the Croydon branch of the Hunt Saboteurs' Association, was a member of the RSPCA – for whom he had worked as an ambulance driver – and was an active member of SLAM, the South London Animal Movement. This was all, of course, on top of extra-curricular activities with the ALF and SEALL. His was by no means an exaggerated example. Indeed, Daley was more than matched by another BUAV committee member, Taggart King, who managed to notch up a combined membership of BUAV, NAVS, Animal Aid, the ALF SG, Hunt Saboteurs Association, Greenpeace, the League Against Cruel Sports, Compassion in World Farming and Zoo Check, in addition to the Bishop's Stortford Animal Rights Group, of which he was founder and chairman.

The point was that if you became seriously involved in the issue of animal rights, you joined just about everything in sight; and if the prevailing philosophy seemed hypocritically 'welfarist', you worked from within to subvert. Some liberationists managed to make a living out of the societies that had been converted to animal rights. Mike Nunn, the former butcher who had been jailed for three years for leading the raid on Wickham, was subsequently employed by NAVS as its Southern Regional Campaigns Organizer. Holding office in an organization was one obvious way of changing its direction, of 'softening' its public attitude towards the ALF every time a new action hit the headlines. Mike Huskisson was at one stage appointed press officer for the League Against Cruel Sports. Staff at the League's south London offices remembered Huskisson as being a dedicated worker, once spending two years under cover posing as the member of an otter hunt; but he was also remembered for a succession of wild and sometimes eccentric ideas. As a piece of ecological voyeurism, at one stage he apparently wanted to install transparent soil pipes in to the League's plumbing system, on the grounds that it would do the staff good to see precisely what their personal ecosystems were producing. As long as his dissent from LACS orthodoxy was confined to this kind of bizarre but harmless activity, Huskisson was welcome: he worked hard, he cared genuinely about animals and knew a great deal about them. But when he was caught red-handed on the SEALL raid on the Royal College of Surgeons laboratory at Downe, he was immediately sacked.

Legitimate, law-abiding but energetic campaigns like the League trod a difficult line with people like Huskisson. They valued his energy and commitment but they simply could not afford the association with direct action. Concerned as they were specifically with blood sports, this was particularly hard for the League, out of all the traditional animal protection societies. The Hunt Saboteurs Association, founded in 1962, had been the first seriously militant group to fight on the animals' behalf, long before anyone had dreamed up the idea of animals having rights of their own. The HSA had given a hard edge to the fight against blood sports and the League welcomed it; there was, after all, a strong class element in the campaign against hunting, conjuring up as it did the image of a decadent and cruel upper class. The League had always taken a tough and often controversial line against, for example, the Royal Family's involvement in game shooting; but they knew where to draw the line. The League's President was the Rev. Lord Soper, the venerable Christian socialist; its vice-presidents were a Labour MP, Eric Heffer, and a Labour peer, Lord Houghton of Sowerby. These people played a vigorous game, but they played it strictly according to the rules of democracy.

But more important was the understanding of the League's staff of the kind of working-class people on whom they relied for support. Richard Course, for many years the League's director, was working-class himself. He saw no point in taking an abrasively censorious line against the angling community, for example: he knew these people, realized that you could not bomb or bully them into a radical rethink about the 'rights' of fish. Where the ALF preached, fulminated and finally fire-bombed, the League cajoled and lobbied. And so, in the process of robustly maintaining its independence from the mainstream of the animal rights movement, the League earned a reputation as being the haven of a bunch of traitors. In the pages of the ALF bulletin, Richard Course was reviled as a turncoat and, when the Merseyside ALF destroyed the Land-Rover belonging to a local angling champion, they left false evidence suggesting it was the work of the hated League. None of this seemed terribly fair on an organization one of whose senior officers had given Ronnie Lee a job at an animal sanctuary after Lee's first prison sentence. Lee had repaid the favour by organizing the sanctuary's first and only strike.

The League had employed animal rights activists, and there were many more within the ranks of its members, but the organization itself remained free of the excesses of the anti-vivisection societies. But these three groups, venerable and comparatively wealthy as they were, were nothing in comparison to the really big prize – the RSPCA. With assets of twenty million pounds, and an annual income of ten million, the RSPCA represented the animal welfare establishment in all its considerable glory. Founded under Royal Charter in 1824, and incorporated by Act of Parliament in 1932, the Society was recognized as one of the great British institutions. It ran its own inspectorate who worked closely with the police in tracking down animal abusers like dogfighters; it rescued pets from cruel and neglectful homes; more controversially, it destroyed hundreds of thousands of animals for whom homes could not be found.

The RSPCA's own research came up with a profile of its average donor that came dangerously close to parody. Eighty per cent were female, predominantly from the Home Counties: they were 3.6 times as likely to live in Surrey than in any other county; they were overwhelmingly middle-class. And yet the Society's membership had shrunk drastically since the 1960s, down from a hundred thousand to a mere twenty thousand. By the early eighties, the Society had fallen on distinctly troubled times: a major scandal involving the misuse of RSPCA funds for the financing of an inappropriately sybaritic life-style had led to the disgrace of one director; within the ranks of the membership there was so much disagreement on the issue of vivisection that a delegation to 10 Downing Street had to include a minimum of ten representatives, on the grounds that 'a smaller number could not represent all the strands of opinion within the RSPCA'.

To the new generation of animal rights activists, the RSPCA seemed like a disgracefully hypocritical monolith. For a start, there was the question of Royal patronage: how could any society that was supposed to be fighting for the animals enjoy the support of the hunting community? There was the issue of meat eating: not only did you not have to be a vegetarian to serve on the Society's governing council, one chairperson had the gall to jokingly admit that without meat in her diet she would not have had the strength to rescue stray animals! Even more heinous were the Society's connections with the vivisection industry: hundreds of thousands of pounds were invested with animal 'torturers' like ICI, Beechams and Boots. Worse than that, members of the hated Research Defence Society actually sat on RSPCA advisory committees drawing up guidelines on the humane practice of animal experimentation; a peer who actually boasted that he belonged to the British Field Sports Society sat on the Society's Farm Livestock Advisory Committee.

But then all these things were perfectly compatible with the traditional British view of animal welfare. People knocked the Duke of Edinburgh for shooting grouse for fun, but this appeared to hold no contradiction with his absorption in the conservation of wildlife. The British attitude towards animals had always been a curious combination of sentiment and practicality, a practicality derived from the realities of rural life. The idea that your faithful terrier and the rat whose neck you sent him to break actually shared the same set of rights in creation seemed little short of barmy. To the animal rights zealot these were the kind of contradictions that made the RSPCA so necessary a target; kick out the Royals and use the cash to finance real liberation ... it seemed a matter of common sense and humanity.

The question that remained was one of tactics. So far had the numbers of the Society's membership shrunk over the years that initially it seemed possible for liberationists to obtain election to the governing Council simply by canvassing like-minded members for support; involvement in animal rights, including the sharp end, had never, as in the case of Tim Daley, precluded membership of the Society: there were hundreds, probably thousands of votes to be picked up simply by identifying yourself as an animal rights candidate. Twelve of the twenty-three members of the Council were elected by national ballot, eight of the remainder being elected by the Society's eight regions, with three members co-opted. In 1983 Angela Walder, BUAV's scientific advisor, put up for election, followed a year later by her colleague Kim Stallwood: both made it on to the Council at the first attempt.

This was a spectacularly successful piece of entryism. The trouble was that, once on the Council, Walder and Stallwood soon fell out over what to do next. Stallwood was the ideological purist, Walder a much more instinctive (and genuinely animal-loving) operator: she liked and admired Ronnie Lee, and supported the ALF, but she would work with anyone who was serious about animals. Stallwood, on the other hand, was not interested in compromise; at the same time he both overestimated the rank and file support in the membership for the cause of pure animal rights, and underestimated the ruthlessness of the RSPCA in dealing with serious dissent. The year after he was elected, Stallwood publicly criticized the Society for allowing vivisectors on to its committees and for continuing to invest in pharmaceutical companies that practised vivisection. For his pains he was abruptly thrown off the Council and deprived of his membership.

This was not so much a defeat, more an opportunity to put into practise some of the sharper lessons Stallwood had learned from his observation of caucus politics within the GLC Labour group. Within a couple of months, the arrival of something called the 'RSPCA Action Group' (RAG) was announced, whose only address appeared to be a Post Office box number in the care of Middlesex Animal Rights Group in Harrow. RAG was in fact organized by BUAV activists, primarily Stallwood and Martin Green, who had taken over from Angela Walder as scientific officer. RAG's plan was to effect a Militant-style take-over of the Society, a long-term game plan that began with the promotion of six RAG-approved candidates in the 1985 elections. The group had the active support of several middle-ranking figures within the RSPCA, including Philip Hale, treasurer of the Brighton branch, and a member of several central RSPCA committees.

None of the six was elected that summer, but RAG was able to work on new tactics for the following year; this time they would be more modest – three candidates would be endorsed, candidates whose brief curricula vitae as printed in the Society's official electoral literature seemed positively anodyne. A National Health Service Administator, a barrister, a solicitor – all three RAG-approved candidates stated baldly that they happily agreed with all the Society's policies. Working from BUAV headquarters and the Middlesex Post Office box, RAG set about the recruitment of animal rights activists who would support their chosen slate. RSPCA membership forms were distributed in the BUAV newsletter, and directly to all those who wrote in, in a kind of animal rights voter registration blitz. But RAG had underestimated the organization of the enemy, and particularly its executive director Frank Dixon-Ward, former chief executive of Lambeth Borough Council. Four months before the ballot, 150 RAG-inspired membership applications were turned down by a session of the Society Council meeting at an exclusive club in St James's. It seemed they were forgeries.

Actually, they were photocopies of bona fide forms, produced in a hurry by the RAG team. For Dixon-Ward and his staff, amongst whom military or local government service was not an unusual background, this was a highly convenient lapse in efficiency, and not one they were going to miss. The forms, said the Society's official spokesman Mike Smithson, had been distributed 'by groups which seek to destroy the way we operate'. The Society was well aware that it had 'extremists' in its midst, but it would fight any take-over. This was all proving a great deal harder than the BUAV and NAVS campaigns. RAG had done its best to maintain anonymity, but the RSPCA's Smithson was prepared to publicly point the finger at the BUAV: 'they are very much the front organization for the people trying to change the Society' he announced.

The tactical outflanking of RAG came as something of a shock to Kim Stallwood; now the real character of the 'ginger group' began to emerge. Following the disaster of the forged application forms he told an interviewer that the RSPCA's allegations of extremism and advocacy of law-breaking were no more than disgraceful smears but then went on, following the inevitable logic of the convinced liberationist, to contradict himself. There was no doubt, he said, that any struggle for freedom had involved some breaking of the law; it was true that at the present animal experiments were legal, but the higher moral law meant that animals had a right to live free from persecution and suffering. 'It's that moral law which we should look towards, not necessarily the legal law of the land.' Some laws were clearly more equal than others.

That summer, none of the three RAG-approved candidates was elected on to the RSPCA's council. The threat had effectively been seen off, at least for the time being. After the fiasco of the forged membership forms, many animal rights activists had joined the Society legitimately, but not enough to make the crucial difference; under its experienced and politically sharp senior staff, the RSPCA had managed to turn out the traditionalists in sufficient numbers to see off the radicals. These, however, were not simply going to fold up and go away; animal rights was a rolling tide, the old guard would get older, the Society would be increasingly vulnerable to the kind of infiltration undertaken by RAG. Philip Hale, who had worked his way into the office of branch treasurer in the Society, said that the radicals would work to a ten or even twenty year plan. This was a lifetime's work.

For the old guard, determined to preserve the RSPCA in its recognizable form, there was always the welcome feature of regular vendettas between the leading individuals involved in the entryist movement. Angela Walder and Kim Stallwood had fallen out as soon as they had been elected to the Council; new pressure groups came and went according to the ebb and flow of these disputes. In late 1987, a new group, 'Watchdog', was established, with the same agenda set by RAG. They claimed the support of five hundred members, though the Society's press officer thought this an exaggeration. More public bloodletting seemed inevitable. This, as Philip Hale had said, was trench warfare and, given the commitment and numbers of the troops at the front, there was no prospect of an early peace.

CHAPTER FOURTEEN

It took us years to get our act together
. . . the big problem was sorting out the
little old ladies from the thugs.
ARNI (Animal Rights National Index) Squad
Detective at Scotland Yard

When the Animal Rights Militia sent four letter bombs to the party leaders in 1982, Scotland Yard's anti-terrorist squad simply did not believe that this was the work of animal rights supporters. Just about any other explanation seemed more plausible – the crazed gesture of a nest of anarchists inspired by the Baader-Meinhof gang or the Red Brigades, a one-off revenge attack by some bitter individual who felt thwarted by the state – than the idea that 'animal lovers' would try and maim or kill other human beings for the sake of cats and dogs. It was to be another three years before animal rights terrorism was judged to be a serious enough threat to merit the establishment of a specialist squad, based at Scotland Yard. Only when the ALF's campaign of economic sabotage began to wreak serious havoc with the balance sheets of some of the countries' largest companies did the police begin to treat Ronnie Lee and friends as an authentic threat to the state.

The single event that changed everything was the Mars Bar hoax. This was warfare on a scale that the giant food combines simply could not tolerate. 'Ben' and his balaclava'd comrades down in Bournemouth had seemed a faintly ludicrous and ramshackle bunch, but the fact was that at a single stroke they had achieved serious recognition for the ALF. What was more, they were neither caught nor prosecuted for the hoax, though if they had been there was considerable confusion as to what they would have been charged with, since the only two bars actually poisoned were the ones sent to the BBC and the *Daily Mirror*. The scale of potential damage to big business by this kind of action belatedly alerted the food industry, the Home Office and the Association of Chief Police Officers to the need for clear and concerted action. These were no longer an obscure bunch of vegan nutcases: they were organized, they were dangerous and it was time for the state to take them seriously.

On 5 December 1984, a month after the Mars hoax, the crime committee of the Association of Chief Police Officers met to discuss the crisis. Officers later drafted into the specialist animal rights squad said privately that this was the direct result of considerable pressure from the food industry, a major benefactor, it was noted, of the Conservative Party in power. The police had already sent a report on the Mars incident – drawn up by Detective Superintendant Colin Hoye of Scotland Yard's Serious Crime Squad – to the Director of Public Prosecutions, but no action had followed. At the ACPO crime committee meeting it was decided to set up a special team, dealing exclusively with animal rights, and to be run by Superintendant Hoye. The ALF had been going in one form or another for more than ten years, and yet the senior policemen who gathered to set up the specialist squad had only the vaguest idea of the kind of people involved and the nature of the ideology they espoused. And then, to their rescue from the reaches of rural Essex came a lone uniformed constable, one Colin Wiggins.

PC Wiggins was later to earn a battery of unflattering 'Bill'-style nicknames from his more sophisticated new colleagues in the Met ('PC Plod' being the most polite) but the fact was that, as the new squad convened at the beginning of 1985, he was in a unique position. What emerged was that, quite incredibly, for fifteen years PC Wiggins alone had been the entire national police response to the animal rights movement: every snippet of information, every press cutting, every random piece of intelligence had been carefully hoarded by this obscure administrative officer at Essex Constabulary headquarters in Chelmsford. It had all been an accident of history. Because several of the early animal rights actions had occurred on his patch, the Chief Constable of Essex had reluctantly been forced to admit the additional responsibility of dealing with animal rights activists: this duty had been delegated to Colin Wiggins.

In his late forties and balding, PC Wiggins was no one's idea of a supersleuth; dogged, obsessively meticulous he was as one of his new colleagues admitted, the 'kingpin' of the new squad. When he moved into his new office at the Yard, a lorry-load of documents came up with him from Chelmsford. 'The thing about Wiggins,' said another squad member, 'is that in his position most people don't bother to keep notes or write up cases: but he'd done all of it . . . every ALF action neatly written up and filed away. He knew all about Ronnie Lee and all the others.' It had been a solitary and utterly unglamorous pastime but now his hour had come: now even Detective Superintendants at the Met were listening respectfully. PC Wiggins could have been excused if, after all those years in Chelmsford, he had developed an obsessive loathing for Ronnie Lee but he hadn't. The ALF were just a 'damn nuisance' – and his job was to put them away.

The squad that convened under Colin Hoye was half a dozen strong, mainly composed of CID officers from the Home Counties. At the beginning it was called simply 'the ALF Squad' and was attached to the Yard's C 11 Branch, which was responsible for intelligence gathering. Later, the name was changed to the 'National Index of Animal Rights Extremists', and a few months after that the 'Animal Rights National Index', or ARNI for short. Some officers thought that the word 'Extremists' should have been retained, on the grounds that not all animal rights supporters were involved in law-breaking, but their seniors felt this was being unnecessarily pedantic. The squad formally became ARNI in January 1986, at the same time being removed from its home in C 11. The Branch was supposed to enjoy a low profile, and the animal rights squad had quickly drawn an embarrassing amount of attention. In its new incarnation, the squad was for the first time organized on a proper national footing: just two days before ARNI formally came into existence, the Animal Rights Militia had planted its sequence of four car bomb devices, and officers were running an informal book on which vivisectionist was going to be the first to die. Brian Meldrum was the odds on favourite.

ARNI was now to be run as an autonomous, national unit, parallel to Special Branch. The core squad, based at Scotland Yard, varied from half a dozen to ten detectives working full time on animal rights, including the now plain-clothes PC Wiggins. What had been treated a year earlier as a kind of joke now carried much the same status as the Anti-terrorist Squad: these were real bombs planted by people who really wanted to kill. It was crazy, but it was no longer funny. Every force outside London was allocated its own animal rights liaison officer, collating information and dealing directly with ARNI;

the role was usually assigned to the Head of CID, who would normally carry the rank of Chief Superintendant. In twelve months things had moved dramatically from the one solitary PC lurking in a Chelmsford basement to a matter of top national priority.

Before the squad had come together, the impression had been that ALF activity was a sporadic and not terribly significant nuisance. With the benefit of PC Wiggins' lorry load of documents, and a properly computerized collation system, a far more worrying picture began to emerge. The ALF itself claimed by the mid eighties to be responsible for six million pounds' worth of damage a year: but the truth seemed to be that this, if anything, was an underestimate of the real cost. The vast majority of liberationist activity was low level, but the volume was enormous – half a dozen raids a night, every night, all over the country. And on top of that, there were the large-scale acts of economic sabotage. Much of the low-level activity had never been reported before the squad had been set up: farmers and butchers had simply accepted the ALF's attention as part of the modern price of staying in business. But, putting the whole picture together, it was clear that in terms of economic sabotage alone, the ALF was outstripping the IRA.

But while the Anti-terrorist Squad by now had a clear idea of the enemy and the ideological background of militant Irish republicanism, ARNI was floundering in the dark. Video observation at the big demonstrations only seemed to confuse the issue: what on earth were all those nice middle-class ladies doing next to punks and anarchists? The sheer multiplicity of organizations and different groups, most of them beset by endemic infighting, was hopelessly puzzling to this small bunch of conventional and largely animal loving Englishmen who now found themselves in pursuit of this peculiar strain of terrorism. The good news, though, was that intelligence was almost pitifully easy to gather; the squad was soon on the mailing list of the ALF Supporters Group, and within a few months a clearer picture began to emerge. Organizations, it emerged, mattered less than individuals: regardless of who claimed responsibility for actions, it was felt that there were probably no more than twenty top-ranking 'planners' within the movement; Ronnie Lee and Vivian Smith, it was clear, were more than just the movement's 'press officers', as they were careful to describe themselves.

Every detective seconded to ARNI, said one of them, went there 'by accident'. None of them was particularly pro or anti blood sports, meat-eating or vivisection. They liked to think that they had a common sense view of the issue: 'sorting out the wheat from the chaff' meant working out who was basically just a harmless animal lover; and who was a potential bomb planter. 'You could always see both sides of the coin' said one member of the squad; 'you could appreciate that there were two sides to the argument, especially when it came to hunting.' But the line was clear: the police were not there to stop people caring, but to deal with those who broke the law. That didn't put them in the pockets of the hunt masters, they were anxious to point out. 'We all care about animals,' said a detective, 'and we could see that these animal rights people started it in all good faith – some of us might even have joined them in the early stages.' Even after the bombs, there was none of the sense of personal antagonism you would find in other branches at Scotland Yard.

Later, at court hearings and when activists had been picked up for interrogation, this even-handed approach seemed close to a curious kind of personal warmth, and even intimacy. Tim Daley had argued quite seriously for the assassination of vivisectors; had regretted that ARM bombs had not succeeded in killing the enemy; had admitted to being deeply involved in ALF activity. And yet this same Daley was, in the view of one policeman, 'a cracking bloke – you could really relate to him'. They would have long, earnest conversations on animal rights when Daley was brought in for questioning, discussing the rationale behind the movement. Partly this was the intimacy of a high intensity surveillance operation, but there was also more than a sneaking regard for the leading activists who genuinely cared about animals. Daley was bright, articulate, and his conventional, suburban background might have stood him in good stead had he, for example, chosen a career in the Met.

He was certainly more alert than most to what ARNI was up to. He had been under continual surveillance, he claimed, since January 1985, the month the squad came into existence. 'The first I noticed was when I was being followed by cars from home. I'd wake up in the morning, I'd look out and there'd be a car sitting up the road. I'd set off from home, and the car would come with me, then shortly afterwards it would disappear and then another car would come with me.'

Daley enjoyed this cat and mouse game with the police. His mail was opened, he said, pouring scorn on the primitive methods used; his phone was tapped, so that he had been able to mischieviously 'plan' a phoney raid on BIBRA Laboratories in Carshalton which led to eight transit van loads of police wasting an entire afternoon waiting for a non-existent mob. This was a game and Daley was good at it, but for someone of his background it was, he admitted, 'very odd' to be under police surveillance. His parents were very sad about it all; he had been brought up as law-abiding, and until he joined the animal rights movement he would never have remotely considered doing the kind of things he got up to now. But now, you had, he said, to break the law to change the law. All this Daley could put across with the same charm that made him enormously successful in his career selling advertising space in newspapers; when he talked about the need for selective killings, 'shootings on the doorstep', the charm never wavered. It was clear why the men from ARNI held him in some respect, even a kind of grudging affection. And in the end, he has never been charged with any offence.

Other activists were suspicious of Daley's charmed life; there were suggestions that the men from ARNI wanted him out in the open where they could monitor his activity. But Daley was a smart operator. He and John Beggs had spent hours together studying the Irish Republican movement, learning the lessons of authentic terrorism; how to maintain tight security on a 'need to know' basis, how to run an effective watertight cell, how to recruit without prejudicing security. Beggs and Daley prided themselves on their professionalism, which they felt stood in sharp contrast to the often chaotic operations of the older ALF hierarchy. Ronnie Lee's anarchistic tendencies, they thought, were hopelessly impractical. 'The only plan is no plan,' Ronnie would boast, as if this were some kind of tactical masterstroke. But, though they were picked up on several occasions, Beggs and Daley were never charged: Ronnie Lee, to the surprise of the men from ARNI, in the end proved an almost ridiculously easy catch.

In the space of three years from the ACPO meeting during which ARNI was first mooted, the squad was responsible for the arrest and subsequent Crown Court trials of four ALF cells responsible for the firebombing campaign against department stores. The first, and by far the biggest success came with the cracking of the Sheffield group, who had run the campaign against Rackhams. It had been the incendiary bomb that caused £200,000 worth of damage to the store in November 1985 that had first drawn the animal rights squad to Sheffield. What they did not suspect at the time was that Ronnie Lee himself was personally involved in the campaign as courier and adviser. 'We were amazed when he started getting his hands dirty,' said one of the men involved; 'we knew he was making up the tune, but we didn't think he'd start playing the instruments.'

The squad's natural instinct had been to see the ALF 'Press Office' in Hammersmith as a kind of equivalent to Sinn Fein; there was no doubt about the connection with the bombers, but it was assumed that the front organization would carefully steer clear of any practical, traceable involvement with activists out in the field. Early in 1986, both the Hammersmith office and the end-of-terrace house in Sheffield where the local cell used to meet were put under twenty-four-hour surveillance. Attempts to disguise the Hammersmith HQ, with its bogus plaque, had been almost laughable and both Lee and his assistant would insist on meeting visitors away from the premises, in local pubs and coffee bars. But as curious journalists had already established, it was a simple matter to trace either of them back to their centre of operations. Later, when Lee was under surveillance on his regular trips to Sheffield, he would employ what he imagined to be sophisticated anti-surveillance techniques, doubling back on himself, and zig-zagging up and down the country on railway journeys of considerable complexity. But, after the IRA, this was elementary stuff to the ARNI squad. 'They were babies at the game' was the patronizing verdict of their pursuers.

In those early weeks of 1986, Ronnie Lee paid several visits to the house in Idsworth Road, Firth Park, Sheffield. Ostensibly this was the home of Brendan McNally, the cell's 'liaison officer', who lived there with his wife Jenny; in fact, it was now in almost full-time use as a bomb factory, turning out the compact incendiary devices, constructed by Ian Oxley, that fitted so neatly into a cigarette packet. By now this was known to ARNI because the flat had been penetrated; a highly sensitive radio microphone 'bug' had been placed under the floorboards of the flat's living-room. At the same time, the house was under permanent watch, so that the squad was able to raid the premises when the entire eight-strong cell was on the premises: 'they were all sitting round the table,' said one of the raiders, 'with the stuff spread out in front of them'. Lee and Vivian Smith were picked up separately in London; under the bed in Vivian Smith's flat the police found a drawer with one of the ALF's bomb-making manuals inside. 'They were genuinely surprised when we went in,' said a detective, 'they really thought they'd been clever, with all the doubling back and general paranoia about being watched.' Vivian Smith had, after all, talked about how she and Ronnie would visit Irish Republican pubs in Kilburn and admire the spirit and the sing-songs; but when it came to the practicalities of terrorism they had proved hopelessly amateurish.

Lee, Smith and the Sheffield cell were put on trial at Sheffield Crown Court in January 1987. It was the first and biggest of what the animal rights movement would refer to as a series of four 'show trials'. Ronnie Lee was just thirty-five, though he looked a great deal older. Now virtually bald and just over five foot tall, it was hard to recognize the charismatic figure that ALF activists held in such obvious awe. Twelve years in the movement, with two gaol sentences already behind him, Lee was not only the longest-serving veteran of the direct action campaign, he was acknowledged as the 'godfather' of the movement. His was the face recognized by millions of television viewers as the public face of the ALF. Younger, more sophisticated 'planners' might be impatient with his impractical, anarchistic view of the campaign, but Lee had always remained the central figure. He was highly regarded by many at the 'respectable' end of animal rights, as well. John Bryant, of Animal Aid and the League Against Cruel Sports, found him exasperating and hopelessly idealistic, but said that the world would be a much better place if it were populated with Ronnie Lees. At Sheffield Crown Court, this charitable view was severely strained.

Passing sentence on Lee, the Deputy High Court Judge described him as a fanatic and a dangerous criminal. He had allowed what might be very worthy ideals to change him into a 'dangerous terrorist'. There was no doubt that under the direction of Lee, in the somewhat archaic phrase used by the Judge, 'fireraisers were abroad'. This had been a widespread, national and dangerous conspiracy, for Lee was also implicated in the fire bomb attacks on Allders in Croydon and Selfridges in London's Oxford Street. He was found guilty of conspiracy to commit arson, commit criminal damage and incite others to commit criminal damage. The detectives in the ARNI squad had no idea what kind of sentence would be handed out; they suspected that, because the issue was animals, it might be on the soft side. Ronnie Lee was given ten years. On hearing his sentence he smiled and, speaking clearly, said 'that's all right', before giving Viv Smith a quick hug and a kiss. For a man whose public behaviour had always been devoid of emotion, this was something close to loss of control.

Vivian Smith herself was described by the Judge as Lee's 'enthusiastic and able lieutenant'. She was twenty-six, a picture of drab anarchist chic – black clothing, jet black hair framing pallid unsmiling features. Sir Frederick Lawton had been shocked by the discovery of the 'horrendous' bomb-making booklet under her bed. It had also emerged in court that Vivian had done much of the laundering of the ALF Supporters Group's funds, £13,000 of which had passed through her personal account, and was now untraceable. In court she seemed to live up to the description given by another leading activist who disliked and distrusted her middle-class, Home Counties background; she was like one of the Baader-Meinhof gang, he said, upper middle-class designer revolutionaries with BMWs, playing the thing as a kind of decadent, destructive game. Other people in the movement disapproved of meat-eaters, he said, but Vivian Smith genuinely and wholeheartedly hated them. It was all too easy to remember the smile of almost seraphic pleasure she gave, sipping her half of cider in the seedy Hammersmith pub, as she anticipated the death of the first vivisector. Vivian Smith was found guilty of committing criminal damage and sentenced to four years' imprisonment.

Of the Sheffield gang, three of the 'footsoldiers' – Baldwin, Cartwright and Oxley – were each given four years, as was 'liaison officer' Brendan McNally. Julia Rogers, who had actually planted the bomb at Rackhams, was given thirty months, the judge recognizing that she had become involved in the conspiracy only because of her love for Kevin Baldwin. Two fringe members of the cell got off comparatively lightly. John Hewson, the sixty-three-year-old retired teacher – a good thirty years older than anyone else in the dock – was singled out by the Judge as 'a bit of a humbug', and was given twelve months. By contrast, the youngest defendant, nineteen-year-old student Isabel Facer, was described as 'the most pathetic of all of them', someone whom the genuine love of animals had caused to embark on a trial of terrorism. Sir Frederick sentenced her to nine months' in youth custody. To the journalists covering the trial they seemed a strangely assorted bunch, obviously identifiable neither as criminals nor terrorists. But the truth was they were a fair cross-section of the kind of people the movement had thrown up. One face, however, was missing from the final line-up in the dock. Roger Yates, the 'northern press officer' of the ALF, sentenced in his absence to four years in gaol, had absconded the week before the verdict. He had not been found. In this postscript, at least, the ALF were beginning to look like real terrorists.

One year after the Sheffield trial, the concerted efforts of ARNI, working with their CID liaison officers in South Wales and Strathclyde in Scotland, produced three further results that saw another six conspirators consigned to prison. But if the police had been pleasantly surprised by the total of thirty-eight years handed out in Sheffield, they were now appalled by a series of what they regarded as light prison sentences. In March 1988 two Scots ALF activists appeared at the High Court in Edinburgh. David Barr, founder of the Glasgow-based 'Vegan Action Group', and his co-conspirator Valerie Mohammed, received sentences of three years in prison and nine months detention in a Young Offenders' Institution respectively. Barr had planted an incendiary device in Jenners department store in Edinburgh in the previous autumn and, together with Mohammed, had sent threatening letters to various branches of the media warning that Jenners and other stores would be burned down unless they stopped selling furs and cosmetics that had been tested on animals.

Three months later, two of the leading ALF hierarchy who had taken over the running of the ALF and its Support Group in the absence of Lee and Smith were found guilty of conspiring to incite others to commit criminal damage (in this case, the placing of incendiaries in department stores in Cardiff and Swansea) but this time the sentences were even lighter: eighteen months each with nine months suspended. Privately, ARNI detectives admitted that they were 'disappointed' by this outcome; compared to Sheffield, the sentences seemed curiously lenient, especially as both defendents were leading activists. Sally Carr was a young engineer from Dorset who had acted as treasurer for the Front, while Lane had taken over as 'press officer' and general co-ordinator. Lane had often used the name 'Chris Oakley' in his dealings with the press, a private ALF joke at the expense of the real Chris Oakley who was the editor of the Liverpool Echo, and a man much given to forthright condemnations of animal rights terrorism in his leader column. In Sheffield, the words 'fanatic' and 'terrorist' had been heavily in evidence, but here in Cardiff Mr Justice Henry, while deploring 'serious offences that had given "the oxygen of publicity" to the Front's activities', said he accepted that Lane and Carr had only broken the law out of their beliefs on animal cruelty.

At the Old Bailey a couple of weeks later, the men responsible for the nine million pound blaze at Debenhams in Luton's Arndale Centre appeared in the dock. Geoffrey Shepherd and Andrew Clarke, both unemployed, had been caught red-handed by the police sitting at a desk in Shepherd's flat in north London, surrounded by clock parts and soldering irons. The police and the army bomb disposal experts had been impressed by the quality of the devices being assembled: 'the stuff [explosive] they were using was very good,' said a detective, indicating that, with more experience, ALF technology was continuing to improve. The judge was less impressed. Sentencing Shepherd to four years and four months, and Clarke to three and a half years in prison, he told the pair in the dock that he wasn't going to waste his time pointing out to them the errors of their ways, 'for the very good reason that you wouldn't pay any attention to what I'd say'. Shepherd, it emerged, had breached a suspended sentence he had been given for smashing a butcher's window. At the Old Bailey, as in Sheffield, the judicial process made no allowance for decent, if misguided motivation.

All in all, setting aside the variation in sentences, the four trials had been something of a triumph for ARNI; within three years of its establishment as a special unit, two squads of bombers had been caught and much of the known leadership of the ALF had been locked away. But two nagging worries spoiled the party. First, the firebombing campaign inconveniently failed to come to an end. Through the spring and summer of 1988 and into 1989, incendiary devices continued to be planted in department stores and in new, secondary targets – businesses that had only an indirect connection with the animal issue. If anything, said the police, the campaign had been played down by the newspapers; almost regardless of how many activists were put away, the level of bombing seemed to remain more or less the same.

But much more worrying was the fact that no one had been either caught or charged in connection with the anti-personnel bombs claimed by the Animal Rights Militia and associated groups. There had now been at least seventeen of these, beginning with the letter bombs to the party leaders. Privately, animal rights squad detectives admitted their frustration but there had been some useful progress. There was no doubt, they said, that the letter bombs were genuinely from people in animal rights, something that had been often dismissed by moderates in the movement, who had argued that they were a piece of black propaganda on the part of the animal abuse lobby. Police had a fair idea who these people were, but not the evidence that would stand up in court; they also had an idea of the group of four or five people involved in the later ARM bombings. They didn't think that there was any separate, more extreme terrorist arm of the movement in existence: that the bombers were well-known ALF activists was the 'strong impression'. But the point that mattered, and not least to the scientists in their sights, was that these bombers remained at large.

CHAPTER FIFTEEN

Action is the lifeblood. Without action,
you're just posing.

Martin Wright, Class War activist

As they queued up patiently to get into the week-long licensed binge that was the annual Bristol Winefair, prospective oenophiles passed a line of chanting demonstrators. This was nothing to do with temperance or personal salvation: for reasons unclear, the Western Animal Rights Alliance had chosen the venue to put on a show of strength. But unless you looked hard at the posters, there were few clues for an outsider about who these people were, or which constituency they represented. A rather threatening skinhead in shiny khaki bomber jacket and Doc Martens stood next to a slight girl in faded jeans, and hand biro'd tennis shoes: her hair was a shock of red, green and blue. A middle-aged man in tweed jacket and worn corduroys pressed leaflets on the incoming boozers, chatting amiably to a couple of elderly ladies in Oxfam chic and shiny Hush Puppies. A young man with a spectacularly tall and rigid Mohican helped with the leaflets; he wore jeans apparently composed of serried layers of ripped denim.

In summer 1987, this was a reasonable snapshot of the new social and political landscape that had been thrown up by the animal rights movement. Trying to find a pattern that could interpret so many apparently conflicting signals was difficult. On the big anti-vivisection demonstrations in London, Manchester, Edinburgh and Cambridge, you would see shaven-headed lads in Union Jack T-shirts, punks, anarchists, right-on leftists of every available persuasion, and alongside them armies of those who might readily be identified as good old-fashioned British animal lovers. This was a movement that existed outside any recognizable political spectrum, where fascism and anarchy seemed to co-exist, jointly subordinate to the cause of the animals. What had happened to the harmless sentimentality of the British love of animals that it should mutate so strangely into this curious hybrid? And why should so many of the young find it so seductive? In the end, what pattern could be interpreted in the political mosaic of animal rights?

Every generation is idealistic after its own fashion. The sixties had produced an optimistic and euphoric sense of the inevitability of things getting better; the harder nosed seventies had seen a commitment to a range of conventionally left-wing solutions to structural economic decline. In the eighties, the young who refused to compete (or were simply not given the chance to compete) in the rigorous rebirth of the enterprise culture were attracted to an intense, non-party form of political activism. They were concerned with 'green' issues, were attracted to vegetarianism and vegansim; were convinced that nuclear power was intrinsically and fatally flawed; were terrified of the imminence of nuclear war. They were curiously pessimistic, took a low view of their own species and its capabilities. Man had been a poor steward of the natural resources he had inherited, poisoning the forests with acid rain, destroying the ozone layer with frivolous aerosols and coldly massacring lesser species for the selfish benefit of their skins, protein and blubber.

There was a strong sense of this pessimism at the anarchists' squat in Brighton; the same feeling of time running out and the last days being at hand of which born again Christians would make so much. 'This system, this concrete jungle that we've made' – it was all rotten and would imminently pass away. The anarchists had no respect for humans, they said, only for the animals; none of the problems of the world were the animals' fault. Man the self-centred and self-styled 'master' species had abused his position in the world, and if he was not stopped then the very planet was threatened. That was why the anarchists were angry, that was why they used the language of violence. 'Ask yourself why we're angry – where it comes from,' said Steve. 'That's why we're going to carry on doing what we're doing: and if that means we get beaten up, if that means we get killed, then personally I'm going to carry on doing it.'

The new animal rights activism was watched with interest by those in conventional politics. Something was happening, and though they didn't really understand what it was, the numbers involved looked impressive. The New Statesman and

Marxism Today ran enthusiastic features exploring ways in which the left could cash in on the liberationist movement, a genuinely mass movement which inconveniently seemed to elude any class-based analysis. *Marxism Today* tried to put this right by developing the theory that animal abuse was the direct consequence of capitalism. 'It was no co-incidence', as indeed it never was with the Marxists, that the relation of people in the West to the rest of the natural world had been so brutally simple. 'Under capitalism, animals are increasingly viewed as objects and commodities to be produced and sold, or as machines for the production of these commodities ... This process culminates in the factory farm, unalloyed greed in material form.' Apart from anything else this was a curiously sentimental view of Soviet and Chinese agricultural practices.

It was also of little appeal to the kind of people who were getting involved in animal rights. One of the first things they would learn in their local animal rights group was that the main political parties had never put animal issues anywhere near the top of their agenda; you got involved in animal rights because you were fed up with conventional politics, and the conventional issues they addressed. You were also angry and impatient; you wanted direct action now, against real, identi-fied animal abusers, not some long-term ideologically correct strategy dictated from above. 'The animals are dying now!' was the cry that echoed from meeting to meeting, the same sense of time passing, animals suffering and the consequent need for action. This violent, personal sense of anger was the common currency of both the new generation of anarchists and also many of the constantly fracturing groups on the far right. From these two wings, nominally so different but actually sharing the same vernacular, many of the footsoldiers of the animal rights movement were recruited.

The traditional face of British anarchism had been theoreti-cal, bookish, quiescent. The movement's most venerable peri-odical, *Freedom*, had been founded as far back as 1886; with a current circulation of around two thousand, it presented no threat to any portion of the state. The first sign that things were changing had come with the Angry Brigade in the early seventies who, though they hadn't actually harmed anybody, had at least detonated real bombs and given the Home Secretary a nasty shock. But it wasn't until the early and mid eighties that a new style of anarchist group began to emerge – popular, street-based, violent and taking the issue of animal rights as one of the most important to be confronted. Confrontation was very much the style: *Class War*, *Crowbar*, *Poison Pen* and *Brighton Bomber* – the names of the lurid new broadsheets suggested that Bakunin and Kropotkin had taken a back seat to comic book caricature.

In fact, they often read like manic adult versions of the *Beano*. The language was violent and personal; the 'rich' were all 'scumbags', the police vicious 'pigs'. *Class War* in particular enjoyed taking on the sacred orthodoxies of both left and right. 'God bless you, Queen Mum' went *CW's* cheerful doggerel on the Queen Mother's birthday, 'your husband rots in hell – the only thing that's wrong with that, is that you're not there as well.' But at the same time, the 'wankers of CND' were just part of the 'parasitical cop-out left', no better than 'rich scum-baggers everywhere'. All this seemed to go down very well with the new generation of young street anarchists: by 1985, *Class War* was claiming monthly sales of ten thousand copies.

Of all the new groups, Class War was most overtly interested in animal rights; on the big marches against the 1986 Animal Act, Class War banners were the most visible. Being anarchists, the group wasn't supposed to have anything like a formal leadership. In effect, a curiously matched pair, Ian Bone, an unemployed sociology graduate, and Martin Wright, a former road-sweeper, ran the monthly paper and set the prevailing tone. Wright came from a north London working-class back-ground, with a history of violence against black teachers at school; he had flirted with National Front ideas for a time, he said, but then got stuck into Bakunin and realized he had really been an anarchist all along. The joy of it was, you didn't have to abjure violence; in fact it was a central feature of the anarchist life, with regular rucks with the British Movement and other ritual enemies. 'We'd have our regular meetings, too,' said Wright, 'but these were more like booze-ups, and generally they ended by smashing up the place.' Class War endorsed the new recreational violence practised by the highly organized squads of football 'hooligans', as the authorities chose to describe them. But the point was to take this violence and channel it in more fruitful directions. 'Every time you crack someone who's exactly the same as you, except they support the other team,' argued Class War's paper, 'you might as well be kicking yourself in the head ... There's some brilliant things that happen at football, like rucking the police and looting from shops, but it's time to go a step further, like thieving off the rich instead of each other, hitting the bastards where it really hurts.'

Ian Bone shared this appetite for violence, but he insisted that it should be developed from a sound theoretical base. With his severely cropped pate and gold-rimmed granny specs, he looked like an intellectual skinhead, and it was the role of tactician and ideologue that he relished: he had a degree in sociology, after all. The son of a butler to a wealthy landowner, Bone said that he had inherited his hatred for the rich from his father. It was rumoured that his involvement in animal rights stemmed from the theft of one of his daughter's pets, but rigid veganism was in any case the orthodoxy practised by the Class War collective. Bone first published the paper in July 1983, the splinter-group of a splinter-group from the Socialist Workers' Party. Its tone was from the beginning one of loathing for any and every manifestation of the state, caring or otherwise: 'We won't rest till the guts of the last social worker have been used to strangle the last probation officer' ran one cheerful headline, echoing identical sentiments in the ALF Bulletin directed at the huntsman and vivisector.

Under Bone and Wright, a series of disruptive events were organized, usually ending in large-scale punch-ups. Class War had rioted in the City of London in an attempt to disrupt trading; a thousand assorted punks and skinheads had taken part, with just under five hundred being arrested for obstruction and damage. Several of the Brighton anarchists had taken part in this 'bash the rich' exercise, and in a subsequent violent demonstration outside a Hunt Ball in Mayfair. This was a near perfect Class War occasion, combining as a target both 'rich scumbags' and evil animal abusers. 'Jostling, well-placed kicks, spitting, and an outstandingly well-placed smack in the gob contrived to ruin many an evening,' the paper later commented. On animal rights demonstrations, the Class War contingent could always be identified by the nest of black banners, some of which incorporated the ALF logo within the anarchist capital 'A', and also by their ritualized chanting of 'scumbag' at every manifestation of state authority. More respectable demonstrators watched all this with some unease and on occasions would engage in slanging matches with their black-clad allies. The trouble was that more often than not the anarchists made up at least half of the demonstration; they might, as the nationalist community would say of the IRA in Ulster, look like a bunch of thugs but at least they were their thugs. Besides, these were also the footsoldiers of the ALF, risking arrest in order to carry out the direct actions that even 'respectable' members of the movement approved of.

Radical animal rights groups like the BUAV enjoyed a difficult relationship with the anarchists. On the one hand, they swelled the numbers at demonstrations, but on the other they represented bad publicity when their violent ranting got out of hand. At one demo outside a laboratory in Islington, Ian Bone led a Class War contingent that behaved in a threatening and bullying manner towards any BUAV supporter who failed to follow Bone's confrontational directions. BUAV office manager Margaret Manzoni said that the anarchists 'threatened us and spat in our faces anytime we didn't do what they wanted'. But the animal rights movement was not the kind of uniform, coherent front that could be contained within conventional political oganizations: it was by definition diffuse, chaotic and troublesome. Organizations like BUAV wanted it both ways: they needed and welcomed the new blood provided by the squats and collectives when it came to votes and demonstrations but they were embarrassed by the physical appearance and violent language that came as part of the package. BUAV supported and financed direct action which involved the breaking of the law: and the hard fact was that these black-clad kids, with their ritualized abuse and dangerous rage, were the ones prepared to go out and break it on their behalf.

Margaret Manzoni had said that Class War showed worrying 'fascist tendencies'. This was not particularly surprising given Martin Wright's background, but it was even less surprising given the common ground that the animal rights issue had provided for anarchists and the far right. So far as most observers could see there was no racist content to the Class War invective, but apart from that, the collective's theory and behaviour seemed to owe more to the far right than the left. And indeed, organizations like BUAV were as exercised about fascists infiltrating the movement as they were about the embarrassing public behaviour of the anarchists. The far right shared the anarchists' view of the purging qualities of violence; many of the newer groups also shared a vision of post-industrial society that was anti big business, rural and zealously conservationist, as well as rigorously nationalist.

The fascists saw the new non-party, issue-based politics as a fruitful way of introducing the idealistic young to their more questionable ideas. They were also attracted by the fact that here was a large pool of activists prepared to take direct action on a matter of principle. But the truth was that English and European fascism had long had a curiously 'greenish' tinge to it. This was rather more than the fact that Hitler had been a serious vegetarian and a teetotaller: the Nazis had, as a matter of policy, passed measures dealing with cruelty to animals and restricting vivisection, as well, of course, as banning 'shehitah' – the practice of kosher butchery. Throughout the 1930s, the issue of ritual slaughter had frequently been raised in the publications of the various strands of British fascism. In April 1937, *The Fascist* – published by the Imperial Fascist League – ran a front page cartoon entitled 'John Bull's Blinkers'. An ox, marked with a Star of David, is congratulating an aged horse put out to grass: 'you will not be sent to hell on earth before you die. But neither Laws nor Animal Protection Societies can save us; they will cut our throats and let us bleed to death because they will not oppose the Jews who govern them.'

In the eighties, the right again seized on the issue of ritual slaughter. 'Stop this evil!' insisted the *National Front News* in 1984, demanding to know 'what type of people can demand such a cruel way of slaughter?' under a lurid photo of a cow with its throat cut. The Front supported the Campaign for Animal Welfare, it said; at its 1983 Annual Conference, the Front had voted to ban all animal experiments for the purpose of cosmetics, and to ban all pursuit blood sports, as well as demanding an end to ritual slaughter, both by Muslims and Jews. 'Unlike Britain's other political parties, the National Front does not rely on the voting support of immigrant communities. It is for this reason,' promised the *National Front News* 'that the National Front is the only political party that can take the lead in the campaign against ritual slaughter without fear of being compromised.'

No doubt the Front hoped that this admirable streak of altruism would go down well with anyone vaguely concerned with 'green' issues. Certainly, there was a concerted effort to infiltrate local animal rights groups and the national organizations. In 1984, the Manchester Council for Community Relations was sufficiently concerned to write warning letters to eight of the main bodies, including the RSPCA, NAVS, the Hunt Saboteurs Association, the Northern Animal Liberation League and the League Against Cruel Sports. Local animal rights groups found that National Front members were turning up for meetings and distributing literature on the issue of ritual slaughter. In Brighton, the local animal rights group had been split over whether or not to join in an NF march, with some ALF supporters voicing the belief that it really didn't matter what the broader politics were, as long as the single issue of animal rights was at the centre of the demonstration. In Blackpool, the local BUAV contact wrote worriedly to headquarters about the presence of NF supporters at meetings, and a deluge of literature that had arrived courtesy of the local NF press officer.

Later, the BUAV took the Front to court after a local council election campaign in Essex, during which the National Front-supported 'independent animal rights' candidate distributed literature lifted verbatim from leaflets printed by BUAV. The printer credited on the pirated leaflets was a well-known Front supporter, driving an embarrassed BUAV to immediately apply for an injunction to stop the material being distributed. The message was fine, but this was not the kind of messenger the liberationists wished to see capitalizing on the issue. Patrick Harrington, an NF spokesman, said the BUAV was just paranoid about being connected with the Front. The party's concern for animals was absolutely genuine: he, for example, had been a vegetarian all his life.

Certainly, the Front's publications continued to trumpet the animal rights issue, and not simply on the question of ritual slaughter. *Nationalism Today* ('The Radical Voice of British Nationalism') gave cover story prominence to a long interview with Hans Ruesch, one of the seminal figures of the animal rights movement. His books on the subject were required reading, recommended by BUAV and most of the other organizations. 'We feel sure that our readers will find his views both fascinating and agreeable' ran the introduction in *Nationalism Today*, going on to plug Ruesch's anti-vivisectionist bulletin, *Civis*.

Ruesch's argument was that all vivisection was scientific fraud, and that there was a worldwide conspiracy to cover up the exciting potential of 'fringe' medicine: the medical establishment and the drug companies were in an unholy and profit-driven alliance. 'Powerful vested interests are intent upon making money whatever the cost in human and animal suffering,' Ruesch told the NF. To its credit, the BUAV wrote to Ruesch after this episode, more in sorrow than in anger: surely he could not have known what sort of people the National Front were to give an interview – had he not thought of the consequences for his image? Ruesch was unapologetic; he thought the piece had come out 'quite well'; he would have preferred publication in a national newspaper but was 'delighted that it had appeared at all'. Ruesch had heard that Mrs Thatcher was supposed to be a secret member of the NF. 'Of course, I don't believe it, but it would be great if she were, so at least she saw the interview [sic]. She'll hardly hear the truth from the British AV [anti-vivisection] journals.'

Ruesch didn't necessarily approve of fascism or nationalism, he said, but he had lost all patience with 'the hypocrisy of the present ruling system that sails under the false flag of liberalism in order the better to exploit man and animals with the spreading of false information and systematic suppression of the truth'. This bleak view of democracy, with its mixture of paranoia and a more general pessimism about the future of the species, was more eloquently expressed by Ruesch than by most. Mankind needed a fresh start, a new contract with the natural world must be struck. The old order had to be swept away. It was a vision of enormous appeal to those out on the margins of the conventional political spectrum.

In its central position as the referral agency and clearing house of almost all groups involved in animal rights, the BUAV did its best to monitor the activity of political extremists who sought to use the animal liberation movement for their own ends. But in all but a few contentious cases it was impossible to identify those who fell into this category; on the big marches and demonstrations, the Union Jack T-shirts seemed just as welcome as the black flags of the anarchists. In any case, this was not simply a matter of infiltration pure and simple. It was true that far right groups saw the animal rights issue as a channel for recruitment, but it was equally true that for many young fascists this was something they cared about quite genuinely.

For months, the BUAV engaged in heated and breast-beating correspondence about one Margaret Flynn, who was actively involved in anti-vivisection, the Hunt Saboteurs and the Eastern Animal Liberation League: she was also involved with something called the 'November Ninth' Movement, a far right group that took its name from the date of Hitler's ill-fated 1923 Munich Beerhall *putsch*. Flynn, a former judo champion, had joined 'November Ninth' – an organization that dismissed the National Front as 'little better than a right wing Tory Party' – after meeting her husband Terry, the British 'Führer' of the group. With uniforms of black tunics and jackboots, this was just about as far out on the right as it was possible to go without being locked up; vicious anti-semitic fantasies and an obsession with Nazi regalia preoccupied the group's members, who went off for regular 'training weekends' in the hills, preparing for the day when Britain would become part of an all-Aryan Europe.

But apart from her 'November Ninth' activities, Margaret Flynn had organized her own group of Hunt Saboteurs in the Bedfordshire and Buckingham areas, joined BUAV, and gone out on actions with the EALL. Clearly, Ms Flynn was a busy lady. Arrested eight times while out 'sabbing' (including one incident which left her with a wound requiring eleven stitches), she had been charged with causing actual bodily harm in the course of an anti-circus demo, and been dragged out of several butchers' and fur shops by the police. If this was 'infiltration', she wrote to BUAV, when her 'November Ninth' persona came to light, it was a pretty noisy and unsubtle form. BUAV and EALL wanted nothing to do with her once her fascist affiliation emerged but the truth was that Margaret Flynn was only a slightly more extreme version of the kind of men and women who relished direct action as the only meaningful form of political action. She appeared to care quite genuinely for animals, taking them into her home and looking after them; but she also like a good 'ruck' and in animal rights found something worth rucking for. Unpleasant as it might have been for gentler souls in the animal liberation movement to contemplate, this was not unusual. Ian Bone and Martin Wright would have understood.

The ALF was never as fussy as the national anti-vivisection societies in its relationship with either the anarchists or the far right. Ronnie Lee's own political background lay in a rather gentler, herbivorous form of anarchism than that of Class War, but over the years he had been persuaded that more rigorous

Indeed, there are times when to refrain from violence would be immoral.'

Prison life is dull but not hard, he says. He has a cleaning job, which takes up the best part of an hour a day, and he is studying French and German. He makes it clear he enjoys the odd status he has in Long Lartin, and there is something of the martyr in his air of quiet self-congratulation. Prison isn't really so much of a deterrent, he says, except for the fainthearted, and the movement is better off without them anyway. Life inside can be an inspiration if you have the right attitude. The police are confident that he is still the brains behind the ALF and the Support Group; in the shabby visiting room, messages are passed on, policies discussed without apparent interference. 'I still express opinions on how things should be run,' he says, with no traceable sense of irony in the voice. As far as the prison authorities are concerned, Ronnie is a model prisoner. With full parole and remission he could be released by 1992.

Vivian Smith was released in August 1988, having served just over half her sentence. She returned to her parents' address in suburban Kent for the duration: colleagues in the movement could not conceive that she would not soon be back in circulation. Of the other leading activists, Tim Daley continued to avoid the attentions of the police, while managing to maintain a successful career in telephone sales; by summer 1988 he had been promoted to manager on a local paper in Godalming, Surrey. He had not modified his views on animal rights; it was still 'a war', and in war people were killed. John Beggs, on the other hand, had tried very hard to go respectable. He was now chair of the BUAV executive committee and responsible for a series of 'designer' advertising campaigns with consumer friendly titles like 'Health with Humanity' and 'Choose Cruelty-free', which used the endorsement of celebrity figures like Lenny Henry and Joanna Lumley to lobby against vivisection. BUAV now seemed very different in style. Kim Stallwood had gone at the end of 1986, after yet another *putsch*, and was now in America running something called PETA, People for the Ethical Treatment of Animals, one of the country's biggest animal pressure groups. BUAV produced seductive videos and wanted to capitalize on the Bodyshop approach to campaigning, but at the same time ALF Supporters Group members still sat on the committee, and John Beggs found it hard to renounce his past; he was now legal officer of the Hunt Saboteurs

Association as well. He said he had nothing to do with direct action 'and never had', but still believed that the movement needed 'a hard, cutting edge' so that the 'opposition' would realize that the threat was still there. Where would Martin Luther King have been without the Black Panthers?

NAVS now seemed, publicly at any rate, the more abrasive of the two main anti-vivisection charities; they were campaigning on the argument that Aids had been 'created in the laboratory' as a result of vivisection, a line that seemed fairly dubious even to veteran conspiracy theorists. The RSPCA sailed on, still apparently fending off fifth columnists; they had, on the other hand, recently unloaded some thirty-nine million pounds' worth of investments in pharmaceutical companies under pressure from a membership that had grown perceptibly more radical. The police were less sanguine than the Society's executive about its future; ARNI detectives said that the extremists had changed their tactics and were now flooding into the local branches up and down the country. In a further round of blood letting, the charity's ruling council expelled Ronnie Lee's friend Angela Walder and other leading members of the 'Watchdog' group at the end of 1988. As the RAG organizer in Sussex had said, it was a ten- or twenty-year game they were playing, and time was on their side. In the meantime, many of the proliferating local animal rights groups had begun to organize themselves into a Federation; the anarchists were heavily involved in this, and Ronnie Lee had indicated his approval from prison. It made sense for this huge informal network to enter into loose co-operation. It was rumoured that Roger Yates, the former northern 'press officer' of the ALF, at that point still on the run from the Sheffield trial, was involved.

Abroad, animal liberation groups had sprung up in the least fertile soil imaginable. In Spain, 'El Front d'Alliberament Animal' waged war 'contra las corridas de toros', and the FLA in France joined in by paintstrippering the cars of bullfight fans in Toulouse; they had also bombed a slaughterhouse truck: 'it was pleasant and beautiful to see the truck on fire!' commented the FLA bulletin in a burst of existential enthusiasm. The French seemed keener on this kind of thing. One group, working under a name that translated literally as 'Commando Four Paws' used plastic explosives to attack the home of a vivisectionist; in the explosion that followed, a policeman lost an arm and an eye. Later, animal rights demonstrators were attacked in the street by angry members of the French public. In America, direct action by animal rights groups was one of the biggest running stories of 1988; a simple – by British ALF standards – rescue operation involving the theft of sixteen beagles from a University of California laboratory was splashed across several pages of *Newsweek*. Who were these masked raiders, and what did they want? What ideology did they represent? The Americans were confused: this was a new and unmapped zone in the terrorist landscape.

In Australia, too, the home of the movement's principal ideologue, Peter Singer, liberationist groups were active from Perth to Sydney. It seemed, though, that Professor Singer was less than happy with the movement to which he had given so crucial an impetus. Ten years ago the message had been one of moral certainty; now doubts appeared to have crept in. He was unhappy, he confessed, about the violence that flourished in the movement. 'By violence, I mean any action which causes direct physical harm . . . and I would go beyond physical harm to acts which cause psychological harm like fear or terror.' All this sounded pretty lily-livered stuff to the ALF, who Singer had once so confidently recommended in the back pages of *Animal Liberation*. A prison-bound reviewer of Singer's second thoughts on the ALF was contemptuous: the tone was 'negative', he complained; there were 'no tactical suggestions for further battle, no promotion of effective tactics, not much at all really'. Professor Singer, it seemed, like so many before him, had been overtaken by the revolution he had helped to begin.

The revolution, however, continued on its own haphazard way, punctuated by the irregular detonation of 'viable devices'. In a spectacular pre-Christmas blitz, Dingles, the House of Frazer store in Plymouth was destroyed, and seven other premises planted with firebombs; another was sent to the house of Professor Ian Glynn, Head of Cambridge University's physiological laboratories, but was disarmed by police. Earlier in the year within ten days at the end of the summer, a fire bomb destroyed a van belonging to a mink hunt in Sussex, five incendiaries set fire to offices belonging to Portakabin in Essex, and an anti-personnel bomb was placed under a company director's car in a crowded car-park in Maidenhead: the timing device had been set for half past nine, but only twenty minutes' warning had been given, and there had been no time to evacuate and seal off the area. Fortunately, the mechanical timer failed.

But why, in any case, attack the construction industry? It was the old IRA trick, said ARNI; Costain Construction were building research labs for Glaxo Pharmaceuticals and they, according to the anonymous caller who gave the warning, 'were involved in animal cruelty'. The car bomb was by way of 'discouragement'. The caller said he was from something called the Animal Defence League: no one had ever heard of them but within twenty-four hours the ADL had become just one more set of familiar initials in a list that was already horribly oversubscribed.

No one had heard of the Animal Abuse Society either, when at the end of February in the new year a spokesman rang the *Daily Mirror* to warn that a bomb had been placed in the Senate House at Bristol University. A police team with sniffer dogs failed to find anything, but a few hours later – at midnight – five pounds of high explosive wrecked the building. For the first time, animal rights activists had used sophisticated plastic high explosive – a quantum leap forward from the incendiaries and the ARM's gas canister car bombs. Animal warfare had crossed a new and worrying threshold. The day after the bomb went off, a caller from the ALF rang a news agency promising a fresh wave of attacks: they would escalate until someone was killed. No one doubted that they meant it.

A BRIEF CHRONOLOGY
OF EVENTS

1962   Hunt Saboteurs Association formed.

1971   Ronnie Lee and Cliff Goodman set up the Luton group of the HSA.

1972   Lee and Goodman found the 'Band of Mercy' from the core of the Luton saboteurs. Campaign of arson and damage begins.

1974   The 'Band of Mercy' destroys seal cullers' boats in the Wash, and burns Hoechst pharmaceuticals plant.

1975   'Band of Mercy' trial at Oxford Crown Court – Lee and Goodman each given three year gaol sentence.

1976   Lee released from prison. Animal Liberation Front formed with a membership of about thirty activists.

1977   John Peel's grave at Caldbeck in the Lake District desecrated by anti blood sport activists.

1980   The Northern Animal Liberation League, the first of the Leagues, formed in Manchester.

1982   Four letter bombs sent to party leaders at Westminster by the Animal Rights Militia.

The ALF's Supporters Group and Bulletin set up.

1983   'Class War' anarchist newspaper first published.

National Front votes to ban blood sports and ritual slaughter.

1984   South East Animal Liberation League raids on Royal College of Surgeons Laboratory, and on Wickham Laboratories in Hampshire. 'Wickham 19' arrested.

ALF Mars Bar hoax: Mars loses three million pounds in lost sales and checking all stocks. ALF cell responsible escapes detection. The hoax is to protest at tooth decay experiments on monkeys.

Hunt Retribution Squad dig up grave of Duke of Beaufort.

1985   Specialist animal rights squad formed at Scotland Yard.

Four scientists' homes are firebombed by the ALF and the ARM. The ARM plants first two 'devices' under scientists' cars.

ALF firebomb Rackhams department store in Sheffield.

1986   ARM representatives give first interview to TVS. IBA bans interview, but allows precis to be broadcast.

ARM plant four car bombs in different parts of the country, timed to explode at hourly intervals. Warnings are given.

ARM plant bomb under cancer vet's car. No warning given.

Allder's department stores are firebombed by ALF, in protest at fur sales.

Ronnie Lee, his lieutenant Vivian Smith, and Sheffield ALF cell arrested.

1987   ALF's 'Young Supporters' Group formed.

Trial of Lee, Smith, and Sheffield cell. Ronnie Lee gaoled for ten years.

Debenhams department store in Luton burnt down by ALF in protest against fur sales. Nine million pounds' worth of damage done.

Rentokil declared 'legitimate target' by ALF.

1988   Department stores in London's Oxford Street firebombed by ALF.

Animal Defence League plants bomb under car of building contractor working for pharmaceuticals firm in Maidenhead.

Dingles department store in Plymouth destroyed.

1989   February: Senate House at Bristol University blown up by high explosive bomb.

GLOSSARY OF ORGANIZATIONS

ACPO	Association of Chief Police Officers
ADL	Animal Defence League
ALF	Animal Liberation Front
ALF SG	Animal Liberation Front Supporters Group
ARM	Animal Rights Militia
ARNI	Animal Rights National Index (Police)
BARG	Brighton Animal Rights Group
BIBRA	British Industrial Biological Research Association
BUAV	British Union for the Abolition of Vivisection
CALL	Central Animal Liberation League
EALL	Eastern Animal Liberation League
HRS	Hunt Retribution Squad
HSA	Hunt Saboteurs Association
LACS	League Against Cruel Sports
NALL	Northern Animal Liberation League
NAVS	National Anti-vivisection Society
NFU	National Farmers' Union
OAR	Oxford Animal Rights
PAR	Pagan Animal Rights
RAG	RSPCA Action Group
RCS	Royal College of Surgeons
RDS	Research Defence Society
RSPCA	Royal Society for the Prevention of Cruelty to Animals
SEALL	South East Animal Liberation League
SLAM	South London Animals Movement

INDEX